HITLER AND POLAND

HITLER AND POLAND

HOW THE INDEPENDENCE OF ONE COUNTRY LED THE WORLD TO WAR IN 1939

NORMAN RIDLEY

FRONTLINE
BOOKS

First published in Great Britain in 2023 by
Frontline Books
An imprint of
Pen & Sword Books Ltd
Yorkshire – Philadelphia

ISBN 978-1-39904-347-2

A CIP catalogue record for this book is available from the British Library.

Typeset by Lapiz Digital
Printed and bound by CPI UK

Pen & Sword Books Limited incorporates the imprints of Atlas, Archaeology, Aviation, Discovery, Family History, Fiction, History, Maritime, Military, Military Classics, Politics, Select, Transport, True Crime, Air World, Frontline Books, Leo Cooper, Remember When, Seaforth Publishing, The Praetorian Press, Wharncliffe Local History, Wharncliffe Transport, Wharncliffe True Crime, White Owl and After the Battle.

For a complete list of Pen & Sword titles please contact:

PEN & SWORD BOOKS LIMITED
47 Church Street, Barnsley, South Yorkshire, S70 2AS, England
E-mail: enquiries@pen-and-sword.co.uk
Website: www.pen-and-sword.co.uk

or

PEN AND SWORD BOOKS
1950 Lawrence Rd, Havertown, PA 19083, USA
E-mail: uspen-and-sword@casematepublishers.com
Website: www.penandswordbooks.com

CONTENTS

I have issued the command – and I'll have anybody who utters but one word of criticism executed by a firing squad – that our war aim does not consist in reaching certain lines, but in the physical destruction of the enemy. Accordingly, I have placed my death-head formation in readiness – for the present only in the East – with orders to them to send to death mercilessly and without compassion, men, women, and children of Polish derivation and language.

Adolf Hitler speech to Wehrmacht commanders
at the Berghof, 22 August 1939

Now, when we talk about countries to our west, we mean Germany; Poland, Romania and the Baltic States no longer count with us – they have not counted for a long time – we will break these countries apart at a given time and under given circumstances.

Marshal Kliment Voroshilov, People's Commissariat
for the Defence of the USSR, 29 November 1938

INTRODUCTION

In 480 BC the Greek naval commander Themistocles lured the massed warships of the invading Persian fleet into the Straits of Salamis and destroyed them, forcing King Xerxes to abandon his campaign to establish Asian dominion over European soil. The whole of European culture and tradition, which to a very great extent emanates from the Greeks, owes much to this famous victory and it may be said that, in a similar vein, the battle of Warsaw in 1920, when Polish forces repelled the Red Army, was comparable by stemming the tide of communism surging out from the newly installed Bolshevik regime in Moscow that threatened to engulf the whole of Europe.

The newly created state of Poland was wedged uncomfortably between the two dominant nations of Germany and Russia with diametrically opposed political philosophies, both of whom plotted continuously to reclaim the lands of Poland that had up until recently been part of the once great but now defunct German and Russian empires. In order to protect itself, Poland was obliged to plot and negotiate with both of its neighbours to try and prevent them from realising its ambitions to eviscerate the country.

The United States had been instrumental in the creation of the Polish state after the First World War but thereafter showed little interest in its predicament. While France was a traditional friend to the Polish peoples and a significant supplier of military aid, its political influence over Eastern European affairs weakened as its own political institutions fell prey to extremes of both left and right and its immediate post-war dominance waned. Britain seemed interested only in commerce and that made Germany and Russia significantly more important as trading partners than the predominantly agricultural and technologically backward state of Poland.

The decisions taken at Versailles created a Europe that seethed with discontent. It is true to say that the problems faced by the decision-makers were almost beyond solution and while very many historians, with good reason, have criticised them, few have ventured to suggest what better arrangements over national borders would have been less contentious. The Allies struggled to accommodate US president Woodrow Wilson's concept of the 'congruity of peoples … and their lands' but there was a big gap between 'ideals and demographic realities'.[1] New countries emerged from the chaos of war and borders were drawn on maps by the victorious powers with arrogance, war weariness and frustration at the seemingly intractable problems of ethnic divisions, ethnic mixing and ethnic aspirations. There were no historical guidelines, only natural markers such as mountains and rivers, and there were certainly no clear divisions between ethnic peoples who had co-mingled, co-existed and inter-bred for many generations within the now defunct imperial dominions. It was inevitable that people who were henceforth obliged to live in a country that did not represent their own nationalistic aspirations would feel cheated and be susceptible to propaganda that told them that they did not have to accept what had been given to them and had every right to rectify what they saw as an unacceptable situation.

For the people it was a sense of national identity that motivated them but for governments it was a question of security and economics. When borders were contested so fiercely there was every incentive for governments to take matters into their own hands and literally push the boundaries to create borders that encompassed what they saw as legitimately theirs and contest jurisdiction over border areas that had significant economic importance. It is with some justification that historians contend that the conditions imposed by the victorious Western Powers at the end of the First World War would be fertile ground in which the seeds of discontent were fertilised by revanchism and grew into the fetid jungle of the Second World War.

This was nowhere more evident than in the struggle between Germany and Poland to redefine their mutual borders. While Poland fought wars over its disputed eastern borders, the areas stripped from Germany at Versailles were not contested militarily but were deeply resented by Germany. Both sides mobilised borderland nationalists to fight not only cultural wars by exaggerating the extent to which areas 'were and always had been' part of whichever of the two nations claimed them but also bloody and brutal terrorist campaigns to achieve ethnic cleansing. Both sides profited politically from border conflicts that allowed them to strengthen their authoritarian regimes and it was this as much as anything else that prevented enduring solutions to emerge and ensured that bitterness and grievance would endure smouldering in the undergrowth until the winds of war blew on them and fanned them into the inferno. Social engineering projects, violence, expulsions and forced assimilation would lead to the final genocidal catastrophe of extreme nationalism.

Despite the dominance of right-wing politics in Poland, the emergence of Nazi power in Germany did little to bring the countries together and even drove them further apart as Hitler ramped up his rhetorical assault on the perceived injustices of Versailles, which were soon to translate into territorial expansion over Austria and Czechoslovakia and with Poland lined up to be the next in line. Britain and France belatedly roused themselves to challenge the Nazi threat and, after the capitulation of the Anschluss and the humiliation of Munich, found themselves in the disagreeable position of seeing no option but to throw its whole weight behind the integrity of the Polish state if they were ever going to make any sort of stand against Nazi aggression.

Chapter 1

NATIONAL RENEWAL

The Imperial region in the East as far as it encompasses portions of the earlier Polish state, belongs because of the facts of history to Germany; also the parts settled by the Poles have become through German endeavour the genuine possession of the German people which can never be renounced.

Bamberg Declaration, 17 February 1919

Europe 1914

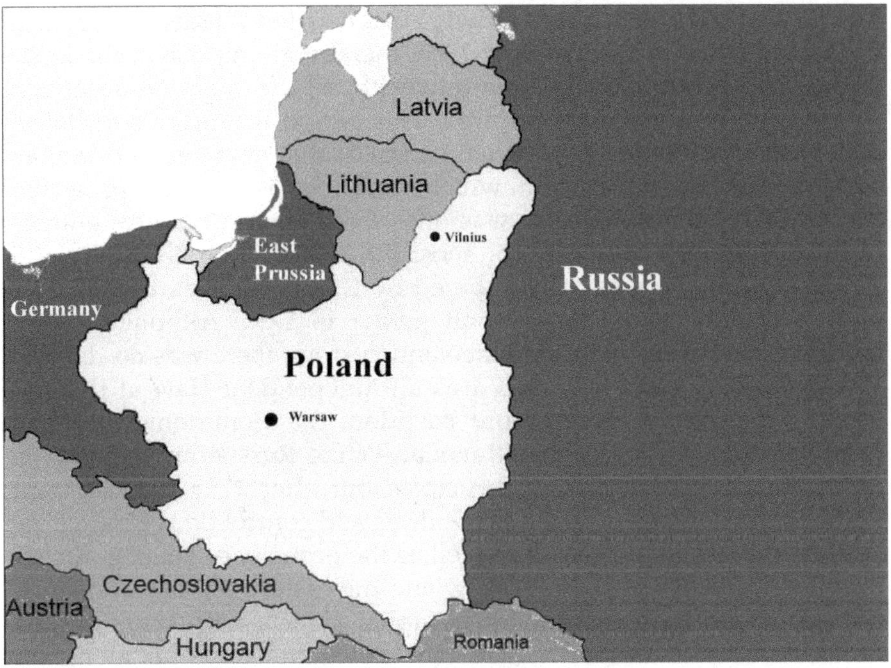

Europe 1922

Map showing the approximate area (circle) where Polish was the main language in 1914

The 12-year-old Polish queen Jadwiga had married Władysław-Jogaila, the Grand Duke of Lithuania in 1386, thereby giving rise to the long-lasting Polish-Lithuanian Commonwealth, which might be described as a sort of 'multinational empire'.[1] This period went down in Polish history as the 'Golden Age' when its political system evolved into an early democratic monarchy in which minorities' rights were protected by law. The Commonwealth was one of the biggest political entities in Europe as well as one of the most influential, both culturally and politically, until it was dismembered by Russia, Austria and Prussia after 1772 and ceased to exist altogether in 1795. Although Polish culture endured through language and custom, there was no defined Polish territory until it emerged as an independent state at the end of the First World War. Before partition, the Commonwealth had been governed by a Polish-Lithuanian-White Russian aristocracy on federalist and decentralised principles but after 1795 the Germans grabbed the resource-rich lands of Silesia and controlled the industrial centres of Posen and Breslau as well as the port city of Danzig, Russia exercised jurisdiction over Warsaw and the eastern regions of historic Poland, while Austro-Hungary occupied Galicia with its culturally important city of Lwów, mineral ore mines and oil fields along the Carpathian Mountain range. The Hohenzollern, Hapsburg and Romanov empires that, between them, had ruled the Polish people were quite relaxed about tolerating their thriving nationalist character both within the aristocracy and the peasantry. The kind of national patriotism that fired Polish identity that was emerging placed rather more emphasis upon the 'people' rather than a geographic region as the embodiment of Polishness. While the idea of independent statehood did exist in the minds of many, it was contemplated more in hope than expectation. This sense of collective identity prized real cultural values and proclaimed a vibrant, flourishing consciousness rather than any adherence to a romanticised, nostalgic past. One of the unfortunate effects of this emphasis on 'Polishness', when the country of Poland was granted independence in 1918, however, was that the new nation embodied a proud sense of self and an almost xenophobic reluctance to allow minority communities within its borders to participate fully in the political life of the country.

Throughout the years of partition and occupation, Polish elites, in various ways, had tried to promulgate a sense of nationhood within the population through various forms of cultural education and had made great efforts to maintain the Polish language in the school system. National pride resulted in tensions between the Polish and neighbouring Ukrainian communities, however, not only because of religious differences but also because of social disparities. Poles in the Russian Empire had remained proud of their aristocratic traditions but were given little political freedom. The upper classes were suppressed and, for the most part, felt 'bitter hatred' for their rulers, while the peasantry lived 'a wretched life' indifferent both to Polish and Russian masters.[2] The Ukrainian populations in the Russian Empire lacked any significant aristocratic component and its predominantly peasant culture was progressively and, with little resistance, subsumed by Russification. Where Poles lived alongside Ukrainians their relations became almost colonial in nature with Poles as colonisers and Ukrainians the colonised.

It was in Austro-Hungary where the Habsburgs had given the greater degree of freedom to all the various ethnic groups within its borders to maintain their own language, cultures and identities, hoping that differences between them would keep them divided and less likely to unite in revolt. While Poles generally found little under Habsburg rule worth protesting about, the state-sponsored movements to encourage the national consciousness of the Ruthenian (Ukrainian) populations of eastern Galicia, a territory long felt to be historically Polish, aroused a great deal of resentment. This region, with its capital Lwów, was to become the home of Ukrainian nationalism, despite more than half of its population considering itself to be Polish, and so became the focus of Polish-Ukrainian tensions. After the First World War with the dissolution of the Austro-Hungarian Empire and the Bolshevik revolution in Russia, both Poles and Ukrainians had hoped for independence and while the former were successful the latter were unable to realise their aims because of the internal divisions and lack of external support. Both nations disputed control of Lwów and the western Ukrainian lands, which were eventually incorporated into the Polish state in 1918. Ukraine up to this time had never been considered to be a political entity and Lwów had for four centuries up to 1772 been part of the Polish Kingdom before being swallowed up by Austro-Hungary.

The province of Galicia, between the Vistula River and the Carpathian Mountains stretching as far east as Brody, had been created in the late 1700s within the Austro-Hungarian Empire. It contained more than six nationalities but consisted mostly of Poles and Ukrainians. It achieved a measure of autonomy with its own parliament, with limited powers, in the 1860s and was allowed to establish several institutions and cultivate its own culture, customs and religion to become a centre of Polish national activity. It was here in a region where Polish political parties were operating freely, and Polish language was commonly used in education, administration and the judiciary, that separatist activists fleeing from the Russian authorities took refuge. Polish national celebrations like the anniversaries of the outbreaks of national uprisings or the passing of the Constitution of 3 May 1791 were celebrated uproariously. In contrast to the rest of the annexed Polish territories, the Austro-Hungarian Empire had a policy respecting local culture and religions on the understanding that all the groups in the empire respect Emperor Franz Joseph as the uniting element of such a large political entity. As a consequence, Polish political activism flourished and the first Polish and Ukrainian political parties gained parliamentary experience through representation in the Austro-Hungarian administration. From 1871 Polish was restored as the official language at both the province's universities in Kraków and Lwów.[3] International crises that erupted during the first years of the twentieth century made a pan-European war a real possibility and preparing for such an eventuality became a priority for Polish leaders such as Józef Piłsudski who, in 1908, founded the Union of Active Struggle (ZWC, *Związek Walki Czyn*) in Lwów. The aim of this organisation was to 'conduct the preparation ... for a future armed insurrection in the Russian zone of partition'.[4] Soon afterwards, paramilitary organisations started to emerge all over Galicia that provided military training for Polish youth preparing them to fight for independence.

By 1914, Eastern Europe was primed to explode with nationalistic fervour and it was the outbreak of the First World War that precipitated it. Prior to this, the question of Polish independence was not one that exercised the minds of the Great Powers but one that existed only for the Poles themselves.[5] The partitioning powers had never shown any willingness to consider the creation of an independent Polish state. When the three great empires that occupied Polish lands were brought down by the war, they left behind a myriad of inextricably mixed populations competing for dominance within disputed borders. Predominantly peasant nations with proud traditions but ruled by aristocrats who owned vast estates, they had been forced to defend themselves for centuries in the spaces separating Western Europe from the vast Asian lands from which invaders had swarmed all through history. When war broke out, however, Poles found themselves in the centre of a battleground as German and Russian armies clashed for the first time since 1762 and regional affiliations became uncoupled under the destabilising effects of war. Mass conscript armies were raised by the opposing forces, both of which tried to outbid the other for the 2 million Poles of conscription age.

The war found Poles on both sides of the battle lines fighting each other in a fratricidal catastrophe. On one side Piłsudski, with Austrian support, was declared commander-in-chief of a Polish National Government, albeit one without a country, and marched his forces into Kraków. He aligned himself to the Central Powers (Germany, Austria-Hungary, the Ottoman Empire and Bulgaria), to whose armies he sent volunteer Polish Legions. It was to the Austrians, however, that his main support went, and his primary effort was targeted against the Russians. Meanwhile, the Polish National Committee (PNC, *Komitet Narodowy Polski*) was formed in Warsaw under Roman Dmowski in cooperation with the Triple Entente countries (France, Britain and Russia) to unite the Polish lands and lead Poland toward regaining its independence. Piłsudski and Dmowski represented different sorts of Polishness and the political divisions they created left Poles in disarray and hindered progress towards independence, at least for the next four years.[6] Piłsudski carried the banner for the Polish Socialist Party (PPS, *Polska Partia Socjalistyczna*), which saw federalism as the way forward with its traditionalist, elitist philosophy of different ethnic groups coming together under the Polish flag. Dmowski had much humbler origins and was much more of a 'modern' Pole who sought to empower the masses in pursuit of a homogenous Polish identity to go along with the new state. His ideas centred on what he saw as the cultural core elements of the Polish people and extended the concept beyond national borders. He had no time for Piłsudski's idea of a new Polish-Lithuanian commonwealth. Differences between the two, who were forced to work together after the war, were to dominate Polish history for the next few years.

Józef Piłsudski had been born in Lithuania, the son of impoverished Polish aristocrats. In 1887, he had been swept up in Russian police operations to unmask the plotters who had tried to assassinate Tsar Alexander III and had spent five years in Siberian exile. After spending some time in England, he was committed to a mental hospital in St Petersburg, from which he escaped and fled to Japan. Back in Poland, he dabbled in revolutionary politics but the crushing of the 1907 revolution in Russia left him yearning for 'elite, disciplined organisation' that he swore to 'realise … or perish'.[7] To finance his ambitions for an independent Poland, he turned to crime and held up a mail train just outside Wilno in April 1908. For years he would bestride Polish life, but he had a complex character. He was 'a conspirator, not a statesman' whose first instinct in any difficult situation was to fight but above all he was a 'wayward, reckless, rude, vindictive, childish, taciturn and unpredictable' maverick whose political life would be 'strewn with blunders and failures'.[8]

Roman Stanisław Dmowski was born to working-class parents near Warsaw in 1864. Like Piłsudski he fell foul of the Russian police and spent five months in prison for political activism before being exiled in Latvia. His disdain for the Polish-Lithuanian Commonwealth with its reverence for nobility and tolerance of minorities, which he saw as weakening national identity, clearly illustrated the political differences between him and Piłsudski. Over time, Dmowski came to favour an accommodation with Russia to form an alliance to combat the threat from Germany.

On 6 August 1914, Piłsudski led his First Cadre Company into the area of Kielce, which the Russian army had evacuated, in the hope of breaking through to Warsaw and starting a nationwide revolution. He established Polish institutions in liberated towns and soon afterwards the Polish Legions were formed in Galicia subordinate to Austrian control. By the summer of 1915, the Legions had expanded to three brigades, totalling 20,000 to 25,000 soldiers. Piłsudski commanded the First Brigade and during the first two years of war, the Legions fought in Lesser Poland, the Eastern Carpathians, Lublin and Volhynia. At the same time, he set up the Polish Military Organisation (*Polska Organisacja Wojskowa*), an intelligence agency to carry out espionage and sabotage missions against Russia, whose forces were devastating whole swathes of Polish countryside with scorched earth tactics as German forces drove them back to the east. The Germans, however, also stripped the land of raw materials and machinery for its war machine but did allow a Polish administration to take control of justice and education. Piłsudski now saw Polish interests being better served by closer ties with Germany, whose banks had historically invested heavily in Polish industry.

In mid-1916, after the Battle of Kostiuchnówka, during which heroic Polish forces were heavily outnumbered by the Russians, and took very serious losses, Piłsudski called on the Central Powers to issue a guarantee of independence for Poland, which Emperors Wilhelm II of Germany and Franz Joseph of Austria were happy to do as they hoped to increase the number of Polish troops available to bolster German forces on the Western Front. On the following day, the Provincial Council of State was created, with Wacław Józef Niemojowski as its president, and Piłsudski as chairman of its Military Commission. In this role Piłsudski insisted that his men be deployed only against the Russians, but the German Military Governor Hans von Beseler took very little notice of his wishes, calling Piłsudski a 'military dilettante and a demagogue'.[9] The Germans showed no inclination to address the question of Polish independence but found themselves having to deal with it due to 'the fate of battles'.[10] They suggested various measures including the radical idea of deporting 16 million Poles into Russia and filling the vacated regions with German settlers to create a buffer zone. In the end Piłsudski set up a Regency Council but it had undefined territorial and constitutional rights, and found itself entirely subordinated to the German military authority.

Despite initial euphoria at the setting up of the Regency Council, there was disappointment that no agreement had been arrived at to define what the borders of the Polish state would be and there had been no discussion about who the future monarch of the new state would be. It soon became clear that the Central Powers' negotiators had been interested only in acquiring more troops and had no interest in the Polish question as such and, in subsequent months, where Polish institutions of public administration, such as the Provisional Council of State, the Regency Council, and even the government, were established they were treated as no more than advisory boards to the occupying authorities.

In 1915, when the Germans had taken Warsaw, Dmowski's PNC had been forced to move to Petrograd (St Petersburg). He soon became impatient with the lack of progress in talks with the Russians over Polish independence, which had foundered on the inconvenient reality that most Polish lands were under German occupation, and turned instead to the French for support to 'internationalise' the issue, but first he went to London. There he wasted no time in denigrating Piłsudski as 'pro-German' and promising to bring 500,000 Polish troops to fight for the Western Allies if they would support the creation of an independent Poland.[11] Neither France nor Britain, however, was ready to think of the Polish question as anything other than an internal matter for Russia but politics there were in flux as the first of the two Bolshevik revolutions swept through Russia in 1917 and forced Tsar Nicholas II to abdicate. The Bolsheviks promised an independent Poland but were in no position to deliver it and never actually defined what it understood by 'Poland'.

The introduction of US troops onto the Western Front and the February Revolution in Russia in 1917 fundamentally altered the dynamics of the war and the Western Allies, albeit reluctantly, stepped up the pressure on Germany by declaring in favour of an independent Poland. In September 1917, the French recognised Dmowski's Polish National Committee as the legitimate representative of the Polish state, with Britain, Italy and the US following suit by the end of the year but not without British reservations over the elevated role of Dmowski as putative leader of the Polish state. The 500,000 Polish troops turned out to be no more than 100,000 and these would later come under the command of Józef Haller, who had commanded Piłsudski's 3rd Legion when he arrived from Murmansk in October 1918.

Piłsudski now felt that it was time to take stock and reassess his decision to support the Central Powers. When von Beseler called for all Polish troops to swear an oath of loyalty that obliged them to transfer their allegiance from Austria to Germany, Piłsudski saw his chance to break away from the hold Germany had over the Poles and ordered his legionnaires to refuse. Despite von Beseler tempting Piłsudski with promises of 'power, fame and money', the Pole replied, 'Do you imagine for one moment that you will win the nation's confidence by hanging Polish insignia on each of the fingers of the hand which is throttling Poland?'[12] As a result, the 1st and 3rd Polish Legions were dissolved and the legionnaires from Russian-occupied territories were imprisoned in camps in Szczypiorno near Kalisz, in Beniaminów near Zegrze, and in Łomża, while the Austrian subjects were incorporated into the Austro-Hungarian army and sent to the Italian front. Only the soldiers of the 2nd Brigade, most of them Austrian subjects, swore an oath and continued to fight the Russians, alongside the Austro-Hungarian army, as the Polish Auxiliary Corps commanded by Józef Haller and Władysław Sikorski. Piłsudski and his chief of staff, Colonel Kazimierz Sosnkowski, were arrested by the Germans in Warsaw on the morning of 22 July 1917. Von Beseler now considered Piłsudski to be a major threat to peace and stability in the country and after the outbreak of the February Revolution in Russia in 1917 much of the fighting had ceased on the Russo Volhynia German front and it was generally accepted in Germany that there was no further necessity to feign solidarity with the Poles. Piłsudski and Sosnkowski were transferred to Gdansk, then Berlin, where they were separated but both incarcerated in the prison in Wilhelmstrasse in Spandau near Berlin. On 6 August 1917 they were again moved, again separately, to the fortress in Wesel on the Lower Rhine near the border to Holland. After only two weeks, as a result of protests by Piłsudski's supporters at the conditions there, he was transferred to Magdeburg.

The internationally famous concert pianist Ignacy Jan Paderewski had become a spokesman for Dmowski's Polish National Committee in Paris. His reputation, especially in the United States, had brought the Polish question to the attention of President Woodrow Wilson, who put his considerable political weight behind the movement for Polish independence. When an uprising broke out on 27 December

1918 in Poznań after a patriotic speech by Paderewski, First World War veterans led by Antoni Wysocki succeeded in taking control of most of the province fighting against the regular German army and irregular units such as the *Grenzschutz*. Fighting continued until the renewal of the truce between the Entente Powers and Germany on 16 February 1917. The uprising had a significant effect on the decisions in Versailles that granted Poland not only the area won by the insurrectionists but also major cities with a significant German population like Bydgoszcz, Leszno and Rawicz, as well as the lands that had historically been part of the Polish-Lithuanian Commonwealth. Paderewski was heralded as the new Polish chief of state by Dmowski; he went on to represent Poland at the Paris Peace Conference and signed the Treaty of Versailles on the country's behalf. President Wilson now took a great interest in plans for the post-war realignment of European borders. He set out his Fourteen Points for the 'autonomous development [of] the peoples of Austro-Hungary' with special attention to a new state 'inhabited by indisputably Polish populations'.[13]

The clamour for Poland's independence soon forced itself onto the agendas of the Triple Entente leaders as well. After the overthrow of the Tsar, Polish units had been created within the Russian army, but they had tried to remain neutral in the Russian Civil War between the White and Red armies. At this time, the Western Allies – Britain, France and Italy – began to accept the Poles as allies in a war that was far from over, so much so that in the summer of 1917 France had begun forming the Polish (Blue) Army made up of volunteers from Western Europe, the United States and Canada, as well as Polish PoWs from the German army, and this Blue Army moved east to engage German forces. France had long been a haven for Polish exiles, many of whom had fought in the armies of the Revolution and Napoleon had briefly fanned the flames of Polish nationhood with the short-lived Grand Duchy of Warsaw (1807–15). The French had made a secret deal with Russia in which they declared its ambitions for a completely independent Poland but, in reality, agreed that Poland would come under tight Russian control. This was hardly a recognition of Polish sovereignty, but it allowed the French to gain influence with the Poles and assure them of its support for independence.

During the year he spent in Magdeburg, Piłsudski was seen as a victim of German persecution and, as such, gradually became a symbol of the Polish struggle against the German occupation forces. Significantly, since he was *hors de combat* and outside the maelstrom of political disputes raging among the Poles, he was not put in the position of having to commit himself to either the Regency Council or to the Polish Wehrmacht (*Polska Siła Zbrojna*). Becoming more and more popular as a party leader, he was seen by many Poles not only as a military leader but also as a leader of the entire Polish people, not least because of a burgeoning reputation as an uncompromising fighter for independence. In view of the catastrophic situation in the country, the German Chancellor Prince Max of Baden sent Harry von Kessler, an officer of the Prussian cavalry, to Magdeburg to deliver a letter from the chief of staff on the Eastern Front, General Hoffmann, offering to release Piłsudski in exchange for assurances that German troops would be allowed to withdraw from the Eastern Front across Polish territory without interference. The offer was rejected because Piłsudski, who realised that large numbers of German troops on Polish soil would make the population uncomfortable, knew that time was now on his side, and he felt confident enough to call the German bluff. He had guessed correctly because, despite his refusal to comply with German demands, a decision was made to release him and Sosnkowski from prison on 7 November 1917. The Germans had enough to worry about apart from Poland as they turned inward to deal with the start of a communist uprising in Berlin. The prospect of Piłsudski reaching the highest office in the Polish state would increase significantly after his return from Magdeburg to Warsaw.

On 8 November 1917, one day after coming to power in Petrograd, Vladimir Lenin issued the Decree of Peace, in which he called for an immediate armistice and the start of peace negotiations with Germany and its allies. The armistice was signed at Brest-Litovsk, 200km east of Warsaw, on 15 December 1917 and peace talks between Russia and the four Central Powers began a week later. The German and Austrian delegations were headed by their foreign secretaries, Richard von Kühlmann and Count Ottakar Czernin, but an influential figure for the Germans was General Max Hoffman, chief of staff of the German army on the Eastern Front. Talaat Pasha represented the Ottoman Empire.

The lengthy negotiations that preceded the signing of the treaty allowed German troops to advance deep into the ethnically mixed region of western Gubernia, called Kresy (borderlands) by the Poles. The whole of Eastern Europe was now thrown into a state of utter chaos with the prospect of occupying forces withdrawing and creating the circumstances for nationalist movements in Lithuania, Belarus, and the Ukraine to take advantage and try to force the international community to recognise its right to independence. Paris, rocked by news of the Brest-Litovsk negotiations that threatened to result in 1 million German soldiers being transferred to the Western Front, lamented that 'this would cure France forever of an alliance with Russia'.[14]

During negotiations at Brest-Litovsk, the Russian delegation, headed by Leon Trotsky, vehemently advocated 'the rights of Polish people to self-determination' and tried to prolong the proceedings by taking full advantage of its time in the limelight to maximise the effectiveness of its propaganda campaigns. Trotsky, believing that he could exploit the fact that German armed forces were totally exhausted through war, called for a recess and returned to Petrograd, where he persuaded Lenin to adopt a policy of 'neither peace nor war' under which Russia would agree to a cessation of hostilities but commit itself to no peace treaty that might force it to give up territory or pay compensation. Count Czernin, in his diary, accused the Russians of 'falsity [and] cunning diplomacy … to oppress decent citizens … and then talk at the same time of the universal blessing of freedom'.[15] While Poland and other Slavic nations were clamouring for independence, Germany, not quite as ready to capitulate as Trotsky had believed, threatened to renew its advance into Russia and sent a German fleet to advance menacingly up the Baltic. It was Lenin who lost his nerve, fearing that if the German advance continued the Russian government would collapse and he argued for acceptance of whatever terms they were offering.

When negotiations resumed, the Russian delegation again tried to stall but the Central Powers had meanwhile concluded a separate peace with the nationalist Ukrainian delegation on 9 February 1918 and all other negotiations came to an abrupt halt while the Russians digested the news. For the Poles, the Ukrainian deal was seen as a sign that the Central Powers did not have the interests of Poland at heart and prompted a severance of ties with them and a move to further its ambitions of realising an independent Poland by appealing to the Triple Entente states instead. The last Polish divisions, no longer having any clear reason to continue fighting alongside the Central Powers, were withdrawn and dissolved. The diplomatic initiative paid immediate dividends when, in his speech addressing the US Congress in January 1918, President Wilson announced the reconstruction of an independent Poland with access to the sea, stating it as one of the conditions for a permanent peace.

At this point the Germans lost patience with Russian delaying tactics and renewed its military offensive in the east, which quickly saw benefits when there was an immediate request from Trotsky to resume peace talks. After all the prevarications, Hoffmann was in no mood for compromise and firmly presented the German demands, which included the establishment of independent states in the Polish and Baltic territories formerly belonging to the Russian Empire and Ukraine. On 23 February 1918, he gave the Russians an ultimatum of two days to resume talks and three more to conclude them. Despite the humiliating terms imposed by Germany, Lenin realised that the new Russian state was too weak to survive a continuation of the war and threatened to resign if the Politburo refused to accept the German proposals. Further pressure was applied to Russia when the French navy arrived in Odesa and British troops landed in Murmansk, while the Japanese sent soldiers up to Russia's Far Eastern border. Behind all this was the latent threat that the Germans might walk away from the peace talks again and resume its invasion of Russia.

The Peace Treaty of Brest-Litovsk was signed on 3 March 1918 in a triumph of German Imperial diplomacy over a helpless Russia, which was forced to give up close to half its European territory. Russian Poland, Lithuania and part of Latvia were ceded to Germany and Austria. The Ukraine, Finland, Estonia and the rest of Latvia were transformed into independent states under German protection. (It was common at the time to refer to 'the Ukraine' rather than its modern title of just 'Ukraine'). Bessarabia was to go to Romania and the Ottomans took the Armenian Kars Oblast areas in the South Caucasus. Russia lost huge areas of prime agricultural land, 80 per cent of its coal mines and half of its other industries. A follow-up agreement in August 1918 committed the country to pay 6 billion Reichsmarks in reparations. The Treaty was traditional in that it did not assign responsibility for the war and included a general waiver for all claims for compensation for the costs and damages of the fighting. Article 3 of the Treaty, rather optimistically given Russia's penchant for propaganda and the export of communism, stipulated that it must not meddle in the internal affairs of ceded territories and gave Germany and Austria-Hungary a free hand to deal with those territories as they saw fit.

At the beginning of October 1918, the Regency Council proclaimed the establishment of the Kingdom of Poland with access to the sea. On 28 October, in Kraków, the Polish Liquidation Committee of Galicia and Cieszyn Silesia was formed to maintain order in these former Austrian territories during the re-establishment of an independent Poland. Similar centres of power emerged in other cities of Western Galicia, while in Eastern Galicia, Lwów included, the Ukrainians tried to take control by declaring Lwów to be the capital of a new West Ukrainian People's Republic. Fierce fighting broke out between Polish and Ukrainian factions and continued well beyond the 11 November 1918 armistice. When the Poles eventually took control of the city, the *New York Times* reported looting and killings under the headline '1,100 Jews Murdered in Lwów Pogroms', although later reports put the figure at 64.[16] A leftist government under Ignacy Dasznski was created in Lublin on 6 November 1918, sparking fears of a Soviet-style revolution. As the Spanish flu pandemic began to take hold, members of the Polish Military Organisation started to disarm the occupying forces and all across the country local authorities began to fill the power vacuum they left but, in the Prussian partition, the Germans held firmly onto power.

The important city of Vilnius also became a focus of nationalistic fervour. Some German troops had remained in the area to fight the Bolsheviks and provided cover for Lithuanian and Belarusian activists to create their own states before the Russians could impose its authority. Anton Lutskevich had claimed the city for the Belarus National Council in March 1918 as it tried to recreate historic Lithuania under the Belarus flag. He was forced to abandon the city in December 1918, however, when the Red Army moved in but many activists stayed behind in Minsk to form the nucleus of what would become the Byelorussian Soviet Socialist Republic. Meanwhile, Lithuanian activists, with tacit German support, opposed Polish claims to Lithuanian territory. With peace talks now going on at Brest-Litovsk, the Lithuanian National Council (*Taryba*) declared independence and called for Polish troops to defend it against the advancing Red Army but failed to get help and was forced to evacuate Vilnius in January 1919. The city was declared the capital of the Lithuanian Soviet Socialist Republic. Piłsudski is reported to have wept at the news.[17] He reluctantly offered to recognise Lithuanian independence but only if it agreed to join Poland in a federation. The Lithuanians refused to consider such an idea.

Freed from his German captivity, Piłsudski had returned to Warsaw to 'find power lying in the streets'.[18] Without any connivance with the Western Powers or the PNC, he took over full civil and military authority from the Regency Council as chief of state on 11 November 1918 by occupying key strategic places like police headquarters and taking over arms warehouses from German troops. He guaranteed them safe passage home and in return, called on them to lay down their arms and not to provoke the Poles. To the Poles he said: 'Avoid bloody fights with German soldiers. Raids on garrisons are out of the question. Let them peacefully leave for their country after they hand over their weapons.' He was counting on the fact that the German soldiers stationed in Warsaw had seen enough of war and were more than eager to go home. In the afternoon, Polish troops began taking over the city's strategic locations, an operation that was carried out relatively peacefully. By the end of the day, most key places were in Polish hands. Five days later Piłsudski wrote to the Western Powers:

> As the commander-in-chief of the Polish Army, I hereby notify warfaring and neutral governments and nations of the existence of an Independent Polish State, encompassing all lands of united Poland ... The Polish State arises from the will of the entire nation and shall be based on democratic principles.

Amidst the collapse of all authority, Poland had created itself out of the void created when the partitioning powers simply left. The Germans had fled Warsaw and simply hoped that, with his authority, Piłsudski would end the chaos, and ensure the peaceful passage of German troops returning home from Russia. Dmowski called Piłsudski's action illegal. The Russians saw the embryonic state as a 'monstrous bastard'; the economist Milton Keynes thought it an 'economic impossibility' and the historian E.H. Carr called it a 'farce'. The British prime minister, David Lloyd George, who would never be a friend to Poland, was particularly disparaging, describing the country as 'drunk with the new wine of liberty supplied by her allies'. Rarely, said Norman Davies had 'a newly independent country been subjected to such eloquent and gratuitous abuse'.[19]

The armistice officially ending the First World War was agreed at Compiègne on the day that Piłsudski returned to Poland and it called for the German army in the east under Hoffmann to remain in position and withdraw 'only when the Allies shall consider this desirable'.[20] The German general, however, ignored this request and thwarted Allied hopes for his men to maintain order against the threat of Bolshevik occupation on the territories. The Poles responded by hastily organising an army to replace the German forces and drive the Russians out of Lithuania at the same time as Ukrainian forces tried to disperse the Red Army in Eastern Galicia. The Russian regime was gravely threatened by the combination of Piłsudski's Polish forces and the internal Russian counter-revolutionary forces led by Admiral Alexander Kolchak and General Anton Denikin, but their fears were not well founded since the Poles and Imperialist Russians, having diametrically opposed ambitions for Russia if they succeeded, could not find common cause. Indeed, the Polish government was trying to get Western financial support for a drive into the heart of Russia, but Britain and France were not yet ready to countenance that. Piłsudski's army drove the Russians back but there was no political consensus in Warsaw over what Polish war aims should be apart from the broad concept of liberating the 'north-east provinces of Poland and Vilnius'.

Meanwhile, Poland was fighting a number of wars concurrently. The West Ukrainian People's Republic had set itself up at Lwów claiming sovereignty over Eastern Galicia but the large Polish populations in the city defied them and called on Polish troops to bring the region under Polish control and become part of the new Polish state. French intervention tried to put an end to fighting but neither side would agree to a ceasefire and so a new Polish offensive began in May 1919 led by Haller at the head of his Blue Army, which had been equipped by France ostensibly to oppose the Bolsheviks. France called for a halt as Romania made its own move to claim the city of Stanislaviv. The Polish Blue Army advance was characterised by extensive looting and anti-Semitic violence. Piłsudski assumed command of the Polish forces in June 1919 and made a final assault pushing the exhausted Ukrainian forces back beyond the Zbruch River, after which the Western Allies recognised Polish control of Eastern Galicia but a move at the Paris Peace Conference to legitimise it was never implemented. After the war, over 100,000 people were placed in concentration camps by the Polish government. In many cases, prisoners were denied food and medical attention, and some starved, died of disease or committed suicide. The victims included not only Ukrainian soldiers and officers but also priests, lawyers and doctors who had supported the Ukrainian cause.

The Polish programme was affected by Piłsudski-Dmowski dualism. Piłsudski's approach was 'federalist' with strong central control, while Dmowski's was 'incorporationist' with regions given powers to make their own decisions. Piłsudski's federal scheme was built around a strong claim to historical legitimacy and, since he saw Poland as being too weak to stand alone against Russia, envisaged a federation between the nations of Poland, Lithuania, Belarus and Ukraine that would cover approximately the same geographical area as the Polish-Lithuanian Commonwealth had done and be powerful enough to withstand Russian aggression. Historically the Commonwealth had been characterised by 'the length to which it went in trying to protect individual and group rights within the confederation'.[21] Ukrainians, and especially the Belarusians, were tempted by Piłsudski's vision, which offered them their own ministries, treasury and coinage that they had never enjoyed before. It would also ensure strategic and military advantages that would protect them from the imperialist ambitions of their Russian and German neighbours, but the idea had been weakened by the political, diplomatic, and military setbacks Poland suffered since the end of the war. It had also failed to get the support of the Great Powers, and it had lost the battle for the hearts and minds of the East Central European population. Furthermore, Piłsudski's federalism bore an uncomfortable resemblance to Polish imperialism and the whole idea of federalism would not survive the Riga Peace Conference.[22] Dmowski, in contrast, saw a centralised Polish state, with its eastern border encompassing Upper Silesia and parts of East Prussia transferred from Germany.

The defeat of Germany and Austro-Hungary, and the collapse of Imperial Russia, encouraged Poland to seek independence under its prime minister, Ignacy Paderewski, who called for territory as far east as Lithuania and German-held territory in the west and along the Baltic Sea to become part of the country. Paderewski had large popular support but lacked experience in politics and diplomacy. He was actually despised by Britain for his anti-Semitic beliefs.[23] In the cases of Silesia and the Baltic coast, he argued that the areas had a majority of Polish speakers and therefore should be Polish. In the east, however, in the case of Galicia he argued that historic Polish cultural institutions, such as universities and churches, proved that the land should belong to Poland despite Poles being in the minority. Two traditions vied for dominance in foreign policy. One, which was basically anti-Russian, saw Poland's destiny as one of expansion and consolidation in the eastern lands of Lithuania, Russia and Ukraine that had once been part of the Polish Commonwealth, while the other looked nervously to the west where Germany, albeit unmanned and boiling with revolutionary fervour after its defeat in war, continued to be the focus of attention. This faction saw Russia as a restraining force on a resurgent Germany and a huge market for trade.[24]

The support of the Western Powers at the Paris Peace Conference, in the form of military supplies, was essential for Poland's efforts to defeat the Bolsheviks and to force German troops to vacate Polish soil. Allied support for Piłsudski's federal solution was strong, with the US declaring that 'Poland and Lithuania are bound together by so many ties and common economic interests that their former political union, lasting for many centuries, should be restored'[25], and the French were happy to support anything that helped to keep Germany in check. The leader of the Polish delegation, however, was Dmowski, who strongly opposed what he regarded as Piłsudski's federal fantasies. He had no faith that Belarus and the Ukraine were sufficiently mature politically for independence and resisted any move to bring them into a federalist union with Poland. His idea was for a partition of East Central Europe between Poland and Russia, in the process of which Poland would be granted only those lands where the Polish language and culture dominated. As a result, the Conference got mixed messages and the delegates were given little incentive to take them seriously, calling the Poles 'a theatre of perpetual intrigues between Germany and Russia [and] a perpetual occasion of European strife'.[26]

Instead, the British looked to the White Russian forces they hoped to manipulate to implement their Eastern European strategy, which at one point looked as if it favoured Poland becoming a province of a new Russia liberated from Bolshevik rule. They argued that any East Central European federation would be little more than weak Austria-Hungary by another name, which would fall prey to German domination in time. The Baltic States were promised to the Whites as part of a post-civil war Russian state that would also include Belarus and the Ukraine, which gave White Russian General Nikolai Yudenich, Kolchak and Denikin little incentive to enter into any talks with Piłsudski.

At that stage the Polish government controlled only Congress Poland and Western Galicia. In the east the Ukrainians, having proclaimed its own republic, battled the Poles until Haller drove them out in April 1919, forcing the leaders to set up a government-in-exile in Vienna. Three million Ukrainian speakers and 1 million Jews now became citizens of Poland, which most of them resented. Protests and rioting were brutally put down. Farther east, the Poles clashed with the Bolsheviks, who were advancing into Belarusian and Lithuanian lands. Both Dmowski and Piłsudski adopted militarism and expansion as core values of the new Polish state, agreeing that the urgent necessity was for Poland to win disputed territory from its neighbours by force if necessary.[27]

The Wielkopolska Uprising, which had erupted in December 1918 when Polish insurgents took the city of Poznán, was followed just one month later by Poland fighting a short war with Czechoslovakia over the Teschen, in south-east Silesia, which the Czechs had annexed. Between November 1918 and July 1920, the Czech and Polish states fiercely contested dominion over the province, some 2,000km^2 of land far from both Prague and Warsaw. This former Duchy of the Austro-Hungarian Empire that housed hugely important rich coal mines, centres of metallurgical and textile manufacture and a vitally important strategic rail link through the Carpathian mountains between Oderberg, Kraków and Slovakia, historically belonged to the Czechs but was mostly inhabited by Poles. It was strategically located between the Czech lands and Slovakia close to Germany. An agreement was reached between 28 October 1918, when the Czechoslovakian Republic was proclaimed, and 7 November 1918 when Polish independence was declared, in which the region was partitioned in expectation of a formal treaty but on 23 January 1919, Czech troops, wearing the uniform of Entente forces to give the impression of legality, invaded large parts of the Polish areas while Polish troops had withdrawn to relieve Lvov. The Poles were further inconvenienced by the fact that they were struggling far more than were the Czechs over establishment of its new state and were particularly vulnerable to pressure. The Czechs rejected Polish claims based on ethnographic criteria given that its whole state was composed of a multitude of minorities. The Entente intervened and enforced the Paris Protocol, which created a control commission, but the underlying tensions prevented a resolution of the dispute. France supported Czech opposition to the introduction of a plebiscite and managed to delay progress until the Spa Conference, when the Entente Powers effectively recognised Czech control of the occupied areas. In the maelstrom of regional conflicts that pervaded Eastern Europe after the end of the First World War, French marshal, Ferdinand Foch, was particularly enthusiastic to utilise Czech forces as a 'dyke against anarchy and bolshevism'.[28] Because he relied on Allied support in the battle against the Red Army in the Russo-Polish War, a humiliated Paderewski had little choice but sign up to the deal on 31 July 1919.

Despite having the cloak of democratic and idealist norms, the resolution imposed by the Entente Powers was 'neither consensual nor compromise' and would persist as a running sore between Czechoslovakia and Poland and a 'powder keg for future conflict'.[29] The settlement spawned enduring animosity between the two countries and became an obstacle to cooperation, but there was much that divided them apart from that. They differed over their attitude towards Russia, who Poland saw as a constant threat but who the Czechs regarded as vital to its security to counteract German and Austrian power. What they really wanted was reconciliation between Poland and Russia to promote Eastern European stability. Meanwhile, Polish forces were taking on the Ukrainians over Galicia and Volhynia.[30] This was a direct continuation of the political contest between Galician Poles and Ukrainians that had started seventy years earlier, in 1848. In November 1918, Ukrainians seized power throughout Eastern Galicia but the Poles refused to accept it as a fait accompli and in Lwów Poles rose up against the Ukrainian state. Street battles in Lwów soon escalated into a fully-fledged Polish-Ukrainian war. Operations lasted until July 1919, when the Ukrainian Galician Army was forced out of west and into east-central or Dnieper Ukraine, formerly part of Russia. This Polish occupation of Eastern Galicia amounted to the destruction of the very foundations on which an independent Ukrainian state might have been built in the post-First World War period.

President Wilson directed his team at the Paris Peace talks to draw borders based on the dominant language of the people in a given area but Britain did not support this approach, fearing that Poland would appropriate too much of Germany's important natural resources and industry in the east and Britain wanted Germany left in a relatively strong economic position so that it would be able to pay restitution for the war and to avoid a communist uprising, like the one in Russia. No aspect of the Versailles negotiations divided opinion more than the German-Polish boundary issue. Dmowski insisted that the Polish Corridor (also known as the Danzig Corridor; known as *Polnischer Korridor* in German and as *Pomorze, Korytarz polski* in German) separating East Prussia from Germany would be bitterly resented and would stimulate revanchism in Germany, which he saw as the greatest threat, while leaving Poland militarily weak. He proposed independence for East Prussia, which might have improved Poland's defensive position but would never be acceptable to a Germany that was already primed to lose so much.

Count Ulrich Brockdorff-Rantzau, the German Minister of Foreign Affairs at the Paris Peace talks, made a number of miscalculations. He failed to appreciate in full the ramifications of his negotiating position by harbouring unrealistic aspirations. An 'arrogant aristocrat, confident that his background, education and twenty-five years of diplomatic experience gave him a special right to conduct diplomacy',[31] he took the somewhat high-handed view that it would be perfectly reasonable to reject any peace treaty if it proved too burdensome for Germany. In February 1919, however, he was realistic enough to tell the Weimar National Assembly that Germany must concede the right of Poland to exist but could retain a hold over its economy by restricting its access to the Baltic.

Danzig was a freeport at the mouth of the Vistula River in which Poland had port and rail concessions but relied on good relations with the port administration. Here was a choke point that could be used to bring pressure to bear by making sure that the theoretically neutral Danzig authorities were under German control. Brockdorff-Rantzau's main diplomatic thrust was to unite Poland and Germany in friendship in the naive belief that the new Germany would be hailed by the Allies as the architects of German democracy and a very useful ally against the common enemy of Bolshevism. The first Weimar coalition cabinet led by Phillip Scheidemann, of which Brockdorff-Rantzau was a member was a melange of centre-left Social Democrats, left-wing

German Democrats and Independents that had no unifying political philosophy and precious little experience in diplomacy. It failed completely to understand the importance of the Polish question in relation to German affairs and seemed quite oblivious to the sacrifices likely to be demanded of Germany at Versailles. Few were able to challenge Brockdorff-Rantzau's position, which essentially gave him a free hand to conduct German foreign policy as he saw fit.

Although there was a tacit ceasefire, German–Polish friction was rife along what Foch had designated as the demarcation line between them. The French had made great efforts to intervene in Romania and southern Russia in support of Denikin but low morale and war-weariness as well as a reluctance to deploy the North African colonial troops in the bitter Russian winter meant that its forces were never able to adequately undertake the tasks that they were set. French troops that had landed at Odesa were frustrated by the lack of coordination between anti-communist forces, whose ranks seemed top heavy with officers and generally lacking in good fighting men, as the Bolsheviks marched towards Kyiv. It appeared unlikely that anything was going to stop the Bolshevik advance and an attack against Poland seemed imminent. General Haller's Polish army in France was needed urgently and Foch wanted to transport them by sea to Danzig but there were not enough ships available, and furthermore the Germans feared that if Haller landed in Danzig, his army would immediately occupy the city. A compromise was arrived at whereby Haller's army was allowed to cross Germany by land but its transit was uncomfortable, accompanied all the way by the threat of conflict between the Polish troops and German populations they passed through.

In May 1919 the Germans cried foul when they saw that Haller, having arrived in Poland, was concentrating his troops along the German frontier and that reliable sources predicted an imminent Polish attack on Posen and Upper Silesia. They reminded Foch that the German government had permitted the passage of Haller's army only after the Allies had pledged that Poland would not undertake any warlike actions against Germany. If Polish forces invaded the Reich, Germany would respond with force but was aware that, in view of the Paris negotiations, it must not allow Haller to provoke German troops to reckless actions that would be hugely counter-productive. The French insisted on claiming that most of Haller's troops were along the Ukrainian front lined up against the Bolsheviks. In April 1919, reports from the east indicated a noticeable immigration of Polish families into areas claimed by both Poland and Germany. German officials realised the importance of this immigration for any future plebiscites and complained bitterly about it. Plebiscites were becoming the accepted way to resolve boundaries where an ethnically mixed population disputed them but while they wore the mantle of authority, they did little to dispel hostility on the ground. Another disturbing factor was the growing number of young Polish men of military age entering West Prussia. The government and the army decided to try to halt further Polish immigration into German territories, while urging the delegation at Paris to keep in mind the section of its official instructions demanding a one-year residence requirement for voting in any plebiscite in the eastern territories.

When the terms of the Treaty were delivered to the Hall of Mirrors at Versailles on 7 May 1919, the German delegation was shocked by its severity and threatened to withdraw troops from the Russian front to line up against Poland. Brockdorff-Rantzau was instructed to inform the Western Allies that the terms were 'intolerable and unrealisable', while the German government urged German people to resist the 'dismemberment of Germany'.[32] Brockdorff-Rantzau wanted to agree to the German-Polish boundaries on condition that plebiscites were carried out in the ceded territories but the German diplomatic corps, hoping for support from the French, was more concerned with retaining densely populated coal mining and industrial centres of Upper Silesia that might just return a majority vote for Poland in any plebiscite. Unfortunately, his position was compromised by his being barely on speaking terms with Matthias Erzberger, the leader of the German delegation at the negotiations, who would be assassinated in August 1921 for his part in signing the Versailles Treaty. The Germans claimed that the region had never been considered Polish for many centuries and its incorporation into the German state would play a huge part in financing German war reparation payments. The separation of Upper Silesia from Germany, they said, would 'endanger the peace of Europe and the world'.[33] In principle, they rejected all of the proposals to cede territory to Poland but Germany's objections to the Danzig Corridor, based upon historical relationships or economic necessity, were dismissed. Germany's insistence on a land bridge between East and West Prussia weakened its argument in opposing the Polish occupation of the Danzig Corridor, which was an essential link between central Poland and the Baltic. If guaranteed rail transit and port facilities were adequate to give Poland access to the Baltic, guaranteed rail rights should be adequate to connect East and West Prussia.

Hostility towards Germany was increasing due to Erzberger's failure to curb Brockdorff-Rantzau's arrogant and cynical excessive use of propaganda as argument and Germany's overall apparent misreading of its parlous state and lack of realistic negotiating initiatives, which were interpreted as merely trying to evade the issues. The Allies had won the war and were committed to restoring an independent Poland with secure access to the Baltic. By failing to understand the necessary consequences of defeat, by outwardly accepting the principle of self-determination while trying to evade its consequences, by deliberately stimulating public opposition to territorial losses, the German government of 1919 made its own important contribution to the failure of the Versailles settlement.[34]

Chapter 2

THE RUSSO-POLISH WAR

> Bolshevism is a disease which is peculiar to Russia. It will never grow deep roots in any countries which are not entirely Russian.
>
> Józef Piłsudski

After denouncing the humiliating Treaty of Brest-Litovsk that the Russians had been forced to sign in order to give more attention to fighting the Whites, they took the first available opportunity to vent their anger and seek retribution for lost lands. The Red Army began advancing into the borderlands gradually being evacuated by the Germans accompanied by Bolshevik teams that sought to establish Soviet republics all across Eastern Europe from the Baltic to the Black Sea. There were clashes between the Red Army and the Polish local self-defence units and regular troops defending Minsk. Vilnius in 1914 had been, culturally, a Polish city with a 40 per cent Jewish population, although its culture varied from that in, say, Warsaw, with most of the land in the surrounding province under Polish ownership. The fall of the Russian Empire opened up possibilities for the creation of Polish and Lithuanian states, both of which claimed Vilnius, but on 6 January 1919, the Red Army occupied the city and on 13 February 1919, the first armed clashes between Russian and Polish forces took place near Bereza Kartuska. A day later further engagements took place in the south-east of Grodno near the town of Vostochnyy Most on the Niemen river (also known as the Nemunas river) in Belarus and it is these skirmishes that are considered to have been the very beginnings of the Russo-Polish War.[1]

The Russo-Polish War was quite separate from the Russian Civil War and neither was the Polish campaign any part of a combined operation by the Western Allies to crush Bolshevism. Piłsudski saw it as a struggle to prevent Russian control of those areas he saw as rightly belonging to a greater Polish-controlled federation of states. For Lenin the war became a vehicle for the export of communism westward reaching out to the proletariats of capitalist Western democracies. It broke out as both sides rushed to fill the administrative vacuum left when the German forces withdrew after Versailles.

At this time, the Ukrainian People's Republic was in conflict with Russia also, but the West Ukrainian People's Republic, despite its formal unification with the Ukrainian People's Republic, retained a separate army (Ukrainian Galician Army) and a government headed by Yevhen Petrushevych, which was at war with Poland, but not Russia. This meant that the Russo-Polish War was fought only in the region north of Pripyat in Belarus, in the Vilnius region and in Latvian Latgale, hence the Poles were able to avoid clashes with Denikin's counter-revolutionary forces that had been weakened by General Nikolai Yudenich's failure to hold Petrograd and Admiral Kolchak's calamitous defeats at the hands of the Red Army commander Mikhail Tukhachevsky in the Urals.

In February 1919, Allied intelligence intercepted the text of an agreement between the Ukrainian forces fighting against the Poles and the commander of the German XXI Corps currently retreating from the East. This clearly showed German-Ukrainian cooperation against Poland, which was a violation of the terms of the 11 November 1918 ceasefire. This left Poland threatened on three sides by the Bolsheviks, Germans and Ukrainians.

Lenin, Trotsky, Stalin and the Red Army leadership had high hopes that post-Versailles turmoil had so destabilised the traditional order in Eastern Europe that Hungary, Romania and even Germany would prove vulnerable to insurrection and communist control. It was against Poland, however, that the Russians were forced to act when Piłsudski challenged the validity of the Curzon Line, marking the temporary separation of Polish and Red Army forces, by taking Vilnius deep inside the Russian zone on 21 April 1919. This was the Polish general's first attempt to take control of the Baltic States under a Polish federation. Piłsudski offered to allow Vilnius to choose its own government, but Dmowski condemned the move, claiming that it was 'absurd' to think of Vilnius as anything but a Polish city. The Lithuanians on the other hand rejected all calls for the city to be anything other than Lithuanian ethnic territory regardless of what the city's population wanted. Piłsudski put the issue behind him and concentrated on fighting the Russians, believing that victory there would bring its own long-term solution for Vilnius.

In April 1919, Poland launched an offensive against Red Army forces in Lithuania and Belarus, taking Baranovichi, Pinsk, Vilnius, Navahrudak and Luninets, and then Minsk, Bobruisk and Barysaw. Lithuanian forces, at first, were not hostile even when the Poles took Vilnius but when, in August 1919, Piłsudski tried and failed to overthrow the existing Lithuanian government of Prime Minister Mykolas Sleževičius to force an alliance with Poland, relations became soured. By November 1919, the Poles had advanced as far as Lepel, Kamien and Ushachy, and in the following months moved west of Vitebsk. The Foch Line was established as a temporary demarcation line between Poland and Lithuania that left Vilnius on the Polish side. At this point Piłsudski halted his advance, fearing that further pressure on the Bolsheviks would be to Denikin's advantage as his forces advanced on Oryol, Tula and Moscow, and he was anxious to avoid giving any help to the Whites. It may well be the case that by refusing to support Denikin at this time he was instrumental in saving the Bolshevik revolution and allowed it to pursue its messianic strategy of exporting revolution to neighbouring countries with the aim of both strengthen its cause and reducing the level of capitalist support for the counter-revolutionary White Russian forces. Bolshevik philosophy insisted that it was through war, when social structures came under the greatest pressure, that revolution found its most fertile environment. Tukhachevsky expounded it clearly when he said that 'over the dead body of Poland lies the shining path to worldwide conflagration'.[2] Already by the end of 1919, Russian troops had held off Piłsudski and occupied large areas of Byelorussia and Lithuania, showing no inclination to halt their slow, inexorable march westwards.

In Poland, Paderewski's administration had fallen to Skulski, which strengthened Piłsudski's position but he still could not persuade the British government, who were happy to give him the support he was counting on to strengthen Poland's defensive capability, to provide the means for them to launch an offensive campaign. Instead, it was the French who came to the rescue when, in early April 1920, they sent General Paul Henrys to Poland to head the French military mission and assume *de facto* command of the Polish army as its chief of staff. Piłsudski welcomed the support but would not have his soldiers led into battle by a French general, so Henrys had to make do with being '*adjoint au Chef de l'État, generalissime de l'Armée Polonaise*'.[3] His mission, however, did bring with it over French 400 officers, who carried out important functions such as military advisors and instructors.

The Polish troops had advanced deep into Belarus and Piłsudski spoke in Minsk about bringing freedom to its people. In Eastern Galicia,

General Joseph Barthélemy, who headed another French mission, called for a ceasefire between the Poles and the Galician Ukrainians, who had been squabbling since November 1919. The French had important economic stakes in the region, especially in the oil industry, and were anxious to bring calm to the region by supporting the Polish advance to the river Zbrucz, the old frontier between Russia and Austro-Hungary forcing the Ukrainian Galician Army to retreat into Ukraine proper. Barthélemy justified the Polish advance on strategic grounds to establish a contiguous front against the Bolsheviks from the north to the south. In Ukraine, Denikin's White Army took Kyiv in August 1920 but could not hold it against the Bolsheviks, at which point the nominal head of the Ukrainian separatist government, Symon Petliura, turned to the Poles for help.

Piłsudski considered a Russian proposal for peace talks that included far-reaching concessions on the part of the Russians, but he chose to play a strong hand by keeping his forces in place until the Russians agreed to desist agitating for revolution within the Polish forces. As an incentive, he assured Moscow that he had, and never would have, any interest in giving support to Denikin's White Russian forces to undermine the Bolshevik administration. For their part, Trotsky and the Russian foreign minister, Georgy Chicherin, got Politburo approval to negotiate an armistice with the Poles but were less than forthcoming with terms that Piłsudski was able to accept and caused him to reconsider, fearing that agreement to the Russian terms might endanger Polish relations with France. He turned belligerent and, in December 1919, threatened that, although he had no wish to allow '[White] Russian reactionaries to triumph', if Lenin would not agree his terms the Poles would 'pick up the glove' and fight, which would inevitably be to Denikin's advantage.[4]

By the time General Edward Śmigły-Rydz (aka Rydz-Śmigły) led his Polish troops into Kyiv, the capital of the Ukraine had changed hands perhaps a dozen times and the only government that had appeared to possess any real power gathered around enthusiastic and vigorous national elements was that of Petliura. Piłsudski offered the Russians terms that would leave the Ukraine in Polish hands but unsurprisingly it was rejected, leaving him three options; to dig in along his current line, which would mean the abandonment of Vilnius, Grodno and Volhynia; come to terms with the Bolsheviks on lesser terms, which invited them to continue their provocative campaign to stir up revolution in Poland; or give full support to Petliura and the creation of a strong ally against Russia, which was the one he chose.

The Russian line was weakly held with Semyon Mikhaylovich Budenny's 1st Cavalry engaged in the Northern Caucasus against the diminishing White forces now retreating into the Crimea. Out of necessity, the Russians had agreed to exploratory talks with the Poles in July 1919 in a lodge in the Białowieża forest dealing with such matters as hostage exchanges but behind this façade, Russian commanders Sergey Kamanev and Vladimir Gittis were making plans to bring their northern and southern forces together for an attack against Polish forces in the area of Minsk. After long interruption, talks were resumed in December 1919 and concentrated on peace and diplomatic relations. The Red Army had now seen off Denikin's White Army and set their sights on exporting the revolution. They suggested making the peace talks official but Piłsudski rejected the move fearing Russian perfidy. 'Lenin,' he said, 'will not hesitate to break even the most solemn word.'[5] He warned the Russians that if the Red Army attacked Petliura the Poles would defend him, but this did not deter the Russians, who poured across the border into the Ukraine. Piłsudski was preparing for war in the spring. Responding to Russian peace offers, the Polish foreign minister, Stanislas Jan Patek, went to Paris and London to canvas the views of the Western Allies. Britain and France saw the Polish advance into the Ukraine as pure imperialism and were critical of Polish intransigence.

In February 1920, a German diplomat in Berlin received information suggesting that the Red Army, which appeared to be concentrating its forces around Kyiv, was, in fact, planning operations around Minsk aiming for an advance towards Warsaw in March 1920 to coincide with internal insurrection by the Polish Socialist Party (PPS). Germany was encouraged by Russian delegates to make preparations to join in the attack on Poland but evidence suggests that the Russians, at this stage, were more concerned with dissuading Germany from joining in a Western Alliance to smash Bolshevism than actually attacking Poland. Indeed at the end of 1918, Chicherin had sent a note to Patek, declaring that the 'Soviet government did not enter into any agreements or pacts with Germany … aimed directly or indirectly against Poland … which would violate Poland's independence and her territorial integrity.' He offered to hold peace talks, an advance that Patek rebuffed.[6]

By March 1920, Lenin was becoming seriously concerned about a Polish attack, however, and he felt the need to threaten Poland with the ultimatum that if it remained silent on peace proposals, they would 'suffer and never forget it'. Trotsky thought that the Poles were manoeuvring to appear the aggrieved party to engender Western support and argued for an intensification of political propaganda both within Poland and the wider European community. Meanwhile, Russian military plans were drawn up for action on the Belarusian front and the situation was approaching the point where war would become an inevitability.

The Poles responded by talking of peace while preparing for war. Piłsudski harboured ambitions to turn Belarus and the Ukraine into self-governing states which, together with Lithuania, would form a federation under Polish leadership with legal status acknowledged by the Western Powers. His stance became ever more demanding of Russian concessions, which diplomatic observers such as the US Envoy, Hugh Gibson, were convinced would never be acceptable to Moscow and would indeed be impossible to implement with many parts of Belarus and the Ukraine already under communist rule.

Eventually Piłsudski responded positively to Russian diplomatic notes on 27 March 1920 and suggested a meeting at Borisov, a small town in Belarus, to open negotiations but pointedly suggested a ceasefire only at this location and nowhere else along the battle front. Sometime earlier, Piłsudski had decided to improve the Polish military position by launching an attack on Mozyr and Kalinkowicki to separate the Russian southern and northern fronts. The choice of Borisov was a provocation to the Russians because it was here that their forces were concentrated and agreement to the ceasefire would weaken their military position significantly. They suggested Grodno or Bialystok, to which Piłsudski disdainfully replied on 26 April 1920 by ordering his forces to resume their advance into the Ukraine with whose military leadership he had, two days previously, already agreed in a secret agreement to recognise Ukrainian independence in return for an understanding that Polish and Ukrainian forces would combine against Russia under Polish command.

On 21 April 1920, the Poles had signed the Treaty of Warsaw with the Ukrainian People's Republic Directorate in which the Ukraine gave up Eastern Galicia, while Poland officially recognised the Ukrainian People's Republic, promising its support in its war for independence and recognition as a sovereign state. The appropriate military arrangements were concluded three days later but the alliance came at a time when the Ukraine was already exhausted after three years of revolution and civil war and it was too late to be of any great use to Piłsudski. The Treaty was not a partnership of equals; rather, it attempted to establish an independent Ukraine under Polish influence. By the terms of the Treaty, Petliura was forced to sign away Ukrainian claims to Eastern Galicia and Volhynia. The agreement was very unpopular with the Ukrainian community, many of whom considered it to be a betrayal of their homeland and Piłsudski's faith in Petliura proved to be misplaced. Ukrainian public support failed to materialise around him in a way that might have helped Piłsudski's cause.[7]

Władisław Grabski, at the time Polish Minister for Agriculture, resigned in protest and Dmowski saw only advantage for his party if, as was assumed, the alliance ended in disaster and he also refused to support it. On 29 April 1920, the Poles defined their war aims as the rooting out of Russian imperialism and ensuring that 'the populations [not of Russian nationality] remain separate from Russia'.[8] The Russians, however, had ambitions to generate class warfare and revolution within Poland, and so on 5 May 1920 Moscow appealed to the Polish workers and peasants to revolt. However, Trotsky's associate Karl Radek, real name Karol Sobelsohn, thought that premature. He warned that there was deep-seated mistrust of Russia in Poland and only a full-scale communist revolution that removed the reactionary classes would allow Russians and Poles to live peacefully side-by-side. Trotsky agreed with his acolyte Radek that the revolution could only start when the war ended. Both urged that communist propaganda within the Polish armed forces should be intensified against the 'shameless bandits of Polish imperialism'.[9]

When the Poles moved into the Ukraine, after two months of preparations in which the French mission took an active part, the population, never sympathetic to the Poles at the best of times, was less than welcoming with memories still raw of fighting them in Eastern Galicia. Although Piłsudski had signed an alliance with Petliura on 21 April 1920, in which he promised self-determination to the Ukraine under Petliura's leadership with agreed borders, the Ukrainian army that had been promised turned out to be a little more than 30,000 men. This did little to balance the large Russian forces massing in the north, but the combined Polish-Ukrainian forces retook Kyiv from the Red Army on 8 May 1920. The British politician George Renwick followed the Poles into the city and found a 'formerly bright and prosperous city in an indescribable condition of filth and desolation'.[10] The Poles advanced south of Kyiv into Podolia and towards Odesa but Russian reinforcements of troops from the Urals and the interior, including the formidable Budenny's 1st Cavalry and a number of mercenary Mongolian units, moved quickly to Dnieper and Dniester on 18 May 1920 and launched a counterattack between the Dvina River and Borisov, following up with further waves over the next days along a 90-mile front from Belarus to Brest.

The main Russian force was to be the XVth Army, under General Kork, driving towards Vilnius with the XVIth, under Nikolai Sollogub, on its flank moving in the direction of Minsk. Sergeyev's northern group was poised to cross the Dvina and strike at the Polish rear, with mobility being the key to success, but the supply chain was becoming severely stretched. Kork attacked on 14 May 1920 but Sollogub was delayed for three days by logistical issues. Kork was fairly well established across the Berezina by 21 May but unable to advance further without reinforcements. The Poles hit back and broke through on 2 June 1920, advancing some 20 miles and shattering the Russian 3rd and 12th divisions in the process. Further south the Red Army failed to break the Poles around Kyiv, where the battle front saw much hard fighting. Polish Kosciusko Squadron aircraft drove back a Russian flotilla trying to enter the city on the Dnieper as the whole Russian front was threatened with being overwhelmed. Stalin was despatched from Moscow to the front to stiffen resolve, with his very presence there threatening execution for commanders who failed to hold the line.

Piłsudski returned to Warsaw to a hero's welcome and proceeded to draw up peace terms, which he expected to offer Moscow before too long. This proved to be embarrassingly premature, however, since the Ukrainian General Ivan Omelianovych-Pavlenko, in cooperation with the Polish 6th Army, failed to hold the Dniester line against Budenny's cavalry army, which had been massively reinforced with artillery. On 5 June 1920, an artillery and machine gun barrage preceded Budenny's attack with Kork and Sollogub, now resupplied, in support. By 9 June Kyiv was threatened and the Poles were in full retreat. The Red Army smashed through Polish lines west of Byelaya Tsirko taking Berdichev and Fastova and entering Jitomir on 12 June. Piłsudski ordered General Śmigły-Rydz to evacuate Kyiv and the Poles were driven towards disaster in the Pripet Marshes but Budenny's Cavalry was halted and attacked by aircraft from Korostyshev as the Poles stabilised their lines along the Berezina.

They were helped to some extent by the White Army's General Pyotor Wrangel, who had exploited the Red Army's preoccupation with the Poles by attacking through Perekop on the Sea of Azov and taking Melitopol in south-east Ukraine. The XIIIth Army of the Red Army was ordered to break off from the Polish front and halt Wrangel's advance but when its 1st Cavalry Corps was encircled and destroyed Wrangel became master of the Northern Taurida, north of the Crimean peninsula.

The Poles could not hold the line against the Red Army advance, however, as further Russian reinforcements arrived. On 14 June 1920, Wilno fell and the Russians handed it over to Lithuania. Grodno was captured on 19 June. The Polish forces were now far too spread out to resist and, under the weight of Russian air attack and cavalry, withdrew. By 4 July 1920, five Red Army groups under the command of Tukhachevsky and Alexandr Yegorov were driving deep into Polish territory towards Warsaw. With an army now mustering some 120,000 men and including an elite cavalry corps, KonKorpus, they had an almost twofold superiority over General Stanislaus Graf von Szeptycki's Polish forces. The Russians offered Vilnius to Lithuania in return for free passage of Red Army troops, which was agreed under secret protocols to the Treaty of Moscow on 12 July.

Between 5 and 16 July 1920, a conference was held at Spa in Belgium to consider how the terms of the Versailles Treaty were being applied. The conference was dominated by the imperious British prime minister, David Lloyd George, who castigated 'Polish imperialism', while the French were caught in their ambiguities of eastern policies. The Polish prime minister, Grabski, who had only been in office for a matter of days, took the opportunity to request that the Western Powers act as mediators between Poland and Russia. Lloyd George interpreted the desperate Polish pleas as weakness and attached onerous conditions to any offer of help. Poland was to withdraw all its troops to the Curzon Line, the ethnic line of the Russo-Polish border, in East Galicia and hand over control of Vilnius to Lithuania. Grabski saw no option for Poland but to 'sign away her control over every international dispute in which she was involved'[11] in return for vague assurances of Western aid. The lack of Western commitment was illustrated by the British pledge to 'assist the Polish nation to defend its existence with all the means at their disposal', which proved to be mere hyperbole.[12] This is not surprising given that on many occasions Lloyd George had denigrated Piłsudski's policies while working behind the scenes to open trade negotiations with Moscow.[13]

The Russians rejected any notion of peace talks in which they might have been obliged to sit down and talk to Wrangel and ignored British and French warnings not to advance into Polish territory. The Western Powers had looked on the prospect of a Polish defeat with some trepidation, undermining as it would the whole basis of the Versailles settlement and opening up Western Europe to communist expansionism. Germany, however, chose to bolster Russian prospects and remove some uncertainty with a firm declaration of neutrality in the conflict in the expectation that a Russian victory would be in its long-term interests.

The Polish forces could not withstand the pressure of the Russian attack and retreated. Tukhachevsky issued an order of the day proclaiming to his armies that 'the fate of the general revolution will be decided in the west'. With twenty-one infantry divisions, he advanced across a 500km front and took Minsk on 11 July 1920 and Vilnius on 14 July. The Poles were outflanked by the KonKorpus at Grodno and on 19 July were forced to retreat further to the next line of defence on the rivers Bug and Narew but they had failed to prevent the Red Army crossing the Niemen river, which had been their last line of defence. Piłsudski sent Grabski to the Allied Supreme War Council with an appeal for help but Britain and France viewed the Polish position as being close to collapse and revolution as the likely outcome. A number of alternatives were mooted, including removal of the 'narrow-minded, tricky and intensely vain' Piłsudski, but caution stayed their hand, fearing that his removal would do no more than accelerate Poland's descent into revolutionary turmoil.[14]

A high-level Franco-British mission including Lord D'Abernon for the British and General Maxime Weygand, whom the French saw as *de facto* commander of the Polish army, arrived in Warsaw on 24 July 1920 ostensibly to assist in an unspecified way with armistice negotiations. As the Polish situation on the front was deteriorating, the British and the French berated Piłsudski and his handling of the war, and agreed to help Poland only if he relinquished one of his two powers as joint head of state and military commander-in-chief. He was, in fact, prohibited by Article 46 of the 1921 Constitution from simultaneously holding both positions. Piłsudski offered to stand down as of chief of staff in favour of Weygand and tended his resignation as head of state and commander-in-chief of the armed forces. Sir Maurice Hankey, Lloyd George's eyes and ears in the mission, told the prime minister that the Polish position was so precarious that he expected Warsaw to fall to the Russians by 5 August 1920. It was he, also, who erroneously thought Piłsudski to be secretly in collusion with Moscow, although how he arrived at that bizarre conclusion was not clear. By putting Hankey at the heart of the British delegation, Lloyd George had tried to maintain personal control of events but succeeded only in 'replacing the advice of trained professionals by that of a bewildered amateur'.[15] The mission achieved little in practice and exhibited its incompetence by failing to report back officially until after the crucial battle for Warsaw had taken place.

A note signed by Lord Curzon had been sent on 11 July 1920 to Moscow proposing an armistice but confusingly included proposals about the Crimea on which the Russians were not prepared to compromise. French forces at the time had landed in Odesa trying to bring some order to the White Russian counter-revolutionary forces, albeit with little success, and it may have been in connection with this that Curzon had muddied the waters. Lenin called the note 'a complete swindle', believing it to be a ruse to gain time for preparations for a new attack on Russia by White forces and their Western Allies and pressed for continuation of the advance on Warsaw.[16] While Kamanev reported a spirit of intense optimism, predicting a final, crushing victory within weeks, Trotsky, not uncharacteristically, took an alternative line and urged acceptance of the British terms given that his Red Army commander at the front expressed grave concerns about continuing the war.[17] Chicherin replied to the Curzon note on 17 July 1920 saying that he could not take it seriously since the Poles had not made the offer directly and implied, in diplomatic niceties, that they could not be trusted to keep to the terms of any armistice anyway. Moscow could only accept a Polish commitment to 'establish a solid foundation for truly fraternal relations between the working masses of Poland, Russia and the Ukraine, Belarus and Lithuania', which was an unequivocal call for communist revolution and not one to which the Poles were likely to respond favourably.

On 22 July 1920, the Polish foreign minister, Eustachy Sapieha, sent a message to Chicherin proposing an armistice. It was agreed that a meeting would be held at Baranowicze on 30 July to discuss terms but, at the same time, the Red Army High Command had issued a directive for an all-out attack against Warsaw to begin on 12 August. Kamanev believed that the Polish forces around Smolensk had 'ceased to exist' and that the road to Warsaw was wide open.[18] The Russian Mozyrn Group was ordered to advance its right wing in the direction of Lublin and join up with the left wing of the XVIth Army in the centre, while Budonny's cavalry would move towards Lwów. Unfortunately, the 'startling impreciseness of the language'[19] of the directive was sufficient to cause a divergence of interpretation among the Red Army commanders in the field, which was not helped by Kamanev's insistence that more forces should be withdrawn to contain Wrangel's White forces in the south and prevent him joining up with Romanian units.

Piłsudski vigorously opposed any deal with the Russians and forced the collapse of the Polish government on 24 July 1920 when Grabski's Popular National Union was replaced by Wincenty Witos' Polish People's Party. Piłsudski replaced von Szeptycki with Haller as commander of the Polish Auxiliary Corps, giving him clear instructions to hold on at all costs while he made a concerted attempt to defeat Budenny's forces in the south. On 1 August 1920, Tukhachevsky's Red Army forces captured Brześć and crossed the Bug, breaching the last natural defence before Warsaw, but the KonKorpus had been weakened by its lightning advance, had got bogged down in heavy fighting as it advanced towards Brody and was forced to withdraw to regroup. Tukhachevsky, who had now been given command of the whole Polish front, had advanced some 600km by utilising the Red Army's principal strength, which was its ability to sow uncertainty and panic by projecting the mystique of an unstoppable and unforgiving horde. Piłsudski called it: 'This incessant wormlike movement by large numbers of enemy troops, punctuated now and again by a sudden leap forward, a movement continuing for weeks on end, gave the impression of something irresistible rolling on like some heavy, monstrous cloud.'[20]

The Polish troops were exhausted by their long retreat in the summer heat, and many abandoned their positions and fled at the mere whisper of encirclement. Panic spread through the Polish capital, with the government on the point of collapse in the face of communist revolution. In anticipation of victory, on 23 July 1920, Lenin had inaugurated a Polish Revolutionary Committee, to be set up as a Bolshevik government for Poland. Leaflets calling for world revolution were printed in German in preparation for the onward march and on the same day he suggested to Stalin that Budenny should continue on through Romania and Hungary to spur Italian communists to revolution. Foreign embassies began packing up and leaving Warsaw. Lloyd George dismissed the Poles to their fate by declaring '[they] have quarrelled with all their neighbours and they are a menace to the peace of Europe'.[21]

Piłsudski gambled that Tukhachevsky's rapid advance must have tired his troops and stretched supply lines to breaking point. In a manoeuvre reminiscent of the Russian Imperial Army's movement in the 1830 Polish Rising, the Russian commander had wheeled his north flank as far as the East Prussian frontier to try and encircle Warsaw but in so doing had weakened his centre. In the south, his left flank offered little support since forces there had been unable to keep up with the Mozyr Group's central thrust. Meanwhile, Piłsudski had built up a volunteer force of over 164,000 men and women, and while many of the men marched barefoot and resembled 'a collection of tramps', their morale was high.[22] He planned to hold the bridgeheads at the Wieprz River with a quarter of his force concentrated to the south poised for a strategic counteroffensive. Haller would hold the centre at all costs while Sikorski would defend the northern flank and, if possible, cut off Russian forces attempting to envelop Warsaw from that direction. Piłsudski's assault group was to spearhead a lightning northern offensive from the Vistula-Wieprz River triangle south of Warsaw and break through between the Russian western and south-western fronts to split the enemy ranks near the East Prussian border. The plan was criticised by Polish and French advisers alike as highlighting Piłsudski's lack of formal military education with Polish troop realignment far too close to the enemy positions and open to attack as they manoeuvred. Piłsudski admitted that it was a very risky gamble, but the desperate situation persuaded other army commanders that they had no choice but go along with it as the only possible way to avoid being completely overrun. When a copy of the plan accidentally fell into Tukhachevsky's hands, its amateurish concept persuaded him that it was a poor attempt at deception and, catastrophically, he ignored it. The Polish lines were strengthened, and forces were regrouped in accordance Piłsudski's plan. On 11 August 1920, Tukhachevsky realised he had blundered when his scouts reported on the new Polish concentrations, which now threatened a flank attack from the south. He ordered Alexander Yegorov, commander of the Russian south-west front, to immediately break off his attack against Lwów and turn north towards Lublin to reinforce his flank but Yegorov, preoccupied with holding off Wrangel, questioned Tukhachevsky's authority to order that. Budenny, whose cavalry were under Yegorov's command, also refused to move having received a written order that was technically invalid since it had only a single signature and not two as demanded by military protocol. By the time a correct, legal order had been passed along on 17 August, Lwów had come under intense Polish attack and neither Yegorov's XIIth nor his XIVth armies was able to disengage.

The final Russian assault on Warsaw began on 12 August 1920 when its XVIth Army attacked Radzymin and on the following day the Red Army made a frontal assault on the Praga bridgehead as foreign diplomats, with the exception of British and Vatican ambassadors, hastily fled Warsaw. On 14 August the Red Army broke through Sikorski's lines. The situation was saved by the Poles taking out the last remaining Red Army radio station, causing the IVth Army to lose contact with its headquarters and continue marching toward Toruń and Płock instead of turning south as Tukhachevski required it to do. The Red Army found Warsaw very well defended, with plenty of troops, heavy artillery, tanks and even aircraft, but a vigorous attack at Wkra on 13 August hit Haller hard while Sikorski's flank held firm. A Russian victory seemed certain on 15 August but early on the following day, Piłsudski launched his counterattack with 3 infantry divisions numbering 27,500 infantry and 950 cavalry under his personal command, while to his right 2 more divisions, under General Śmigły-Rydz, numbering 25,000 infantry and nearly 3,000 cavalry, moved out in a north-easterly direction.

The Red Army was only 13km from Warsaw when the tide of battle turned. Tukhachevski had marched across the Vistula in the north into sparsely defended territory, leaving only token forces to hold the centre. The Russian situation was dramatically weakened by Budenny's refusal to break off from Lwów after receiving an order from the chief political commissar of the south-western front Josef Stalin to stay put.

Tukhachevsky's forces north of Warsaw was forced to retire, while the XVIth Army was encircled and annihilated. Russian reinforcements were held up in the dilapidated rail network and only on 20 August 1920 did Budenny eventually move north towards Lublin but he was too late. The Russian IVth Army was trapped and many of its forces fled across the German border into internment. Red Army units simply disintegrated under the force of the five Polish divisions. The KonKorpus fled west across the border into East Prussia rather than face capture by the Poles.

Budenny attempted but failed to counter with an attack on Lwów and by 25 August 1920 Tukhachevsky's front had ceased to exist, having lost over 100,000 men to death and capture, as well as most of his artillery and equipment. The IVth Army had been preparing to attack the Polish left flank when Sikorski suddenly advanced but their hesitation deprived them of any chance of success. Their half-hearted efforts against Sikorski's left had little effect, and it was not until 20 August that Tukhachevsky's order for a general retreat had reached them. On 22 August they forced their way through Polish lines at Mława and again on 28 August at Chorzele but on 24 August at Kovno they ran up against Pilsudski's main force and chose internment in East Prussia as an alternative to destruction. In retreat, Budenny suffered heavy defeats in the Battle of Komarów in August 1920 and later in the Battle of Hrubieszów.

Meanwhile, on 14 August 1920, before the Battle of Warsaw had taken place, the Polish undersecretary for foreign affairs, Jan Dąbski, had arrived in Minsk in response to a Russian invitation to discuss armistice terms. It was soon clear that Moscow had no intention of making peace and were simply creating a façade in anticipation of the imminent collapse of the Polish state. The Polish negotiators were treated with disdain, even being denied communications with Warsaw when events around the city turned in favour of the Polish forces. Delegates on both sides were told that Warsaw had fallen to Russian forces.[23] Using this as pressure on the Poles, the Russians demanded a reduction in the Polish army to no more than 50,000 men and freedom to create a civilian militia inside Poland recruited from within the working classes and this militia was to be armed with surplus army weapons. Polish war industries were to be closed down and the government would not be allowed to purchase armaments from abroad. Finally, Russia would be given total rights of free passage across Polish territory. Agreement to such terms was tantamount to accepting that Poland would, in effect, be transformed into a vassal state of Russia but before any concessions were even considered news started to filter through of the Polish victory at Warsaw and the whole mood of the negotiations, on both sides, changed dramatically.

While peace talks continued in Minsk, the Poles had continued their advance and had taken Brest-Litovsk on 20 August 1920. In nine days the lead units of the Polish 2nd Army had advanced some 200 miles. The Polish 4th Army averaged 25 miles a day, which meant that Polish supply lines were stretched to breaking point and the troops existed as they could upon the exhausted countryside. By this point Russian resistance was so completely broken that there was little fear of counterattack and the Polish units had ample time in which to reorganise.

The Western Powers warned Piłsudski not to advance beyond Poland's ethnographic frontiers, but he ignored them, claiming that it was impossible to take up a strictly defensive position. The alternatives as he saw them were continued advance or peace negotiations. He much preferred the former and prepared for a new offensive, which began on 12 September 1920. Rovno and Tarnopol were taken immediately, with Grodno falling on 26 September. Red Army reinforcements with fresh troops from the Russian interior at the beginning of September allowed Tukhachevsky to make a stand along the Niemen river but he was again driven back in late September. Polish troops now occupied large areas of Belarus, Podolia and Volhynia. The Moscow-sponsored Polish government-in-waiting headed by Julian Marchlewski, Feliks Dzerzhinsky and Feliks Kon, which had been held at Bialystok, was forced to flee back to Moscow. Even after the signing of the armistice in October 1920, the Russians delayed peace talks for over six months in the hope that circumstances might improve and give some hope of gaining more advantageous terms. Only the outbreak of the Kronstadt Rebellion in March 1921 and the threat of a wider uprising would eventually force Moscow to conclude a final peace agreement.

Hankey had written to Lloyd George on the day that Tukhachevsky launched his assault on Warsaw saying that 'there is no sign of improvement in the [Polish] military position … if the Poles refuse [to negotiate] we should wash our hands of the whole business'.[24] In this he believed he was reflecting his prime minister's view that the Poles were 'troublesome, their leaders feckless and their administration chaotic'.[25] After the Russian defeat at Warsaw, however, Lloyd George tried to distance himself from Hankey's views and on 25 August 1920 instructed the Allied mission to remain in Warsaw and assist peace negotiations but by the time his instruction was delivered they had already left. Hankey, meanwhile, claimed that the Allied mission, and especially the French military aid, had been instrumental in galvanising the Poles into their heroic resistance at Warsaw.

Later, Lord D'Abernon called the Battle of Warsaw 'the eighteenth decisive battle of the world'. The rightist opponents of Piłsudski ascribed victory to higher powers by calling it the 'Miracle on the Vistula', and did everything to deny the marshal the authorship of the victory, attributing it instead to Weygand's leadership. Subsequent analysis suggests that the battle was won by professional officers in the Polish ranks, who had been trained in the Austrian and Russian armies.[26] Piłsudski, however, was not to be outdone and won popular acclaim as the saviour of Poland and the father of victory. The general appeared touched by the enthusiasm of the crowds wherever he went, and lost no opportunity to play on Polish sentiments by declaring in an interview to Paul Genty, a correspondent of '*L'Information*', on 21 August 1920, 'I beg you to fix French opinion on this important point. This is a purely Polish victory. The preliminary operation was carried out in accordance with a Polish plan by Polish generals.'[27] Unfortunately, victory at the gates of Warsaw was to have profound and debilitating consequences for Polish military doctrine, which, over the next two decades, retained a doomed faith in the supremacy of cavalry and failed to understand how mechanisation would revolutionise the battlefield.

Now in the ascendent, the Poles demanded that peace negotiations be transferred to Riga and conducted on a completely different basis. They opened there in the Blackheaded Hall on 21 September 1920 with the Polish delegate Dąbski calling for 'a peace based on mutual understanding' and the Russian leader Adolph Ioffe, described as a prosperous banker and successful businessman, in marked contrast to the Russian position in Minsk, urging 'a just and democratic peace … without victors and vanquished'.[28] When the main sessions got under way, Ioffe diverted attention from the Russian debacle by accusing the Western Powers of conniving a winter war aimed at the destruction of both Poland and Russia. When it came to actual negotiations, however, he had few cards to play. He was forced to concede the principle of self-determination for Byelorussia, Lithuania and the Ukraine and agreed to free elections in Eastern Galicia. However, he threatened to break off talks if agreement was not reached within ten days, claiming that Russia had made huge concessions compared to their Minsk position and aware that both sides were anxious to bring the war to an end before winter set in when 'the burden ... would fall on the working class of both countries'. Dąbski shared Ioffe's sentiments and diplomatically conceded that any agreement must be on the basis of the 'vital interests of both powers'.[29]

Despite a strong desire on both sides to reach a compromise over their demands and end the war, negotiations were prolonged so Ioffe and Dąbski agreed to settle the main questions in private session with dialogue in German, a language in which they were both fluent. By 5 October 1920, agreement had been reached on all basic issues with plans to deal with unresolved issues later but the Poles prevaricated with their troops closing on Minsk, where a number of prominent Poles were imprisoned and some important documents needed to be retrieved.[30] It would also be a strong bargaining chip if Russia chose to continue the war. In what was a personal triumph for both Ioffe and Dąbski, the seventeen articles of the Treaty of Riga were signed off on 12 October 1920 and ratification concluded by 2 November 1920. As part of the agreement, most of the Ukrainian lands would become part of the Ukrainian Soviet Socialist Republic under the control of Moscow, while the eastern borders of Poland now enclosed Eastern Galicia, Volhynia and western Byelorussia (Kresy). The Treaty established a new stable frontier between Poland and Russia and played a significant part in containing the latter for nearly two decades.

The Treaty of Riga was greeted with varying degrees of approbation and criticism. Grabski, who had been Dąbski's second-in-command, was called a 'traitor' but much of Europe heaved a sigh of relief, with one newspaper saying that when the Russian armies stood at the gates of Warsaw, 'the fate of civilisation [had] hung in the balance'. England and France, neither of whom particularly liked the settlement, were condemned for allowing Poland to incorporate 'thousands of square miles and millions of people to which it had no ethnographic claim'. Britain took no pleasure in seeing an enlarged Polish state that would 'complicate [its] relations with Germany and Russia', while France saw no advantage in emasculating a Russia that might yet throw off 1919 the Bolshevik yoke.[31] It was the overwhelming international opinion that Russia was to be honoured with making the peace by offering concessions that were 'the most humane condition ever demanded by one protagonist by another'.[32] A British trade journal at the time claimed that Britain had put huge pressure on the Poles to agree terms in order that Britain might conclude 20 million dollars' worth of trade agreements with Russia that had been held in abeyance awaiting signature during the fighting.

Radek saw no downside, believing that 'not a single vital interest of Russia had been injured by its terms'.[33] Dmowski welcomed it but it had, in his view, created a Polish state 'too westerly to be a federation but not westerly enough to remain a national state'.[34] It had left hundreds of thousands of Poles in Minsk, Kamieniec, Podolski and surrounding lands under Russian control, many of whom would later be sent to internal exile in Siberia, but their exclusion from Polish elections greatly diminished Piłsudski's political support and threw into doubt his ability to pursue his federalist agenda.

A month later new talks began to iron out the remaining points of contention. The Polish delegation this time was composed of technical experts rather than politicians. The Russian negotiators now held a stronger position due to the better disposition of their armed forces and the support of international public opinion as Western countries competed for trade agreements with them. This time, the Poles applied time pressure. They were almost bankrupted, desperate for foreign credits and facing criticism for their spat with Lithuania over Wilno but there was little urgency to complete the tasks. The central and most complex issues were economic and financial especially over the apportionment of the wealth of the former Russian Empire, with the Poles claiming twice as much in compensation as the Russians would concede. Dąbski and Ioffe went into private session again to progress negotiations. Dąbski settled for a lesser sum but demanded gold bullion and not equivalents. Ioffe offered Imperial Russian jewels as well as forestry and mining concessions but these were transient and could be terminated at will and, anyway, Poland did not have the infrastructure to transport bulk materials. In the case of jewels, the Poles felt moral objections to taking and selling treasures that the Russian communists had acquired by murdering the Romanovs. There was also the question of whether or not Moscow could be relied on to ever pay whatever amount was agreed.

Eventually, Ioffe was instructed to close a deal that would ensure a better working relationship with the Poles, especially since Polish forces had now been much reduced from their peak wartime levels. The Russians could then concentrate on extending their influence and control in Poland through propaganda and infiltration of worker organisations to work towards communist insurrection. The Treaty was agreed and signed on the eve of elections in Upper Silesia, which was one of the main aims of the Polish delegation and thus deprived Germany of a propaganda tool able to argue that the Poles were still at war with Russia. At the same time Russia signed a Treaty of Alliance with Turkey and a trade agreement with Britain, bringing it some way into the fold of European nations. Goods manufactured in Western Europe could now be transported safely across Poland to Russia. Lenin described the Russian defeat as 'the early frost' that had blighted 'the growth of the revolutionary flower'.[35] The Allied Powers continued to shed authority as all sides in the conflict had seen their abortive and half-hearted attempted interventions as little more than 'preaching'.

In July 1920, as Polish forces had retreated, the Lithuanians had followed them to secure their lands, which they claimed according to the Soviet-Lithuanian Peace Treaty of 12 July 1920. The Red Army, however, reached Vilnius before them but after the Battle of Warsaw Polish troops advanced and came into contact with Lithuanian forces along the disputed Polish-Lithuanian border. At the Battle of the Niemen River the Red Army forces tried to hold a line centred on Grodno but they were outflanked and forced to retreat, leaving the Poles facing the Lithuanians. After the League of Nations intervened the Poles were forced to sign the Suwałki Agreement on 7 October 1920, with a demarcation line leaving Vilnius open to flank attack. A serious provocation to Piłsudski saw the armistice line between forces putting Vilnius on the Lithuanian side and he was not about to allow that. On 9 October he sent 15,000 Polish troops under General Lucjan Żeligowski to occupy Vilnius against minimal Lithuanian opposition and with the general approval of the city's population.[36] When he failed to advance as far as Kaunas, he halted and proclaimed the Republic of Central Lithuania with its capital in Vilnius, which was incorporated into Poland as the Wilno Voivodeship in 1922. While the annexation of Vilnius was a personal victory for Piłsudski's federalist cause, it was bitterly resented by the rest of Lithuania.

The treaty that had ended the Russo-Polish War was ratified by the Poles on 15 April 1921 and in Moscow on 22 April, and registered with the League of Nations on 12 August 1921. In the end, the Poles failed to detach Belarus and the Ukraine from Russian control, but they were nevertheless criticised by the Russian leadership for taking too much former Russian territory, a view shared by most of the European Left and most Western governments. As part of the Riga agreement, Moscow had officially recognised the Russo-Polish frontier but the Comintern (the association of national communist parties) continued to support the principle of self-determination and questioned Poland's right to both its western and eastern frontiers. Riga was hailed as a 'great victory' for Russia by the government newspaper, but the reality of its defeat had repercussions in Moscow, not least for Lenin who, against vociferous criticism, was forced to defend his decision to order the disastrous attack on Warsaw. It had been necessary, he said, to try and destroy the Versailles Treaty and in so doing undermine the whole post-war structure of international relations. Grigory Zinoviev would concede that the war was lost due to a political failure to revolutionise the Polish peasant to rise up from within the country and overturn the social structure. Peasants who should have welcomed the Red Army with open arms as liberators were alienated from, them not least because of their looting and pillaging as they advanced on the capital. Tukhachevsky denied that his soldiers had been culpable and blamed strategic errors made by those far from the front, while others saw the Red Army advance as the prime motivation for galvanising patriotic resistance to communist propaganda. The Red Army leaders blamed Trotsky; Trotsky blamed Stalin and so it went on.

In its first three years of existence, the Polish state would fight no fewer than six wars of varying length and intensity with the Ukrainians in November 1918, the Germans over Poznania a month later, the Germans again in Silesia in August 1919 to July 1921, the Lithuanians in July 1919 to October 1920, the Czechs in January 1919 and finally the Russians.

Chapter 3

UPPER SILESIA

Upper Silesia is indispensable to the life of Germany.

German *paxkonference* memorandum in response
to President Wilson's 'Fourteen Points'

Nowhere was the perceived injustice of the Treaty of Versailles more apparent to Germany than in those former Imperial German territories now under Polish dominion, even though the treaty had included provisions for the new Polish state to 'protect the interests of [its inhabitants] who differ from the majority … in race, language or religion'. All inhabitants were guaranteed life, liberty and religious freedom, irrespective of national or religious affiliations. Furthermore, the Poles were obliged to offer primary education in their native tongue alongside Polish to children in areas with a large minority population, Although numerically only the fourth largest minority in Poland after Ukrainians, Jews and Byelorussians, it was the Germans who posed the greatest challenge to the state. Many Germans, however, felt that they been demoted from masters to second-class citizens and, much against the wishes of both Warsaw and Berlin, responded by migrating to their homeland. It was those Germans who had previously lived within the borders of Imperial Germany who bitterly resented being placed under the control of those whom they had once ruled and felt the pull of home the most. Within a decade, the numbers of Germans in these western areas of Poland would reduce by a half to just under 400,000, while those in central Poland, mostly in the cities, would see an increase.

The influence of Germans, especially in the western part of the country, bore little relation to their numbers, however. Although few in numbers, they dominated the economic life of the region.

Land ownership, especially of the larger, more productive estates, was mostly in their hands and German capital financed much of the industrial and mining sector.

Of the Germans who stayed, a militant, secessionist minority in western Poland favoured cultural and political independence, and also a reversal of the process that had imposed alien status on them. However, in central and eastern Poland there was little agitation for change, where minorities were more comfortable with each other and the state and were concerned only to achieve and maintain social and economic equality. The mood of rebellion in the west was nurtured by the German language press, that in 1922 wrote: 'Everything that we do, whether it concerns economic or educational aspirations … is valuable only in so far as it contributes to a strengthening of nationality cohesion.'[1] Pomerania, the area that stretched across northern Poland bordering the Baltic Sea, was served by the *Deitsche Gesellschaft fur Künst-und-Wisenschaft,* while the central region had the *Historische Gesellschaft fur Posen,* both of which expanded German consciousness and cultural life with lectures and periodicals.

German youth were catered for by the *Deutscher Kulturbund fur Oberschleisein* and *Wandervogel in Polen,* who specialised in lectures, outdoor pursuits and national festivals. Libraries of German-language material were set up and numbers continued to increase over the next decade. As many as sixty German language newspapers were distributed in Poland in 1921, many of which brought condemnation from the Polish authorities for their outspoken anti-Polish tone. All of this was initially financed directly from Berlin but opposition was soon expressed by the Poles and more indirect funding through ostensibly private institutions took its place. The main purpose and indeed the outcome was that leading members of the German population in Poland were encouraged to remember their German heritage and culture and this filtered down through the whole German-speaking population.

Religious organisations also played a prominent part in fomenting German nationalism. German Protestants were entirely chauvinistic in the way they proclaimed that 'Germanism and Polonism stand opposed to one another … One must forget about religious cooperation along with any other kind of interaction.'[2] Pastors exhorted newly married couples to raise their children as Germans and frowned upon mixed marriage. They even went as far as to say from the pulpit that 'it won't be long before the day comes when we shall take up arms … if the German standard is raised'. Neither were the German Catholics slow to attack the Polish state for what it called a hostile attitude towards the Germans.

Private German schools flourished and were so popular with such good reputations that even Polish families sent their children even though the language barrier made it difficult for them to understand what they were being taught. Families who worked for German companies were encouraged to send their children with the offer of free school meals and uniforms. A joint German-Polish initiative as early as 1919 had set up a fund to develop German intellectual life in Poland but that did not prevent continued criticism of 'persecution' of the German school network by teachers who, for their own part, began to disseminate virulent anti-Polish propaganda through the schools.

While the Poles had traditionally suffered from the superior, high-handed attitude of the Prussians, there had been little friction between them and the Germans to the west during the years of co-existence within the German Empire until after 1871, when Prussia became the dominant force in German politics. After that time Poles were increasingly subjected to intimidation with a view to driving them from German lands but when the First World War had ended there was an opportunity to reset Polish-German relations. The armistice found German troops on Polish soil but generally they were allowed to withdraw without too much fuss. It had been assumed in Poland that Prussian influence would decline after the demise of the Hohenzollern dynasty with the myth of Prussian military might exploded. This was not the case, however. Even though Prussian stubbornness and lack of imagination had contributed to the German failure to win the war, they somehow managed to retain their reputation as heroic defenders who had been undermined by political chicanery. Prussian influence prevailed in essence because of admiration in Germany for militarism itself, because of a willingness within the middle and lower classes to give unquestioning support to the military, which had been the driving force for German unification in 1848 and which had retained its grip on the German psyche.

The view that Germany could only recover from the Treaty of Versailles by casting off any vestige of militarism and welcoming Poland as a strong and reliable neighbour had its advocates but even the Western Allies failed to recognise the opportunity and did too little to encourage that movement and, whether intentionally or not, tended to take the side of those forces inside Germany that were hostile to Poland. Under the influence of a residual Prussian elite, a German state riven by internal factionalism was united by fierce opposition to the loss of territories stripped from it at the end of the war and this victimhood was one of the few things that held the Weimar Republic together. As German political strength slowly recovered it was the new Polish state that became the focus of irridentist fervour long before the Nazis got anywhere near to the levers of power, but political elites in Poland also harboured ambitions to redraw its boundaries with Czechoslovakia.

At the Paris Peace Conference much emphasis had been placed on President Wilson's 'Fourteen Points' that laid out his ideas for a post-war continental re-alignment of borders:

> An independent Polish state should be erected which should include the territories inhabited by indisputably Polish populations, which should be assured a free and secure access to the sea, and whose political and economic independence and territorial integrity should be guaranteed by international covenant.

It was clear that should President Wilson's recommendations be implemented the economically important region of Upper Silesia, according to the Prussian census of 1910, would come under scrutiny as one of the areas that should be included in the new Polish state. The census showed an overwhelmingly Roman Catholic, Polish-speaking population but that belied the strong German cultural influences that had overtaken the region since it had been incorporated into Prussia after the 1870 Franco-Prussian War. On 8 January 1918, when Wilson had outlined his proposals for a post-war settlement to the US Congress, the German government, unaware of the parlous state of its army on the Western Front, had not been too concerned about how they would be affected by them and certainly had no indication that its ultimate defeat would lead to its humiliation at Versailles.

By 12 October 1918, however, the picture was quite different and the Germans, now fully cognisant of Allied supremacy, had conceded all of Wilson's terms. Polish deputies withdrew from the Reichstag and claimed that all Polish districts of Prussia must be included in the new Polish state, whose borders were being drawn up. Initially, the region of Upper Silesia had been seen as an obvious candidate for inclusion but the German industrialists and aristocracy that dominated Upper Silesian society used their impressive political clout to challenge any notion of separation from Berlin. The British conceded that the region had been 'ethnographically Polish from time immemorial' but that it was also 'of the utmost economic value to Germany' and its coal mines, especially, would play a crucial role in contributing to Germany's war reparation payments and the economic recovery of Europe as a whole.[3]

The state secretary of the Reich Economic Office went as far as to say, 'If we lose the Upper Silesian coalfields then Germany will fall apart completely.'[4]

On 22 July 1913 in Berlin the *Reichs- und Staatsangehörigkeitsgesetz* (Nationality Law of the German Empire and States) had determined that only descendants of those defined as Germans in German law, irrespective of whether they felt themselves to be German or spoke German, could be German citizens. In Upper Silesia, many of the locals did not feel themselves to be German, despite fulfilling the legal criteria in terms of ethnicity. Previously, the rise of Prussia to great power status had resulted in territorial changes that affected the ethnic balance all across Central Europe and in some areas, such as East Pomerania and Upper Silesia, Germans found themselves in a numeric minority where they had previously been part of larger areas in which they belonged to the ethnic majority. To make matters worse, these minorities found themselves being subjected to external nationalist propaganda competing for hearts and minds. In 1886, the Prussians had brought in laws allowing them to reduce the Polish element of the population in areas in which they formed a majority through officially sanctioned discrimination, particularly in education and agriculture. With the recreation of Poland, the new state found itself host to sizeable German minority populations. At Versailles, discussions over the economic viability of Poland had led to the territories being ill-defined in terms of their ethnic composition, creating a situation that precluded any stable and political and economic development in Germany and allowed revisionist politicians plenty of ammunition to create tensions for political purposes.

There was a discernible split in Upper Silesian society between the wealthy landowning and mine-owning German civil authorities and the Polish peasant and mine-working communities. Even the lower echelons of the German population tended to get the better-paid, less-arduous manual occupations. All through the First World War there had been strikes and demonstrations, exacerbated by food shortages, against the social and working conditions of the Poles and this continued after the Armistice. However, this time, the authorities clamped down hard on the strikers with street battles resulting in the industrial areas. A US mission in the middle of winter found 'the faces of the workers haggard. The women and children pitiably emaciated [and a quarter of them] on the streets barefoot.'[5]

After fighting had broken out in Poznania and East Prussia, fearing similar conflict in Upper Silesia, the authorities there came down harder still on the striking miners and brought in paramilitary *Grenzshutz* and *Freikorps* units fresh from their crushing of the Spartacists in Berlin. Orders were issued from Berlin to 'use all available military and paramilitary forces to end the Upper Silesian strikes'.[6] A proclamation announced that any activity aimed at promoting the inclusion of Upper Silesia in the new Polish state would be considered a treasonous act. In response Poles were encouraged to boycott the upcoming elections for the German National Assembly.

The Poles were less than pleased to see Lloyd George's 'perplexing and alarming instability' now contribute to the dilution of hitherto British enthusiasm for the Polish cause.[7] The British prime minister, halfway through a premiership that would see Britain go from 'a position of acknowledged world leadership in 1919 to near complete isolation', became convinced that, in view of German and Russian opposition, only a Polish state comprised of a homogenous Polish population could be viable. This view was supported by an Allied commission, backed up by French, British and Italian troops, that arrived in Warsaw in February 1919 and reported that tensions in the region were increasing the risk of all-out war between Germany and Poland. Germany, it said, gambling that Britain was eager to distance itself from any involvement in further military conflict, was provoking a Polish uprising in Upper Silesia that would justify German armed intervention. The Poles, themselves, were anxious to see that the situation did not escalate beyond their control and were successful in quelling industrial unrest but that simply allowed Germany to re-establish authority by bring over 225,000 regular troops into the region. When the Poles responded by creating the *Polska Organisacja Wojskowa* (Polish Military Organisation, POW), an underground group of several thousand members, many of whom were armed, the tinderbox was full and just waiting for a spark to ignite it.

The Paris Peace Conference, which was drawing up the new Eastern European boundaries, began to feel that they had been a little over-generous to Poland. Their deliberations over Polish borders had begun with including areas with clear Polish majorities and then had taken into account natural features such as rivers and lakes, and then, incrementally, they started including any territory deemed strategically essential to Poland, all from areas with wholly German populations. The Germans, already prepared to defend their territory by force, now employed diplomacy to promote Germany's historic and economic claims while decrying Polish attempts at illegal annexation. Many different arguments were put forward, with some success, to emphasise the Germanic character of the Upper Silesia, even among the Polish community and, in the absence of strong counter-arguments, these began to sway the Paris delegates. Lloyd George, whose main concern seems to have been making sure that Germany could afford to pay its war reparations, urged delegates to be lenient with Germany in the one area where the French would allow it; on the other side of Europe.

Intelligence reports suggested that the German industrialists of Upper Silesia had persuaded the German government to oppose any attempt to join the region with Poland and as part of their strategy had agreed to a plebiscite, confident that the outcome would be in Germany's favour. With significant numbers of German and Polish troops in the region, Paris delegates came under severe pressure to agree to the plebiscite in principle. There had developed a sense that if Germany's wishes were opposed in Upper Silesia, it might well inflame the whole of Poznania and Danzig as well. The draft peace terms issued by the Western Allies on 6 May 1919, however, conceded little to Germany but under the circumstances that was no surprise. German aspirations were well known and no doubt the authors of the draft treaty, prepared for German indignation at whatever they were presented with, had staked out an extreme position giving themselves room for the inevitable compromise. However, faced with blunt German rejection and the prospect of prolonged military occupation of Germany if terms could not be agreed, the Allies duly moderated their terms and saw Poland as the one area where concessions could be made to Germany without risking a complete breakdown of the talks. Judging by his remarks at the peace conferences, Lloyd George had little time for the Poles, calling them impetuous and childish, and there was hardly any sympathy for them in British politics as a whole.[8]

When Paris delegates visited Upper Silesia in May 1919 they met with huge pro-German rallies in Katowice and other urban areas. It should be remembered that for the four or five months up to spring 1919, Upper Silesia was part of Germany over which it had total control and, although Allied forces came in to assume security duties, it remained German soil at least until the results of the plebiscite became known.[9] Given that much of the Polish population was poor, unorganised, and spread widely over the country areas, it is not hard to see how the delegates concluded that a plebiscite would result in a German victory, especially since under the prevailing law any expression of a public show of support for Poland was a punishable offence. It may well have been a result of their willingness to see what they had hoped to see and choosing not to look any further but it is inexcusable that a mission whose purpose was to find facts should have been so dilatory in purpose and so biased in its conclusions. When the report was published critics called it 'German propaganda' and 'grossly misleading' but more influential voices such as that of the South African prime minister, Jan Smuts, who was on the British delegation in Paris, characterised the idea of handing over Upper Silesia to Poland as 'reversing the verdict of history'.[10]

Given all the uncomfortable repercussions of sticking to the draft peace treaty and the immense benefit to Germany in terms of its ability to pay its war debts if Upper Silesia remained in German hands, it is no wonder that Britain came down heavily in favour of holding a plebiscite. However, if the British thought that would be the end of it they were sadly mistaken. For a start, the French objected, saying 'the more concessions made, the more the Germans would demand' and reminded everyone that a strong Poland would create a barrier between Germany and Russia. The Americans also spoke for Poland in saying that a free and fair plebiscite could not be held while German troops were conducting what amounted to a reign of terror in Upper Silesia where people found it 'dangerous to express opinions'. President Wilson saw the British as being in what he called a funk (a state of fear or panic) but Lloyd George was able to carry the day based upon his confident but quite disingenuous assertion that a plebiscite would favour Poland. This was despite his gratuitous insult that he would no more give Upper Silesia to Poland than he would 'give a clock to a monkey'.[11] His whole strategy had been based not on any particular ambition for Upper Silesia either way but on finding a way of persuading Germany to sign the proposed treaty and be done with it. The other Allies had considered his pessimism misplaced and that Germany would have signed without a guarantee of plebiscites but all were anxious to avoid a split in the Allied position that might well have been exploited by Germany to the point where they would walk away from talks and leave the whole Paris negotiations in limbo.

The Poles were not pleased, fearing that the political stranglehold the German elite had in the region would make a free vote impossible, but they had absolutely no support in Paris, where even the French seemed to have deserted them despite their assertion that the Germans would continue to cause trouble 'whether there was a plebiscite or not'.[12] Paderewski was able to wring one concession, however, which was that the vote was to be counted individually in each of the 1,500 communes, but lamented that the plebiscite would cause bitter disappointment in Poland. Lloyd George agreed and then secretly instructed that it was to be carried out en bloc, but when the regulations were agreed, it was the commune option that prevailed. German troops were to evacuate the area and Allied forces would be brought in to keep the peace during the two years envisaged to prepare for the plebiscite.

It had been a primary consideration of the Allies to strip Germany of its heavy industrial manufacturing capacity to prevent its resurgence as a military power. In this regard they had given Alsace-Lorraine to France and the Hultschin area of Upper Silesia to Czechoslovakia. Plebiscites in areas such as Masuria, Warmia and Schleswig had favoured Germany and there seemed to be no reason for them to resist another plebiscite in Upper Silesia, which was dominated by German-speaking peoples. Now that the plebiscite had been agreed to, the Germans stepped up their attacks. Cross-border artillery fire was threatening to provoke a Polish reaction, especially when one such destroyed railway lines around Czestochowa and German aircraft fired on Alexandrov and Konin. When one of the aircraft was shot down over Herby, German troops stormed the town and left it in flames. Mass arrests of Poles were still being reported but the German government denied any responsibility for the area now under Allied protection. German industrialists were closing down their plants causing mass unemployment and public disorder, which they then advertised as Polish troublemaking. By August 225,000 miners, both Polish and German, were striking against rising prices that were far outstripping wage rises. The crisis reached a new level when German troops fired on marching strikers in Katowice and Myslowice. Widespread fighting erupted in Pszczyna and Rybnik when military units of Polish émigrés crossed into Upper Silesia from Germany. The conflict became a mélange of class struggle between workers and bosses and nationalist feud between German and Pole.

The effects of the strikes were spreading well beyond the region, with France experiencing shortages of coal, which Germany had been contracted to supply after deliberately destroying French mines in Alsace in 1918. Fighting raged with German troops, now barely under the control of Berlin, accused of 'taking very few prisoners' during fighting and arresting 'anyone they could lay their hands on' at other times.[13] Huge demonstrations in Warsaw demanded government action but Piłsudski was reluctant to send in troops. Paderewski favoured sticking to the terms of the peace treaty and appealed to the Allied Commission to intervene. A high-powered military delegation from four countries in September 1919 found that the situation was actually quietening down and the mines were starting to produce coal again. They could not say where the blame lay for the trouble but called for an immediate cessation of brutality by German troops, a return to work by the miners and a general amnesty for all not accused of offences under common law. It was made clear in their report, however, that the deep underlying grievances would not allow the situation to remain quiescent for long.

The three Allied commissioners given responsibility to implement the plebiscite arrived in Opole on 11 February 1920. From the start, however, they lacked sufficient means to create a calm and stable atmosphere essential for a fair vote in communities where 'the population was split into two elements of such different mentality and tendencies that they will only accept the new condition of affairs with reluctance'.[14] Despite Lloyd George's commitment to supply British troops, his secretary of state for war, Winston Churchill, and the US president, Wilson, whose patience with European machinations was waning rapidly, had persuaded him to withhold them on the pretext of imperial commitments and a more pressing need at home to support the civil administration on issues such as the nationalist unrest in Ireland and the specious internal communist revolutionary threat. Other areas of Eastern Europe too demanded an Allied military presence. Danzig and Memel were under Allied occupation and plebiscites had been authorised on the German-Danish border, on the Polish-Czech border at Spisz and Orava, in East Prussia at Olsztyn and Kwidzyn and at Cieszyn. This left France, the country most strongly opposed to any weakening of German containment, to carry the bulk of the military burden and almost sole responsible for administering and policing the plebiscite area. Already the British and French attitudes to implementation of peace terms with Germany were diverging. The situation was not helped by the Russo-Polish War that was raging in the background and creating more instability and, perhaps more importantly for France, the desperate shortage of coal Germany had been required to supply. France refused to accept the strikes in Upper Silesia as an excuse for Germany defaulting on its quotas. Neither was it helpful that the French were allies of the Poles and had just emerged from four years of war with the Germans. It was a fine line for French soldiers to protect communities from harassment without being drawn into violence.

Local elections held in Upper Silesia in November 1919 had gone less well for the Germans than had been anticipated and might have been worse for them if, as a small Allied scrutiny commission reported, 'the Poles had enjoyed absolute freedom' to vote.[15] As a result, the

German state commissioner, Otto Horsing, was forced to resign by the nationalists who, having been required to withdraw all their *Grenzschutz* and *Freikorps* forces, now brought in the heavily militarised *Sicherheitspolizie* (security police) made up of ex-army personnel armed with machine guns and mortars. Over Polish protestations, this force was tolerated by the Allied Commission, who in reality felt that they could do little about it, as long as it was restricted in manpower and armaments. The Upper Silesian German elite had also recruited bands of professional ultra-nationalists hidden away on their country estates away from Allied scrutiny or operating in their mines and factories as security guards.

German funds flowed in from Berlin through the *Zentrale* organisation in Wrocław for the organisation of the German plebiscite campaign. The Poles were necessarily much less well organised given their social and financial constraints but they were compensated by the covert support of the leader of the Allied Commission, the French general Henri Le Rond. The British, whose sympathy was for the Germans, now showed a little more of their growing antipathy to the French, which had started over their differing views on implementation of Versailles, by undermining Le Rond at every opportunity and criticising his apparent abandonment of impartiality and determination to 'obtain the greatest possible share of Upper Silesia for Poland by fair means or foul'.[16] The British were succumbing to extreme German propaganda warning of the dire consequences for the German economy if the plebiscite favoured Poland.

In the spring of 1920, violent incidents arose between French troops and German Silesians around Opole. French cavalry was called onto the streets to disperse crowds and keep order. Wojciech Korfanty, a Polish member of the *Reichstag* and head of the Polish Plebiscite Committee who was intensely disliked by the head of the British contingent, urged disbandment of the *Sicherheitspolizie,* the halting of some Polish food exports to Germany and a crackdown on German agitators. Korfanty was described as 'a demagogic dictator … a brash, assertive figure', and blamed for later Polish atrocities but he had rather less influence over the Polish community and activists than was supposed at the time.[17]

The plebiscite battle lines were being drawn for the votes of those Upper Silesians who had no strong affiliation and were looking to see which side offered them the greatest political or economic advantage. The Germans argued that the Polish state was unviable and unsustainable and would collapse in a short time, either through internal strife or invasion. Industries in Upper Silesia, they claimed, would become run down under inefficient Polish management. The Poles countered by pointing out Germany's weakness under Allied domination and its vulnerability to internal communist insurrection, in which case foreign investment would flow into Poland instead.

Beyond Upper Silesia, in July 1920, the Red Army was poised to take Warsaw, which would effectively tear the new Polish state apart, in which case the plebiscite would become an irrelevance and the Allies would look favourably on Germany as the last bulwark to communist expansion in Europe. Lloyd George used up all his remaining credit with the Poles by advising them to accept Russian peace terms. On 17 August 1920, before news arrived of Piłsudski's counteroffensive that had driven the Russians back from the gates of Warsaw, a general strike had paralysed Upper Silesia provoked by the German decision to remain neutral in the Russo-Polish War, which was interpreted as favouring Russia.

The streets of Katowice filled with German demonstrators, who attacked French soldiers, killing four of them, while the *Sicherheitspolizie* stood by. It was left to Allied troops to try and restore order by firing on the crowds, killing at least ten. When relative calm was restored the next day the troops handed over control of the streets to the *Sicherheitspolizie*, who again failed to intervene as Polish shops and property were vandalised and pillaged. Korfanty called up Polish armed paramilitaries, fired up now by the news of the Red Army retreat from Warsaw, to oppose more destruction. They occupied villages around Mysłowice, Rubnik, Pszczyna and Bytom. The Poles extended their control, murdering indiscriminately and burning down the German village of Holdunów. Leading German citizens were taken back to Poland as hostages.

Both sides were in the grip of 'a witch's brew of spies, counterspies, bribery [and] death threats'.[18] The prominent Polish dissident Theophil Kupka, a journalist who had campaigned against Korfanty's 'corruption', was shot four times and killed on his doorstep in front of his wife and children. Polish propaganda was quick to blame Karl Spieker to divert attention away from persistent rumours that it had been Korfanty who had ordered Kupka's murder. Spieker was an agent of the Prussian State Commissariat for the Supervision of Public Order, which had been set up to monitor and counter the activities of radical and subversive groups. They now manoeuvred to claim part of the substantial budget that had been allocated to propaganda activities in Upper Silesia. Spieker, who worked in the shadows, used the money at first to set up a network of agents and publications but soon came up with the idea of a secret *Rednerschutz* (defence force) made up of *Freikorps* veteran volunteers 'of the most extreme type'.[19] It seems certain, however, that although the 100 million Reichsmarks sent from Berlin paid some of the wages of the *Rednerschutz* and was used to buy weapons, it is likely that much of it 'went to line the pockets of the many individuals through whose hands it passed'. Indeed Spieker, an 'impecunious journalist', in 1919 emerged from the two years of plebiscite involvement as a wealthy man.[20]

When the French appeared to be fraternising with the Polish insurgents and disarming the *Sicherheitspolizie,* a number of British administrators in the area resigned, complaining somewhat disingenuously of abandonment by the French of 'British standards of justice, impartiality and integrity'.[21] Very soon evidence of Polish atrocities surfaced and forced Korfanty to intervene to disband the Polish militants in early September 1920. However, violence had by now become a regular feature of life in Upper Silesia, with extra-judicial executions, arson and kidnappings committed in equal measure by both sides. The uprising, however, had forced the Allied Commission to ethnically balance the local security forces and take tighter control of the security arrangements. Demonstrations were banned and public displays of inflammatory material were prohibited. The extra British troops eventually arrived from the Rhine but the occasional atrocity was still perpetrated.

Germany's failure to protect its people during the second uprising brought home to them the very real possibility of losing control of the plebiscite process and the plebiscite itself. Even with a split the important mining and industrial areas were looking to go strongly for Poland and it was these upon that the whole issue revolved. Berlin now reassigned its funding of the campaign through the Silesian Committee.

There was considerable criticism of Le Rond for the way his troops had handled the second insurrection but not enough to have him removed. His influence was, however, diminished by increased British control of the decision-making process. Attention now focused on the administrative problems associated with the plebiscite. Having agreed that votes would be counted by communes, the next issue was deciding who was eligible to vote. The Paris delegates agreed that anyone born in Upper Silesia would be eligible to vote regardless of where they now lived. Locating such eligible voters and counting their votes securely was obviously going to be time-consuming and far from straightforward. The vastly better financed German activists would be much better placed to organise their remote voters who, in any case hugely outnumbered the Polish ones. The Poles demanded that such voting, which they claimed had skewed figures in the East Prussia plebiscite, be banned despite the fact that it was they who had called for it in the first place, but their objections went unheeded. The French complained that their security forces in Upper Silesia were quite inadequate to deal with the unrest that out of area voting would cause and also called for it to be abandoned. When Britain promised to hold 2,000 troops, currently on the Rhine, on standby in case of trouble, the issue was resolved but it was the bare minimum requirement and the French continued to ask for more. As well as out of area voters there was the question of what period of residence qualified for voting rights. Eventually it was agreed that only those people resident since before 1904 would qualify.

The date was fixed for the vote: 20 March 1921, and the secret ballot was carried out under such peaceful conditions that the atmosphere was described as 'one of the quietest days experienced in Upper Silesia [for six months]'. The population was offered a simple choice of Germany or Poland with no voice for the German-leaning movement for independence (*Bund der Oberschleisier/Związek Górnoślązaków. BdO*). Overall Germany took 59.6 per cent of the vote with the geographical distribution going as expected, but when it was discovered that around 200,000 ethnic Poles had voted for Germany the first accusations of fraud emerged. In his authoritative and meticulous analysis of the results, Professor T. Hunt Tooley finds that there is little evidence to show that the voting was influenced to any great extent by intimidation or coercion and Richard Blanke concluded that the result was a 'fairly accurate reflection of the desires of the populace … who placed their allegiance on the basis of social, economic, cultural and historical considerations' rather than ethnicity.[22]

In addition to Poland winning Upper Silesia's vital coal fields in Pszczyna and Rybnik, the German vote in the industrial area was confined to four large towns and the industrial triangle had been isolated from the solid German-voting regions to the west. Britain took the view that Germany had won the plebiscite and toyed with the idea of giving the whole of Upper Silesia to them in return for their acquiescence to British terms for repatriations but that was quickly abandoned when it was clear that France would never agree.

The Central Polish Plebiscite Committee published its criticism of the plebiscite in Upper Silesia in May 1921. It concluded that the plebiscites, resulting from the Versailles Treaty, showed that 'a plebiscite is perhaps the worst method possible' to redraw the frontier lines according to the principle of self-determination of nations, and to remove of the causes of future international conflict. In the case of the Polish plebiscites, one part of the population was permitted to perpetrate outrages and to cheat 'grossly and flagrantly'. The result of massive emigration was that that 'swarms of emigrants', brought in at the expense of the German government, were able to terrorise completely the poor Polish population in the northern and western districts of the plebiscite. The system of voting, as used in this plebiscite, that of handing to every voter two official slips with 'Poland' and 'Germany' written on them respectively, facilitated the Germans' use of bribery by openly buying the slips marked 'Poland' and destroying them. The fact that the German bureaucracy was left in place enabled its members to terrorise the Polish population. 'We have seen the national hope of a people long oppressed crushed once more under the iron heel of Prussian Despotism,' the report concluded.[23]

Throughout late March and April 1921 the heads of the Allied Commission, Le Rond for France, Colonel H.F.P. Percival for Britain and General Alberto De Marinis for Italy, discussed various ways of partitioning the region according to the vote but struggled to find common ground. Eventually on 30 March they submitted two proposals for consideration to Paris. Le Rond favoured a line that gave most of the industrial region to the Poles but conceded that it would put majority populations of German voters in the urban areas inside Poland. Percival and De Marinis allowed only Rybnik and Pless to go to Poland, leaving all the developed industrial area to go with Germany. Before these could be given due consideration, however, the Le Rond report was leaked to Korfanty's *Oberschlesisiche Grenzzeitung* newspaper, which published it on 1 May 1921, inflaming the Poles. Polish miners immediately took strike action. When the commissioners imposed martial law there was an armed insurrection along the eastern border on 2 May with Polish Silesian paramilitaries crossing the border to join up with POW units. By 3 May there were 60,000 highly organised, armed irregulars advancing on north and west of the River Oder in a manner that 'left little doubt that it had been carefully planned in advance'.[24] British troops, which the British government did not want there anyway, had been withdrawn immediately after the polls had closed. When Lloyd George suggested that German troops should be allowed to restore order, the French foreign minister, Aristide Briand, acerbically replied that instead of 'a lot of advice [it would be better if Britain contributed] men'.[25] The Italians, who had a small but committed force, saw twenty of their ranks killed by Poles, while the French, heavily outnumbered, simply fell back to avoid a massive confrontation, leaving almost half of Upper Silesia under Polish arms.

In Germany, the military commander Hans von Seeckt was preparing a counterattack with *Freikorps* units, fresh from putting down the Kapp Putsch and the Spartacist uprising with unflinching violence, but he recommended caution in a chaotically unstable situation that could easily get completely out of hand with potentially catastrophic consequences. Unfortunately, von Seeckt's military authority did not extend to the many paramilitaries who crossed the border despite his calls for restraint. At this moment, the French, with British connivance, created a crisis in the Rhineland by threatening to march in and occupy the Ruhr to force German agreement on reparation terms. This prevented all three countries from moving regular troops to Upper Silesia, leaving the German irregulars and the rapidly reinstated *Schutzpolizei* as the only force capable of standing up to the Polish volunteers army but neither of the paramilitary forces had any legitimacy.

By 11 May 1921, a new German government under Joseph Wirth had accepted the reparation terms in the hope that it would persuade the Allied Commission to take Germany's side in Upper Silesia.[26] Given that Wirth had a financial interest in Upper Silesia, having been a prominent sponsor of paramilitary units, it was no surprise when he ignored von Seeckt's advice and appointed General Karl Höfer as overall commander of the German volunteer and *Freikorps* forces. Korfanty hit the panic button and called on the commissioners to come up with a deal that would allow him to call off the uprising without losing face. A deal of sorts was struck that might have ended the violence except that Britain suspected Korfanty of bluffing to get a ceasefire while the Poles controlled most of the region and even doubted his authority over the Poles. Instead, Germany was urged to halt rail transport and withhold food supplies to the Polish areas. The Allied Commission was forced to change its position and refused to have any further talks with Korfanty.

The conflict had grown over the early months of 1921 to the point where, after a Polish armed offensive designed to annul the German plebiscite victory, a state of open warfare now existed with the British much more involved that they had ever imagined they would be. A report in *The Manchester Guardian* accused a British officer of actually commanding a *Freikorps* unit, forcing the British into a denial and explanation that the officer had merely been assigned to collect intelligence. A Polish newspaper accused the British of treating the Poles in the same manner that they had treated 'Hindoos, Kaffirs, Persians and the like.' In the House of Commons, Lloyd George called on the French to restrain the Polish paramilitaries and restore order or let the Germans do it for them. Tensions rose as the French attitude moved from 'passivity ... to near active cooperation with the Polish insurgents' and French security forces became hostile to British officials by harassing them at road blocks, which brought the British delegation in Poland 'close to disintegration'.[27] A number of them resigned and others, including Percival, were recalled having suffered 'nervous exhaustion'. The Italian forces quietly withdrew to the west side of the River Oder and kept well out of the firing line.

While the military conflict had calmed somewhat, food shortages were becoming acute owing to the refusal of German railwaymen to run trains into industrial areas, and workers' wages remained unpaid due to the Reichsbank bowing to German industrialists' pressure and withholding funds. Germany urged the British to bring back the four battalions that had been withdrawn to the Ruhr. Britain agreed but only if the request came through from the French. Foch refused to consider such a thing, but he was overruled by Briand and so the 2,000 British troops on the Rhine, reinforced by the 2nd Battalion, Prince of Wales's Leinster Regiment (Royal Canadians) and the 2nd Battalion, The Connaught Rangers, returned on 23 May 1921 and were deployed around Opole. Unfortunately, they were seen by both sides as pro-German, especially given their near total control of the German plebiscite police. Passions on both sides were still running very high with daily reports of murders and atrocities that were almost impossible to verify one way or the other.

On 24 June 1921, Korfanty agreed to a phased Polish withdrawal of insurgents from the whole of Upper Silesia over a seven-day period, but urged calm in the areas vacated where local officials would be reinstated and peace-keeping forces would move in. Germany bowed to immense pressure to take Korfanty at his word and comply with the terms of the withdrawal when Höfer signed up to it on 26 June. The plan was executed as agreed and by 5 July 1921 the third and bloodiest uprising was over.

Control of the Upper Silesian coal mines, and to a lesser extent its industrial manufacturing capacity, had been of the utmost importance to both Germany and Poland but the peaceful resolution of disputed ownership had been forced upon them by the Treaty of Versailles and that crucially required close cooperation between Britain and France. The issue had been not only a battle of power between Berlin and Warsaw but also a battle of wills between London and Paris.

All through June and July 1921 the Allied Commission had tried to get the Allied Supreme War Council to agree to a final division of Upper Silesia. Britain and Italy tried to force acceptance of their solution by isolating Briand but he resisted sufficiently to threaten British-Franco relations and eventually the matter was put before a meeting of British, French and Italian prime ministers on 8 August 1921. Lloyd George, with his usual bombast, and Briand, employing guile and sweet reasonableness, grandstanded in front of US and Japanese observers, giving no ground and getting nowhere. As ever, it was the 'industrial triangle' that proved so difficult to apportion and nobody really wanted to partition that. Lloyd George suggested that the Poles lacked the necessary acumen to manage the industries efficiently and accused the French of using the issue to further punish Germany. With no compromise in sight, the matter was fobbed off to the League of Nations to sort out. The League faced its first real opportunity to 'demonstrate its ability to settle a key issue among the great powers',[28] considered the matter and presented their findings to the Allied Supreme War Council on 12 October 1921. Their solution was to draw a boundary line right through the industrial area, leaving most of the resources in Poland. This 'seemingly arbitrary, antidemocratic and punitive'[29] decision by the League of Nations to award Poland rather more than the plebiscite had warranted ensured that the public resentment in Germany against Versailles was reinforced. Extreme German nationalist movements, including the *Bund Deutscher Osten* and, later, the Nazi *Ostforschung*, would voraciously feed off this bitterness. A wave of protests broke out in Berlin, bringing the government down, but there was little choice for either country in the end but to accept the Allied Supreme War Council's decision.

Poland was awarded most of the coal mines and industrial plants, along with the largest urban centre of Kattowitz and Konigshutte, which had actually opted to remain German in majorities ranging from 65 to 75 per cent. The League of Nations essentially nullified the overall 60 per cent vote in favour of Germany and, coming after Versailles when, after plebiscites, Poland had been awarded all the former Prussian provinces that the Germans had hoped to retain, the judgement fuelled a growing German sense of injustice. The region became one of the prime centres of 'nationalism and social utopianism' fuelling ideological conflicts over the next two decades.[30] The Weimar Republic that had signed off on Versailles was losing much of its authority and legitimacy and would struggle to retain the confidence of the German people in the years to come. The German-Polish Accord on Upper Silesia was concluded on 15 May 1922 and this officially divided the region, but it remained a breeding ground for irredentist militant nationalism in both Germany and Poland, who both denied the region's multi-ethnic character in favour of simplistic homogenous identities.

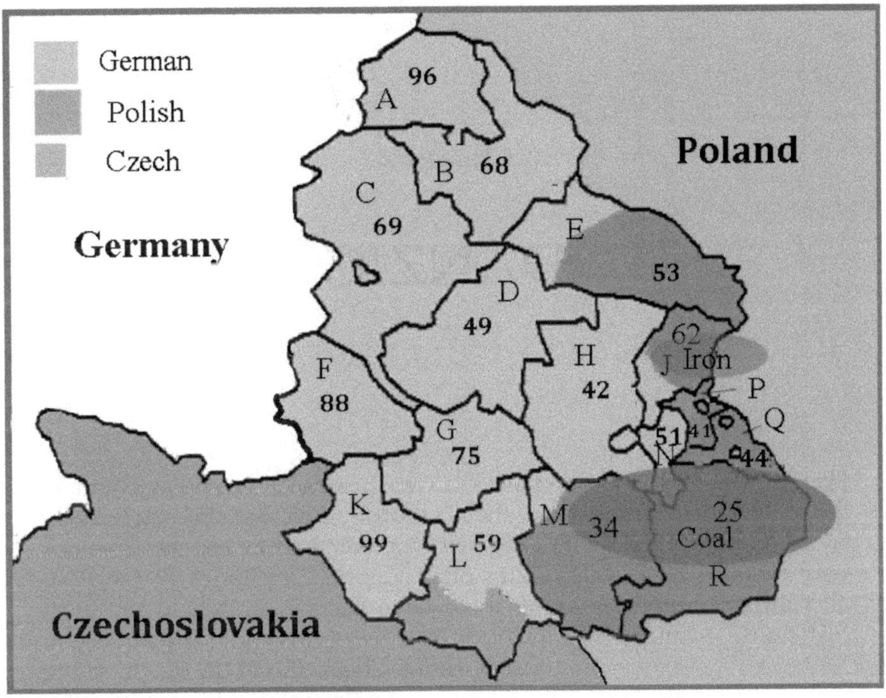

A	Kreuzberg	J	Tarnowitz
B	Rosenberg	K	Leobschütz
C	Oppeln	L	Ralibor
D	Groß Strehlitz	M	Rubnyk
E	Lublinitz	N	Lublinitz
F	Neustadt	P	Beuthen
G	Kosel	Q	Kattowitz
H	Tost-Gleiwitz	R	Pleß

Map showing the percentage of population that voted to go with Germany in each province of Upper Silesia. The dark regions became Polish and the lighter regions German. Note that even in regions such as Katowice that voted 56 per cent for Poland, the city itself gave 85 per cent of its votes to Germany and other urban areas showed a similar preference.

The region of Upper Silesia was to remain a tinderbox throughout the rest of the 1920s and all through the 1930s. When Hitler turned his full gaze on Poland after his 'bloodless victory' in Prague, border disputes became a convenient tool of his aggressive diplomacy.

Chapter 4

DANZIG

> Danzig was and is a German city. The Corridor was and is German. Both these territories owe their cultural development exclusively to the German people. Danzig was separated from us, the Corridor was annexed by Poland. As in other German territories of the East, all German minorities living there have been ill-treated in the most distressing manner.
>
> Adolf Hitler, Chancellor of the Reich, before the Reichstag, 1 September 1939

After initially refusing to do so, Germany had been forced to sign up to the Versailles Treaty in 1919 but consistently saw it as unjust. 'We came to Versailles in the expectation of receiving a peace proposal based on the agreed principles,' they said at the Paris negotiations in May 1919 and decried 'the victorious violence of our enemies'. In their view the reconstruction of their economic life was rendered impossible and the international Reparation Commission, with its economic and cultural dictatorial powers, crushed any semblance of German self-determination. They noted how previous peace treaties had been a factor in originating and prolonging future wars and presciently declared that the 'strength of the hatred and bitterness which this war has engendered' would prolong that process. The Treaty, once signed, gave Poland the Poznań province as well as Pomeralia, separating East Prussia from the rest of Germany. In a compromise that infuriated Poles and Germans alike, the port of Danzig (the Free and Hansa Town of Danzig), in a narrow strip of Polish territory known as the Danzig Corridor, with its majority German population, was put under the administration of the League of Nations and placed within the Polish Customs area.

The League established special Polish rights in regard to the use of docks, wharves, waterways, railways, etc., provided against any discrimination within the Free City to the detriment of Polish citizens or those of Polish origin and speech, and entrusted to the Polish government the conduct of the foreign relations of the Free City and the diplomatic protection of the interests of its citizens abroad. The Constitution of the Free City, under the guarantee of the League of Nations, provided for the appointment (by the League of Nations) of a high commissioner 'with the duty of dealing in the first instance with all differences arising between Poland and the Free City of Danzig in regard to this Treaty or any arrangements or agreements made thereunder'.[31]

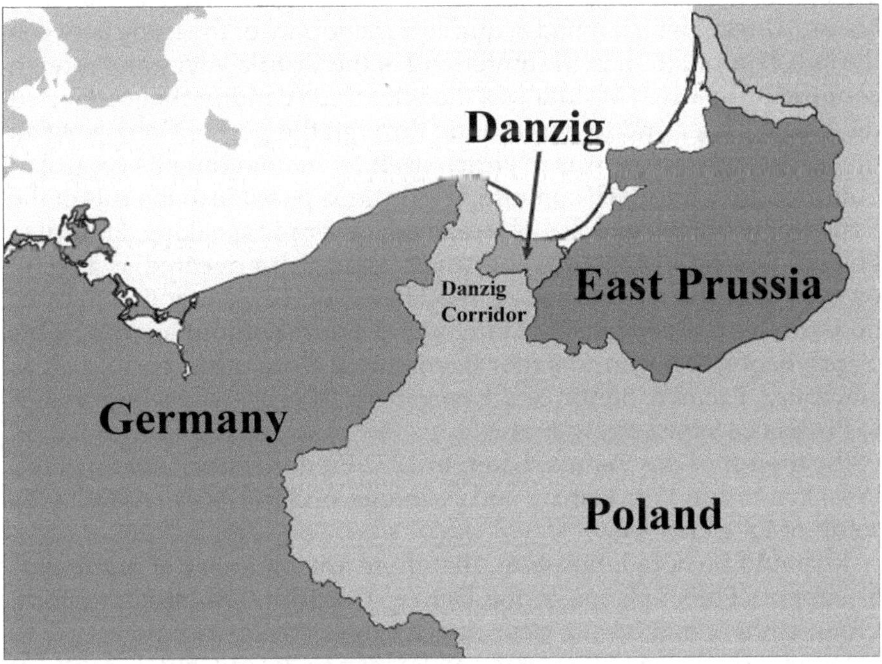

The Danzig Corridor

In the tenth century the Polish Kingdom of Boleslas the Brave had extended from the Elbe to the Dnieper and from the Baltic to the borders of Hungary. After two centuries of almost endless wars, the Order of Teutonic Knights conquered West Prussia and Danzig in 1309, thus cutting off the Polish State from the sea.

Frederick the Great said: 'Who rules over the mouth of the Vistula and the City of Danzig will be more master of Poland than the king who rules there.' He clearly intended that it would be he who would have this control and by so doing 'have a bridle on the Poles and be in a position to dictate to them'.[32]

Danzig had for centuries been a crucially important city. In 1360, as a result of growing trade between Danzig and the Hansa merchants, the city had formally become a member of the Hanseatic League, making it one of the richest and most powerful of the Hansa towns with a charter confirming its ancient rights and liberties. In 1410, however, the Battle of Tannenberg saw the knights defeated by an alliance of Poles, Lithuanians and Russians under the leadership of the Polish King Wladyslaw and the Polish State regained control of the Vistula, Danzig and West Prussia, while East Prussia became a feudal fief of the Polish Crown. The period 1500–1700 was a golden age in Danzig's history, during which it had acquired a monopoly of the trade between the Polish population in the hinterland of the Vistula valley and foreign countries. The River Vistula was the vital trade conduit that connected the Polish hinterland to world trade through the port of Danzig. At all times Danzig's policy was to enrich itself by maintaining its control of Polish trade, while itself submitting as little as possible to the rule of the Polish king, but the merchants remained, generally speaking, faithful to Poland. Danzig's prosperity, however, almost disappeared as a result of wars and the dissolution of the Hanseatic League and it became no more than a provincial capital and seaport without special rights or privileges. It began to suffer competition from other ports such as Hamburg, Bremen, Stettin and Königsberg, after which its importance to Prussia became largely strategic, in view of its geographical situation at the mouth of the Vistula. Later, in 1772 Frederick the Great secured West Prussia, in 1793 Danzig and Poznania, and in 1795 territory to the south of East Prussia.

It should be noted, however, that there are a number of arguments to support Polish claims to the Danzig Corridor. On ethnographical grounds there had been a clear case for the Paris Peace Conference to recommend cession of Pomorze and Poznań to Poland, but that did not necessarily apply to Danzig. The question now was what to do about Danzig. A compromise solution was arrived at which, it was hoped, would do justice to the reasonable claims both of the Danzigers and of the Poles. Article 102 of the Treaty of Versailles placed Danzig under the protection of the League of Nations and provided for the appointment (by the League of Nations) of a high commissioner. It placed the Free City within the Polish Customs area, established special Polish rights in regard to the use of docks, wharves, waterways, railways, etc. and provided against any discrimination to the detriment of Polish citizens. Because the population of Danzig was mostly German it was not incorporated into the new Poland and was left in a position 'similar to that it occupied during so many centuries'.[33]

The Province of West Prussia, within which were located Poznania and the port of Danzig, was established as part of the German Empire in 1878 and reassigned to the Free State of Prussia within the Weimar Republic, and then became part of Poland after the Treaty of Versailles. In 1910, a census had shown that Poles constituted 58 per cent of the population, which was a huge underestimate given that all bilingual inhabitants were deemed to be German. In elections to the Reichstag, the area consistently returned Polish deputies right up to 1912. In the months before the declaration of Polish independence huge numbers of Germans had fled the region that, together with other factors, is strongly indicative of the fact that German efforts to Germanise the region since 1772 had failed and its Polish character had prevailed, giving the Danzig Corridor a distinctly historical Polish character.[34]

After the Treaty of Versailles, there were a number of issues tied up in German-Polish relations over Danzig and the 'Corridor'. Germany demanded an entirely free passage between Germany and East Prussia. Poland demanded free and secure access to the sea given that Poland's foreign trade relied on the River Vistula and the port of Danzig. One of the problems for Danzig was that it was predominantly a linguistically and culturally German city whose prosperity and economic interests were dependent on close relations with the surrounding Polish hinterland. Similar problems existed in the predominantly Polish province of West Prussia (Pomorze), where extensive colonisation and Germanisation had been started in the days of Bismarck and continued before the war.

Despite its defeat in November 1918, Germany was still the greatest industrial power in Europe and concentrated the minds of all European foreign ministers. France feared Germany but needed its coal and steel, while Britain looked to the German market for its goods. Britain was also anxious to see peace in Europe so that it could devote its limited armed forces to the defence of its Empire. Eastern Europe was not seen as a sphere of vital British interests, all of which contributed to the belief of all British governments that the Polish-German frontier should be revised in Germany's favour and the port of Danzig should be returned to them along with the region of Poznania.

In the light of President Wilson's Fourteen Points, a British delegation went to Poznań on behalf of the Allies in December 1918 to see for themselves what the situation was like on the ground. The Poles themselves seemed split between Dmowski and Piłsudski but it was Paderewski who met them in the city, which was awash with demonstrations of Polish nationalism. The incendiary situation was soon made evident to the delegates when pro-German activists opened fire on Paderewski's hotel. Polish militia tried to calm the streets and take back control but fighting erupted all across Poznania and West Prussia. It was only in February 1919 that a ceasefire was finally established with Poznania firmly in Polish hands, but its transfer would not go unchallenged. The seemingly impossible task of establishing conditions for a permanent settlement included holding a plebiscite after the peace had been concluded, voting by communes and permitting ex-residents to return to vote. Ever since Versailles, Danzig had been dangerously sandwiched between Germany proper in the west and German East Prussia.

The Danzig Corridor was an area in the coastal district of Pomerelia that was formerly part of East Prussia. This strip of land provided the Second Republic of Poland with its only direct access to the Baltic Sea and was one of the guarantees proposed by President Wilson. While Danzig and the territory immediately adjacent to it were predominantly German, the majority of the population of Pomorze (West Prussia) and Poznań was Polish. On ethnographical grounds as well as on historical grounds, therefore there was a clear case for the cession of Pomorze and Poznań, but by the same criteria Danzig could not be ceded to Poland. On the other hand, the economic ties between the city and Poland, its history, and its strategic importance were such that neither was it considered feasible to leave it under German sovereignty.

The authority of the Polish state in Danzig was written into the Treaty of Paris on 9 November 1920. This had established a Port and Waterways Board to administer the port and so deprived Poland of port revenues. According to a Transit Convention, Germans were allowed to travel across the Danzig Corridor between West and East Prussia upon presentation of a passport and any goods traded between the two were subjected to fees. Transport of German troops and weapons between West and East Prussia was permitted but only 'if Germany found itself in a defensive war'.[35]

The Danzig Corridor separated Germany from the province of East Prussia and Danzig itself was separated from both Poland and Germany. The term 'Corridor' was first used in 1919 and appropriated as German nationalist propaganda in 1920 but reference to the region as a corridor came to be regarded as offensive by interwar Polish diplomats. The majority of the population in the Danzig Corridor was Polish and the Poles argued that without direct access to the Baltic, Poland's economic independence would be impossible and be dependent upon the goodwill of Germany. Danzig, however, was placed under the protection of the League of Nations without a plebiscite in the hope that the city might retain its essentially German character while allowing Poland full use of the port.[36] The Danzig administration, however, attempted to deprive Poland of important rights granted under Versailles, which it was allowed to do by the Allied Supreme War Council, who were insufficiently concerned to make an issue out of it. While Danzig was to have been included within the Polish customs area, in practice, it became mired in a complex system resulting in many disputes between the city administration and Poland, which Germany was quick to use as propaganda against Polish involvement. After the dock workers of Danzig harbour had gone on strike at a critical moment during the Russo-Polish War, refusing to unload ammunition, the Polish government built a new seaport at Gydnia in the territory of the Danzig Corridor, and connected this seaport to the Upper Silesian industrial centres by a new railway, thus challenging the economic status of Danzig.

The Prussian king, Frederick the Great (Frederick II), had settled around 300,000 colonists in the eastern provinces of Prussia in 1772 after the annexation of the region during the first partition of Poland aiming to replace the Polish population, and another attempt at Germanisation was attempted in 1832. By 1910 almost half the population was German but after the end of the First World War this had dropped dramatically to less than one fifth. This exodus continued and was the result of a number of factors including coercion to leave by the Polish government, fear of a Russian takeover in 1920 and to avoid conscription in the Russo-Polish War. It is also true that a number of repressive measures were taken by local and regional Polish authorities as reprisals for former discrimination against Poles.

There had been an East Prussian plebiscite on 11 July 1920 over self-determination of the regions of southern Warmia, Masuria and Powiśle, which had been in parts of Allenstein and Marienwerder, in accordance with Articles 94 to 97 of the Treaty of Versailles. This was at a time when Poland faced almost certain defeat by the Red Army. In the period leading up to the German-conducted plebiscite there were serious disturbances and many claims of German intimidation of the Poles. In return, the Polish authorities tried to prevent traffic through the Danzig Corridor, interrupting postal, telegraphic and telephone communication. The British representative on the Marienwerder Plebiscite Commission, H.D. Beaumont, complained of disruption by Polish officials and ill-will between Polish and German nationalities, which meant that, in his opinion, it was impossible to believe that any settlement could have any chance of being permanent. 'Not even the most attractive economic advantages would induce any German to vote Polish,' he said. The whole issue of the frontier was left in a mess with no natural line to follow and cutting Germany off from the riverbank within 1 mile of Marienwerder, which was certain to vote German. When the votes were counted, there was an overwhelming vote in favour of joining East Prussia, with Olsztyn / Allenstein region voting 98 per cent in favour and the Marienwerder / Kwidzy region voting 92 per cent.

Relations between the Polish and German populations were generally not particularly bitter but political decisions taken by the Polish government would become sufficiently troubling to the German population that by 1922 about two thirds of Germans from the former West Prussia and Poznania had left for their German homeland. Following a plebiscite in the vitally important Upper Silesia it was partitioned into the German (Western Upper Silesia) and the Polish (Eastern Upper Silesia). Under international pressure, the opposing sides agreed to sign the Geneva Protocol on Upper Silesia in which the Polish right to exercise their culture and language freely in Western Upper Silesia was thus guaranteed. The protection of minorities, particularly in the context of German-Polish relations, had been a key feature of the Paris Conference and the Versailles Treaty, which had endeavoured to strengthen the conduct of international relations. With almost 1.5 million Germans living in the new state of Poland, the fate of these minorities was soon to become particularly relevant. Poland had been forced to sign up to what became known as the Little Treaty of Versailles to protect minorities who differed from the majority population in race, language or religion.

Of the 32 million inhabitants of the new Poland, some 10 million had non-Polish nationalities. These included 5 million Ukrainians who fiercely resented their fate and responded with terrorist activities that were answered with brutal repression. One and a half million Byelorussians lived in miserable poverty, which the Polish government did little to alleviate. Three quarters of a million Germans, however, were quite a different matter with powerful support from their homeland and a strong cultural, intellectual and nationalistic character. The 2.5 million Jews found life particularly hard, living within an intensely anti-Semitic culture that thrived under conservative administrations. The League of Nations was constantly bombarded with complaints about Poland's treatment of its minorities.

Germany did everything it could, within its very limited means, to search for lenient interpretation of the Versailles terms by exploiting the growing differences between Britain and France over implementation of the Treaty and played upon the almost universal fear of Soviet communism spreading from the East. Internally, calm and stability were slowly established in Germany through a group of officers who were the remnants of the Imperial High Command under the leadership of Generals Wilhelm Groener and Hans von Seeckt. This group of men provided a bedrock of authority for the government as the only force capable of challenging the political chaos that was sweeping the country. The two leaders, however, while working together to give Germany the stability it desperately needed, had differing visions of how the country should develop as it emerged from the catastrophe of the war.

Groener believed that Germany could regain its relevance and power by appealing to the Western Allies and offering itself as a leader of the anti-communist crusade. His concept involved German reoccupation of Poznań and a commitment from the Western Allies that Germany would 'not be bullied on the Polish question'.[37] He did not oppose the Versailles terms but warned that if Poland was allowed to become a viable state it would eventually subsume East Prussia. At the same time he saw a Russia freed from communism as the best hope Germany had of keeping Poland in check but this hope also dissolved when General Rudiger von der Goltz's *Freikorps* army fighting alongside White Russians in the Baltic was forced to disarm, leaving the Bolsheviks firmly in power in Moscow.

Von Seeckt, on the other hand, had no intention of meekly accepting the Versailles terms and while his views on Poland matched those of Groener, his attitude to Soviet Russia was quite different. He had become head of the *Truppenamt* and chief of the German general staff with a single-minded ambition to restore Germany to its pre-war eminence economically, militarily and politically. In this he saw 'close understanding with Russia' as the 'immovable goal' of German policy.[38] He refused to back Poland in its war with Russia, calling it 'a mortal enemy of Germany, [an] ally of France [a] thief of German soil [and an] annihilator of German culture'. He appeared sanguine about the possibility of Poland collapsing and allowing Bolshevism to perch itself on Germany's borders, apparently seeing not conflict but an open road towards a glorious 'union with Russia'.

The prospect of Poland surviving the war with Russia seemed, to von Seeckt, to be highly unlikely. He saw the huge communist propaganda drive within Poland as weakening it internally, even in the army, rendering its capacity for resistance 'to be rated as insignificant'.[39] The Western Allies would do little to help Poland, he believed, because they lacked both the means and the will to intervene. Germany would certainly resist the passage of French or British troops if they tried to cross German soil to reach Poland. Torn between his hatred of communism and his need for Russian support against the Western Allies, von Seeckt had a 'compelling duty to [encourage] danger or even destruction to this most unbearable neighbour of ours [Poland]', and 'viewed with gratitude' the prospect of its demise.[40]

When a Soviet attack against Poland seemed inevitable in March 1920, von Seeckt proposed that Germany should refuse to give any help to either side but must be ready to reach an agreement with the Russians that they would respect the 1914 borders and hand over all Polish territories ruled by Germany at that time. Of course, the war did not develop as von Seeckt had predicted and all this came to naught after the 'Miracle on the Vistula'.

Another important view was that of the German foreign minister, Baron Ago von Maltzan, who because of his political role had a more nuanced vision but he, too, was conflicted between opposition to or cooperation with the Russians. While trying to persuade the Allies to accept the principle of employing Germany as a foil against Bolshevism, he was also meeting the Russian diplomat Victor Kopp, Trotsky's man who had been captured and imprisoned in Germany during the First World War, in Berlin to discuss economic relations. Kopp was enthusiastic to promote agreement of non-intervention in each other's internal affairs and an immediate exchange of prisoners of war. Von Maltzan was not prepared to go as far as establishing diplomatic relations but was receptive to the idea of trade negotiations.

Meanwhile, in April 1920, the German chancellor, Friedrich Ebert, in anticipation of a Russian victory, spoke out against the 'hateful policy of Poland towards Germany', predicting that soon the Red Army would take over the country, but at the same time he was confident that the need for the Russians to remain on good terms with Germany would prevent a Bolshevist revolution there. Poland responded by condemning the universal desire across all German political parties for revenge against Poland and their irreconcilable opposition to the very existence of Poland as an independent state. Clearly one of the things that drew Russia and Germany into a closer alliance was their anti-Polish sentiments.

The Russian attitude to Germany during its war with Poland was twofold in that on the one hand it had ambitions to foment communist revolution in Germany but was, at the same time, fearful that the

Germans would succumb to Western influences by joining with them in an anti-communist crusade. Its policy towards Germany at this time, therefore, was to maintain very friendly relations and to try outbidding the West by holding out the prospect of fruitful cooperation in those areas currently denied to Germany by Versailles. Moscow, however, was confused by Poland's withdrawal of troops from its border with Germany to join in the attack on the Ukraine. The Russians took this as a sign that they had come to a secret agreement with Germany that they suspected included a pledge for German troops to enter Poland to quell any communist uprising that might occur while Piłsudski's troops were fighting abroad. There was precious little trust in public or in private.

Germany saw the evolving war as creating the sort of instability on its borders that would allow it to take advantage of the chaos and find an excuse to move troops into those areas stripped from it at Versailles. For instance, at the height of the Russo-Polish War, it made a request of the Entente to double the size of the German army to 200,000 as a precaution against a Soviet victory but it was made clear that 'any support of the Poles against the Bolsheviks was out of the question'.[41] Lord D'Abernon, at the Spa Conference in July 1920, seemed sympathetic towards the Germans, stressing the importance 'of obtaining [their] cooperation against the Soviets', and Winston Churchill wrote about 'the dark future should Poland succumb' and agreed that a more lenient attitude should be adopted towards Germany if it was 'willing [to stand up] against the Bolshevik onslaught'.[42] The French, however, wouldn't hear of it. Their interest was in keeping Poland strong against the possibility of a resurgent Germany and they would not countenance strengthening Germany at Poland's expense. At that time, the only country that really wanted to see Poland destroyed as an independent state was Russia. Germany hoped to exploit this by treading a fine diplomatic line that might eventually result in the reclamation of Poznania and the Danzig Corridor.

On 31 July 1920, Russian troops had reached the border with East Prussia and were ordered to halt in anticipation that German troops would march into western Poland to re-establish the pre-war German-Russian border. At the same time, activity was intensified to bring about proletarian revolution in Poland. This did not appeal to von Seeckt, who was not prepared to make such a drastic breach of Versailles fearing French retaliation, but he hoped that the situation might allow Germany to 'establish the groundwork for the recovery of lands snatched from us', and with that, to emphasise his disinclination to get further involved, he packed his bags and went off on holiday.[43]

The German government formally declared neutrality in the Russo-Polish War but, in reality, while it denied transit of French military aid to Poland across its territory, it was giving its own direct aid to Russia.

The Poles, fearing German intervention in the war, were unnerved by reports of six Zeppelin airships passing through Polish air space in a north-easterly direction towards East Prussia and by evidence that the Red Army was using German ammunition. They also recorded instances of German officers serving in the Red Army. Polish agents intercepted letters between German nationalist *Friekorps* detachments and Kopp that promised Germany would be allowed to occupy Danzig and Upper Silesia if they agreed to provide military assistance by invading Poland from the west as soon as Red Army forces entered Warsaw.

The threat of German intervention eventually dissipated with Piłsudski's victory in the Battle of Warsaw but it had shown clearly that Germany was prepared to move in any political direction that offered a loosening of the bonds of Versailles. The lessons for Poland were clear. Russia would do its utmost to bring about proletarian revolution in that country either directly or by first fomenting revolution in Germany and then gripping Poland in a vice, or it would work with a capitalist Germany to maintain a simmering hostility towards Poland in the hope that future events might allow them both to benefit from any instability that might arise.

The Polish victory against Russia, while maintaining a hostile stance towards Germany, was a huge boost to national morale and self-confidence that was not entirely warranted. There simultaneously grew a sense of military power that could withstand the danger that continued to lurk on two fronts alongside a bitterness towards the Western Powers, who had obfuscated and prevaricated over the question of sending aid to Poland during the war. It was especially galling for them that it had been the French, theoretically Poland's closest ally, who had refused to compromise on the issue of bolstering German democratic institutions that, in the long, run would curb Moscow's ambitions to export communism all across Eastern Europe. Polish confidence in Western support was at a low ebb and showed little signs of recovering. At the same time the growing, if clandestine, military cooperation between Russia and Germany posed a long-term threat based to some extent as it was on a common hatred of an independent Poland, whose very existence seemed to be a provocative affront to them both.

Chapter 5

THE TREATY OF RAPALLO

> The Two Governments undertake to give each other mutual assistance for the alleviation of their economic difficulties in the most benevolent spirit.
>
> Clause V of the Treaty of Rapallo signed between Germany and Russia, 16 April 1922

Two days after the signing of the peace treaty between Poland and Russia at Riga, on 7 October 1920, the Polish foreign minister, Sapieha, declared that 'it seemed to him unlikely that the peace about to be concluded would be of very long duration, or that its territorial provisions would be of a permanent character'.[1] He saw little likelihood of a friendly understanding or rapprochement with Russia, whatever happened in that country. It was essential, therefore, for Poland to conclude alliances with the other Western neighbours of Russia but General Tadeusz Rozwadowski, chief of the Polish general staff, expected that the war with Russia would be renewed in the spring. The German foreign minister, Dr Walter Simons, was of a similar opinion, saying 'recent events have diminished considerably the hope for an early end to the conflict between Poland and Russia', with the Soviets now apparently preparing for a new attack on the Lithuanian border. Appealing to the Western Allies, Simons said that Germany was 'the barrier against Bolshevism and disorder'. and despite having achieved a notable victory over the Red Army, the Poles were now 'far too weak' to fill that role.[2]

The Russians viewed things from a different perspective. In a speech on 2 October 1920, Lenin called Poland:

> a buffer state ... designed to safeguard Germany from Soviet communism and ... an instrument to be used against the Bolsheviks ... An independent Poland is very dangerous to Soviet Russia, it is an evil which, however, at the present time has also its redeeming features; for while it exists we may safely count on Germany, because the Germans hate Poland and will at any time make common cause with us in order to strangle Poland.[3]

The French, he said, were coming to Poland's aid in order to recoup from Russia the billions of roubles they loaned to the Tsarist government. Lenin clearly viewed the Treaty of Riga in the same light as the Treaty of Brest-Litovsk, the terms of which would be ignored as circumstances dictated. While Russian leaders still harboured the expectation of an imminent outbreak of communist revolution in the countries of Central Europe, the Poles looked forward to the demise of Bolshevism.

Poland had found it difficult to follow a consistent foreign policy because Piłsudski and Dmowski once again had diverging views on the path Poland should tread. Dmowski was happy with Riga and thought that Poland should consolidate its position in the east while Russia was weak and preoccupied with the Far East, where both Japan and the emerging power of China were giving them pause for thought. This ensured that Russia would look for good relations with Poland. Piłsudski, on the other hand, wanted to expand Polish influence by helping Byelorussia and the Ukraine to achieve independence and thereby become Poland's natural allies. To achieve this he needed French support and so, on 2 April 1921, he secretly approached the French minister, Hector de Panafieu, and warned that the Russian government would not, or could not, fulfil certain provisions of the Treaty of Riga having lost much of its authority and power. The best thing, therefore, would be to maintain calm on Russia's western borders while the regime collapsed from within as a result of civil war and on no account give it cause to restore its prestige through a new military offensive that would re-establish national unity through xenophobia.[4] Poland should strive to demolish the notion of Russia as a great power, both internationally and internally. To this end Piłsudski advocated support for the dissident Boris Savinkov anti-Bolshevik faction in Russia and Petliura in the Ukraine, even though Savinkov had lost the support of the Polish government and Petliura's group had been theoretically liquidated at Riga never to be reformed. Polish military intelligence proceeded to put this into practice in a clear violation of Riga without reference to the Polish cabinet, which put Piłsudski in a difficult position, but he gambled that if he was successful then the French would support him. He resorted to subterfuge by using his power as commander-in-chief of the army and blithely ignoring the extreme gravity of Poland's economic and financial situation by concluding military agreements with both Savinkov and Petliura that infuriated Moscow.

Petliura would end his life on Rue Racine near the Boulevard Saint-Michel in Paris on 25 May 1926. He was approached by Samuel (Sholom) Schwartzbard, a Jewish watchmaker whose parents had been murdered in one of the pogroms in Odesa allegedly on Petliura's orders. A nurse, Haia Greenberg, testified at Schwartzbard's trial that she had witnessed the murders in 1919. The jury was out for less than one hour before returning with a verdict of 'not guilty' of murder on the grounds that the killing was not premeditated. *The New York Times* reported that the 400 people in the public gallery cheered the verdict. The court would not condemn him for avenging the deaths of so many Jews (some claims put the total at 30,000) and even though the fact of his murder of Petliura was not contested, the court declared him insane and he walked free from the courtroom.[5]

France had lost its main pre-war ally, Russia, after the communist revolution and looked for new ways of building an alliance against Germany. The new Polish state had successfully fought off a Russian attack and seemed the best option to challenge both German revanchism and Bolshevism. For Poland, the incentive was to have an ally to monitor Germany from the West and support Poland in case of future conflict with Russia. A Franco-Polish Alliance was signed in Paris on 9 February 1921 by Sapieha and Briand. The agreement brought the two countries together in economic agreements and a mutual assistance pact in the event one of the signatories became a victim of an unprovoked attack by either Germany or Russia although it fell short of requiring France to enter a war on Poland's behalf or indeed of sending any troops at all. Meanwhile, Poland concluded a raft of agreements with Germany dealing with the practicalities of administration in the territories ceded to Poland at Versailles and, as a result of plebiscites, even the thorny issue of Danzig was subject to initiatives from both sides, giving hope of some stability and acceptance of the situation by the populations. For its part, Germany was coming to terms with the parlous state of the Red Army after its defeat by Poland and realised that German hopes of recovery, in the short term, lay with the Western Allies, which inevitably meant refraining from antagonistic actions against France's ally, Poland.

One month later Poland concluded a similar alliance with Romania by signing the Convention on Defensive Alliance. Like Poland, Romania wanted to create a cordon sanitaire against Russia as well as strengthening its position against the Bela Kun regime in Hungary. Romania had also set its sights on the annexation of Bessarabia, to create more of a protective barrier against Russia. Hungary and Romania had already fought alongside Polish forces in Western Ukraine, whose independence they both opposed. Poland valued a deal with Romania that would allow transportation of war material in the event of war with Germany. The treaty with Romania allowed that in the event of an unprovoked attack on either state's eastern border, the other would come to its aid. This now gave Poland two treaties and alliances with one partner to the West and another in the East to establish a security strategy against both Germany and Russia, which it would strive to maintain it at all costs.

In May 1921, after the Russians had seized Georgia, the new Polish foreign minister, Konstanty Skirmunt, pressed the Baltic States to join Poland in a defensive alliance. Like Sapieha, he disagreed with Piłsudski over the implementation of Riga, favouring non-involvement in Russian internal affairs and distancing Poland from anti-Russian activity in general. Peaceful coexistence was his ambition, but he had no illusions about how difficult that would be given the hostility between the two countries. He was able to arrange diplomatic relations on 4 August 1921 at a time when famine in Russia and organisational chaos in the Red Army threatened to bring down the government. Despite its internal contradictions, however, the Bolshevik regime was sufficiently confident to begin flouting some of the terms of Riga while Western governments brought pressure to bear on Poland to stop harbouring Russian dissident leaders such as Savinkov, who were agitating against the Bolsheviks and adding to the chaos and uncertainty. This did not prevent the Russians from actively supporting communist movements inside Poland, however, and sending troops into eastern Ukraine. Piłsudski was not impressed by Soviet activity, which he saw as the last death throes of a doomed regime, but the Polish government was forging ahead with commercial agreements and the implementation of Riga. The official policy was to encourage the reconstruction of the Russian economy, upon which much of Poland's future trade and prosperity relied. The chief of the Polish general staff, Władysław Sikorski, argued for a prolonged period of peace by reinforcing the status quo, especially by peace treaties with the Baltic States to deter Soviet expansionism.

The Russians, however, were much more interested in Germany, their policy towards whom was to prevent any reconciliation between them and the Western Allies. To this end they had entered into conversations with German industrial leaders and also the Wehrmacht, both of whom took little convincing of the huge advantages of political and military cooperation. In December 1921, Trotsky and the Russian chief of staff, P.P. Lebedev, told Colonel Hasse 'that the Red Army would attack Poland in the spring of 1922 if Germany made immediate all-out efforts to rebuild Russia's war industry'.[6] Radek urged von Seeckt to send German officers to Russia to train Red Army officers. To impress the Germans, the Red Army began massing troops along their western borders on the pretext that an attack by Poland and Romania was imminent but at the same time, to play both sides against the middle and placate the Poles, the Soviet government opened trade negotiations ahead of the Genoa Conference.

Piłsudski feared that the increased military activity might spiral out of control and spill over into another frontier war. Sikorski sent reinforcements up to the Russian front to deal with armed bands who crossed from Russia to pillage and burn, even though Russia said that these were bands of Polish Byelorussians and Ukrainians agitating against Polish oppression and that they had nothing to do with Russia. To ease tension, Poland suggested that Russia send delegates to the Baltic Conference in Warsaw. This and a marked change in Soviet attitude towards Germany, whom they saw as procrastinating in their negotiations for cooperation, softened the Soviet approach to Poland at the start of the Genoa talks but any hopes Poland might have had for developments in this area were firmly quashed when the German and Russian delegates at Genoa peeled off and had secret talks. In a very short time these led to the signing of the Treaty of Rapallo on 16 April 1922, resulting in the re-establishment of normal relations between the two countries. They agreed to cancel all financial claims against each other and strengthened their economic and military ties. Rapallo was the first agreement concluded by Germany as an independent agent since the end of the war.

The Soviets had been keen to prevent any rapprochement between Germany and the Western Powers and had secretly sent Radek with Leonid Krasin and Khristian Rakovsky to Berlin in January 1922 to prepare the ground for Rapallo. Radek had tried to panic the Germans by implying that France was working towards a policy of 'holding Germany down'[7] and was willing to end its support of the Poles in return for Soviet agreement to recognise the Versailles terms as binding upon Germany. Radek also urged his old friend von Seeckt to supply Russia with arms to enable it to launch an attack on Poland in the spring. Fearing isolation, the Germans took Radek at his word and made arrangements to come to a formal agreement with Russia when they met at Genoa. The German ambassador to Warsaw, Herbert von Dirksen, was 'rather enthusiastic' about a treaty that would 'impress [intimidate] the Poles'.[8]

The German Chancellor Wirth, von Seeckt and Brockdorff-Rantzau were as one in their hatred and contempt for Poland. Wirth saw an alliance with Russia as the sensible course for Germany in order to once again become a great power, which meant that Poland, in his view – which he claimed was in accord with von Seeckt's on this issue – had to be destroyed.[9] Brockdorff-Rantzau was a little more circumspect and argued that against any pact with the Russians that eliminated Poland would put the Bolsheviks on Germany's border and at the very least Upper Silesia would be lost. While his approach to the Russians softened somewhat due, not least to a desire for its support to ward off an attack by France, he viewed with dismay any actual alliance with the 'unscrupulous' Bolshevik government that might at any time attack Poland and leave Germany defenceless against any French move in the west. If Poland was destroyed, Brockdorff-Rantzau feared that Germany would then become the battleground for a mighty conflict between east and west.

Passivity was not part of von Seeckt's philosophy, however. He called the mere existence of Poland 'unbearable and incompatible with the vital interests of Germany'. This 'vassal' and 'power outpost' of France must either be allowed to collapse through internal strife or be destroyed at the hands of Russia, with Germany's assistance. He wanted to make clear to Russia, whose 'hostility towards Poland cannot be increased' that Germany was of like mind and Poland threatened from both sides would be crushed by instability. France also had to know that if it supported Poland in any war with Russia, it would be taking on Germany as well. Von Seeckt's confidence in German arms was clearly at odds with that of Brockdorff-Rantzau but the diplomat was winning the political war and gradually limiting the general's role in the political sphere as pragmatism became the order of the day and war-like rhetoric was discouraged to promote better relations with the West.

Brockdorff-Rantzau was born Ulrich Karl Christian, Count zu Rantzau, in 1869, the elder of twin brothers in an ancient Holstein family. He later added the surname Brockdorff on inheriting the estate of Annettenhoh near Schleswig from an uncle on his mother's side. His demeanour was aristocratic to an extreme and his intolerance of those he considered to be less than equal to him, intellectually or socially, unguarded. As a qualified lawyer he had been appointed German foreign minister (*Reichsminister des Auswärtigen*) in 1919 and led the German delegation to the Versailles peace talks, where he vehemently challenged the charges that Germany and Austria had been solely responsible for the war; a stance that angered the Western delegates, especially those of France, whom he treated with scorn. When the final swingeing terms of the treaty were agreed, a disgusted Brockdorff-Rantzau resigned in protest. In November 1922, he was appointed to the Moscow embassy, a post for which his experience and ability made him ideally suited, where his policy was to pursue rapprochement between Germany and Russia without sacrificing German links to the West. He became convinced that Germany's political future required compromises with a lesser devotion to militarism and more emphasis on democratic ideals that would come about through economic growth and cooperation with both Russia and the West.

Brockdorff-Rantzau was one of two men who would play crucial roles by influencing Polish affairs from outside the country. The other was Chicherin, the absent-minded, fidgety, nervous and scruffy Russian commissar for foreign affairs.[10] Chicherin's father had been a diplomat and his mother, whose maiden name was Meyendorff, came from Baltic nobility. He was brought up by an English nanny in Karaul and, as a child, despite being 'undisciplined and eccentric' showed 'outstanding intellectual qualities'.[11] He grew up speaking fluent English, French, German and Polish with some command also of Italian and Serbian, which gave him an excellent grounding for a career in diplomacy. In 1914 he lived in London at 12 Oakley Gardens, where he joined the Communist Club and became involved in campaigns against conscription. It was here that he gained a reputation as 'a singularly tiresome guest … a pacifist, internationalist, and anti-imperialist … not content to keep his opinions for his own delectation'.[12] His activities eventually saw him end up in Brixton Prison in August 1917 charged with 'hostile associations [and] pro-German activities'. When Lenin let it be known that Chicherin was to be appointed Russian ambassador to Britain, however, his incarceration was terminated, and he was put on a steamer at Newcastle and, to the relief of all concerned, shipped out to Norway.

Chicherin, an accomplished pianist, and Brockdorff-Rantzau were well suited, finding a common interest in intellectual pursuits and fine wines, a commitment to sound Soviet-German relations, rejection of the League of Nations, mutual dislike of France and, most of all, the thing that brought them closest together was their utter contempt for Poland. The elimination of Poland as a power in Eastern European politics was second only to the unshackling of Germany from the chains of Versailles as the centre of Brockdorff-Rantzau's strategy when he arrived in Moscow. In both cases they agreed that the main obstacle to the progression of their agenda was France.

The Polish foreign minister, Skirmunt, condemned Rapallo as a violation of Riga but Chicherin brushed that aside by saying that Riga had only been a protocol and had never been a binding agreement. The Polish General Staff saw Rapallo as a dangerous development and a threat but the Polish government, who were trying to cut the military budget, took a more sanguine view, choosing to believe that neither Germany nor Russia the Soviet Union was in any fit state to start a war. For Piłsudski, the treaty was a failure of Polish diplomacy and he forced Skirmunt to resign in favour of his own man, Gabriel Józef Narutowicz. This proved to be a short-lived success for Piłsudski when Narutowicz was assassinated one week after taking office by a right-wing fanatic, Eligiusz Niewiadomski. His death came as a bitter blow to Piłsudski, whose retreat from political life accelerated at this point. Russia responded by, once again, softening its line on Poland and inviting it to join in serious talks over the future of the Baltic States but the Poles remained unconvinced by their solicitude and argued that the Soviets should implement the terms of Riga, especially in relation to plundered works of art, before discussing any new deal.

Meanwhile, Mustafa Kemal's victory over the Greeks at the Battle of the Sakarya River in the Greko-Turkish War had galvanised the Western Powers to enter into talks with Piłsudski to build an Eastern European alliance, ostensibly to oppose Turkish expansionism but, in practice, to put up a block to the Soviets also. If Romania moved against Turkey, Chicherin warned that Russia would not stand by and would be duty bound to act against Romania, which, in turn, would draw in Romania's allies, the Poles. Piłsudski urged calm and a return to normalisation of border conditions to avoid a skirmish escalating out of control. His reading of the situation at the time was encapsulated in his address to his staff in October 1922:

> I am convinced that Germany will rise again and become very powerful. Poland should base its policy on Germany. To me the future of Poland seems possible only in alliance with Germany, directed against Russia. When Germany and Poland jointly overthrow Russia, Poland will be established for good, otherwise ruin awaits us. I do not believe in the alliance with France ... I am convinced [that] England and France, in competing with Germany for Russia's riches, will forget all about us and will abandon us entirely to the tender mercies of Russia, which,

> sooner or later, will be utilised by the same France and England as a counter-weight against Germany.[13]

In the meantime, Polish efforts had succeeded in persuading a number of the Western neighbours of Russia, Finland, Latvia and Estonia, to attend a meeting at Tallin on 3 August 1922 to agree a common policy when they attended the Moscow Disarmament Conference, invitations to which had gone out from Maxim Litvinov, the Soviet deputy foreign commissar, in June 1922. Invitations were later extended to Lithuania and Romania but after the five invitees met in Warsaw on 21 September 1922, Romania chose to decline the invitation in protest at Moscow's refusal to recognise the demarcation of their mutual border. All agreed, however, that the disarmament proposals the Russians were putting on the table were probably no more than a disingenuous initiative to encourage them to disarm to reduce border threats to Russia. The dire state of the Russian economy demanded a reduction in its own armed forces, which it could not safely bring about unless it reduced the external military threat. The Warsaw meeting concluded that talks could go ahead to discuss disarmament but only if Moscow agreed to sign up to a non-aggression pact first. Poland, with two long borders to protect, was particularly concerned about any reduction in its armed forces and was under no illusions about how difficult it would be to monitor any reduction that the Russians might agree to in principle. While the prospect of a fighting war breaking out was not considered to be great, the continuous movements of Russian troops along the frontier, the presence of both Russian and Lithuanian armed bands close to the frontier, and the threat of cavalry raids to pillage the fruits of the Polish harvest made life for border populations distinctly uncomfortable and meant that constant vigilance on the part of the Polish General Staff was the order of the day.

The Moscow Disarmament Conference opened on 2 December in an atmosphere of deep mutual distrust. The head of the Soviet delegation, Litvinov, proposed that Russia and its Western neighbours reduce their land forces by 75 per cent within two years, limit military expenditures to an agreed maximum, disband all irregular military formations and establish neutral zones along their common frontiers, but none of the other participants were interested in going along with that until other outstanding political questions had been addressed and an atmosphere of mutual confidence had been established. Prince Janusz Radziwill, for the Poles, submitted a draft treaty of non-aggression and arbitration to which Poland and the three Baltic States had previous agreed. The Russians went along with it but wanted a disarmament treaty to be signed at the same time. However, their suggested cuts in forces were not acceptable to the others and could not be agreed before a thorough study of the effects was made. Goodwill was in short supply and progress was slow, leaving delegates exhausted and frustrated to the point where, on 12 December, the conference adjourned without agreement. Enthusiasm ebbed away and with nothing new to offer they never found any motivation to restart the talks. It is assumed that the Russians had been satisfied to demoralise the other delegates and wanted only to win a propaganda victory. They probably never had any intention of cutting their forces to the extent discussed simply because that would have severely jeopardised their negotiations with Germany and the implementation of Rapallo, which essentially rested on their mutual hostility towards Poland.

Elsewhere, Poland was finding that implementation of the 'complex and unsatisfactory' agreement over Danzig that had come out of the Paris Peace talks was becoming very contentious.[14] The free ports of Memel, Königsberg and Danzig had been intended to assure Poland of a direct outlet to the sea but it was proving impossible, in practice, to reconcile Polish rights of full access to the port with the intransigent attitude of the mostly Prussian officials, whose political affiliation to Germany outweighed their obligations to Polish commerce. This would prove to be an enduring and steadily worsening problem that was encouraged to deteriorate by the Nazis when they came to power in 1933. Important rights of access were denied the Poles but their objections were considered trivial and more often than not rejected by League of Nations arbitrators. Management of the port, which should have been under Polish control, was handed to a board of administration composed of equal numbers of Polish and Danzig representatives. Germany was quick to use the huge number of, often minor, disputes that arose as propaganda to accuse the Poles of mismanagement and reinforce German opposition to the whole Danzig agreement. The Poles seemed too exhausted by their internal reconstruction to give sufficient attention or investment, either financial or cultural, to counter the increasing German discriminatory application of rules and regulations. Despite all the feuding, Danzig began to achieve a modest increase in wealth and importance as a trading port but Poland became increasingly frustrated by German obstructionist tactics and, in the winter of 1920, began channelling much of its trade instead through the small fishing village of Gdynia, which it developed into a modern port through the Gdynia Seaport Construction Act of 23 September 1922. It was ironic that German dock workers in Danzig, who had so infuriated the Poles by refusing to unload Polish ammunition ships at the height of the Russo-Polish War, were now being made redundant as trade slipped away from Danzig to Gdynia.

German-speaking minorities in countries all over Eastern Europe had been encouraged in their ambitions for political, economic and social autonomy by propagandists such as Walther Adolf Franz Heinrich arousing folklore sentiments and advocating the alignment of ethnic German-language speakers through *Volkgruppensprecht* and *Volkstumslehre*, which went far beyond any measures enshrined in Versailles for the protection of minorities. There were a number of powerful organisations in Poland that were politically active in this area, financed and encouraged by German industrialists and landowners in Upper Silesia, Poznania and Pomerania eager to reclaim the privileged position they had enjoyed before 1914. It was the ambition of German statesmen such as Gustav Stresemann to sign up to the League of Nations to acquire a platform to air German concerns over the alleged ill-treatment of minorities.

The question of minorities had plagued Eastern Europe for years and would continue to do so. The German-Polish border was never officially accepted by Germany and ever since Versailles German foreign policy had been aimed at revision of the treaty to push back the Polish frontier and reclaim lost land. Inside Poland, a significant number of ethnic Germans in Polish Silesia became Polish citizens but all former citizens of Partitioning Powers (Germany, Russia and Austria) who rejected Polish citizenship were made to leave the country by 10 January 1923. Germany used the existence of the German minority in Poland, the persecution of whom it highlighted continually, for political purposes and as part of its revanchist demands, prompting Polish countermeasures. The Polish prime minister, Sikorski, ordered that the de-Germanisation of these territories had to be ended by vigorous and quick liquidation of property and eviction of Germans to emphasise to German nationalists that they were wrong to view Poland's borders as being temporary. By the time of the Vienna Convention on 30 August 1924, both governments had agreed on the eviction of 28,000–30,000 Germans living in Poland who had chosen German citizenship and of 5,000 Poles living in Germany who had chosen Polish citizenship.

The League of Nations had enshrined in its constitution the two main principles of equality of states and collective security but had proved to be quite incapable of sorting out the vexatious questions of national borders in Eastern Europe, leaving the states to try and impose their own unilateral solutions. This had resulted in accusations of 'intrigue, propaganda, tyranny and terrorism' against Poland, which had to defend itself continuously in endless petty arguments.[15]

Slowly, however, Poland was able to take a greater part in the League of Nations meetings and gain international recognition of its eastern borders, but Danzig and the question of German-speaking minorities continued to burden them.

The Military Inter-Allied Commission of Control's solution to the Upper Silesian border dispute had by no means ended strife in the region and the German government began an unrelenting propaganda campaign to force its revision, while local leaders sought to exploit the running sore of grievances for political gain. Both Polish and German political leaders in Upper Silesia were endorsed and afforded considerable support by their respective national governments in their attempts to legitimise their respective claims. Activists who had taken part in the battles before, during and after the plebiscite were in no mood, either, to accept the status quo. The Polish Insurgent League (*Związek Powstánców*) flourished under Korfanty's patronage, with its members reluctant to relinquish the status they had achieved as heroes of the insurrections. They fanned the flames of popular insecurity by constant reference to the 'German threat' of invasion, which in turn gave leaders of the German minorities ample justification to counter with accusations of Polish discrimination and injustice. A significant aspect of opposition to the partition was the introduction of public demonstrations and rallies, the first of which took place on 25 February 1923 in Katowice's municipal square to demand the whole of Upper Silesia be 'reunified' with Poland. More rallies, with government support, followed on both sides of the border, with each emphasising the threat from the other side, and these served to fuel and legitimise the border disputes. The Polish government-endorsed rally held on 3 May 1923 was significant for the fact that it was held on Polish Constitution Day commemorating the 1794 Tadeusz Kościuszko rebellion against imperial occupiers but more importantly it was the third anniversary of the first insurgency. In response, the Germans held their own revanchist festivals to commemorate their plebiscite victory and planned a big event in response to the anticipated fourth anniversary of the insurgency planned for 3 May 1924. Upper Silesia was going to bubble away as a simmering stew of ethnic conflict for many years but in early 1923 it slipped a little way down the international agenda as a new crisis emerged.

At a conference of representatives of Soviet Republics in December 1922, the USSR (Union of Soviet Socialist Republics) was created and henceforth in this book, unless part of a direct quotation, Russia will now be referred to as the USSR or the Soviet Union.

Chapter 6

THE RUHR CRISIS

> The French occupation of the Ruhr had swung German opinion to the Right. That encouraged Hitler and his Fascists in Bavaria and, on November 9th [1923], they struck and tried a coup from the Right.
>
> Morgan Philips Price, *My Three Revolutions*

The dire economic state of the German economy at the beginning of 1923 had left it unable to keep up its reparation payment to France that had been stipulated at Versailles. In particular, it had defaulted on deliveries of timber during the winter of 1922–23. As a consequence, on 11 January 1923, French and Belgian troops, in an act of disputed legality,[1] occupied the Ruhr industrial region to force other Western governments to face up to German default, which, if allowed to continue unchallenged would, they argued, undermine the whole Versailles agreement and release Germany from any of its obligations to that treaty. The French action sent shockwaves all across Europe, with Germany especially not only being deprived of its revenues from its Ruhr coalfields and steel-making industries but fearing that Poland might take advantage of the crisis to invade and occupy Upper Silesia. The Soviet Union welcomed the social, economic and political repercussions, which stirred discontent within Germany, as a stimulus to hasten the revolt of its proletariat and the establishment of a communist government but was also nervous about the possibility of Poland, energised and motivated by the French action, attempting an occupation of East Prussia. Both Germany and the Soviet Union were equally concerned to prevent any aggressive action by the Poles.

Germany had certainly anticipated some sort of French reaction to its default on reparations, which were anyway being reduced rapidly by Germany's rampant inflation, but were shocked by its scale. Seeing the devaluation of German repayments, always assuming that they would continue to be forthcoming, France demanded payment in kind and in order to guarantee that carried out the occupation of Germany's biggest industrial region. Brockdorff-Rantzau had warned Trotsky in December 1922 that Germany was about to default and asked what the Soviet Union's response would be. Trotsky advised against confronting France militarily, whatever action they took, but, employing the language of diplomatic ambiguities, assured the Germans that any Polish moves against Upper Silesia would be met with resolve by the Red Army, whatever that might mean.

When the French occupation took place, the Soviet Politburo member Nikolai Bukharin warned openly that if Poland attacked Germany then the Soviet Union, with the support of Lithuania, would not hesitate to move against Poland. At the same time a vigorous Soviet propaganda campaign was launched against Poland and again it was made clear by Moscow in direct contacts with Berlin that it would not stand idly by if there was any Polish intervention in German internal affairs.[2] This all proved to be little more than hot air when Trotsky assured the League of Nations representative that only in the extreme circumstances of a direct threat to the Soviet Union itself would the Red Army move against the Poles; a declaration that left Berlin wondering just how much it could rely on the support of the Soviet Union in any crisis.

As for the Poles, the army would only move on a command from Piłsudski and he was becoming ever more disillusioned by political infighting in a country that was on the verge of economic meltdown. He had already, in 1921, refused to consider standing for the presidency of Poland and retired completely from the political scene in June 1923 when he resigned as chief of state, leaving the way clear for Wincenty Witos to become prime minister. Sikorski pleaded for political unity and gained a little solace when, in May 1923, to show support for Poland, Foch made an official visit to Warsaw, which brought Radek and Brockdorff-Rantzau together to condemn it as a hostile act. To counter the French initiative, Radek launched a virulent propaganda initiative to condemn it.

Meanwhile, the League of Nations' arbitration process awarded the territory of Vilnius to Poland over Lithuanian protests. Moscow sympathised with the Lithuanians and offered to mediate in the dispute, presumably on their behalf, which did not go down too well in Warsaw. The Soviets also revived the contentious issue of East Galicia, which it accused Poland of having taken by force. Arguments over the implementation of Riga continued to simmer and angry diplomatic exchanges kept alive accusations of the persecution of minorities in Belarus and the Ukraine. It was clear that the Soviet Union was working closely with the Germans to keep the Poles off balance to minimise any support they might want to give to the French action in the Ruhr. Brockdorff-Rantzau was not slow to show his appreciation when he called the Soviet Union's attitude to Poland 'unalterably loyal' but may have been exercising diplomatic hyperbole if he ever expected the Soviets to act in anything other than their own interests.[3] Throughout the crisis, however, and despite official support for Germany, Chicherin was, all the time, in secret talks with Warsaw continuing to explore the possibility of reaching an understanding at the expense of Germany.

The summer of 1923 saw further dramatic events in Germany as inflation raged untamed and strikes ravaged the economy. The German government of Wilhelm Carl Josef Cuno fell on 12 August 1923 after only 264 days and was replaced by Gustav Stresemann's German People's Party, who declared a state of emergency in the country. In Saxony, Thuringia and Hamburg communist-inspired revolution broke out financed by Moscow. A separatist government, supported by the French, was declared in the Rhineland Palatinate and Adolf Hitler launched his abortive Munich Putsch. The Communist Party of Poland, which Radek said was 'of great importance to the German revolution', was put on alert and readied for action when the German crisis reached its peak. Zinoviev, Chairman of the Third Soviet International, called for an independent communist Poland in 'alliance with the workers'–peasants' republics of Russia and Germany'.[4] Moscow, however, was not totally convinced that the reactionary forces in either Poland or Germany would succumb to the revolution and so continued to maintain clandestine contact with the official governments of both countries so that irrevocable diplomatic breakdown would not result if the revolutions failed.

Brockdorff-Rantzau actually had documentary evidence that the Comintern was giving material support to the German communists in their bid for revolution but his protests to the Soviet government were comfortably batted aside since neither Zinoviev nor Radek, the main instigators of revolt, held government posts and Radek, in particular, was adamant that he was not acting as an agent of, nor would he accept instructions from, the Soviet government. Chicherin was ever ready to express deep regret for Germany's internal problems but this was no more than diplomatic niceties. Despite this, relations between the Soviet Union and Germany continued more or less in a constructive fashion, not least because Brockdorff-Rantzau, who had the full confidence of the German government and the notional confidence of the Soviets, was totally committed to cooperation and made every effort to keep diplomatic relations on track.

By pursuing its dual official and covert dealings with both Germany and Poland, the Soviet government was risking what small reputation it had achieved to date. In the case of Germany it offered support to the government while aggressively promoting revolution inside its borders, and in Poland it was secretly sounding out Sikorski's views on allowing the transit of Soviet forces over Polish soil to support the German revolution if the government of that country was teetering on the edge of collapse. The inducement to Poland was that, in the aftermath of any disintegration of the Weimar Republic, the Soviets would not oppose Poland grabbing some German territory such as East Prussia. In a flurry of diplomatic initiatives, Kopp was also despatched to Riga as the representative of the People's Commissariat of Foreign Affairs to offer them a non-aggression pact in return for Latvian agreement for free transit rights to Soviet forces in the event of a German revolution. He then met the Lithuanian government to negotiate its neutrality in the event of Soviet forces entering Poland. At last, he reached Warsaw and had to shuffle his briefs to see what version of Soviet plans he would present to the Poles. When he decided on the line to take he addressed his message to the whole of Europe. The Soviets, he said, would remain neutral towards Germany's internal affairs but only if the rest of Europe did the same. From the Poles he requested unlimited transit rights of Soviet troops in return for recognition of Poland's existing borders and vague promises of Soviet support for greater Polish influence in Danzig and East Prussia. A memorandum from the Polish embassy in Paris noted that the 'Polish government did not give any consideration to these suggestions', although the Polish chargé d'affaires in Moscow intimated to Radek that the question of East Prussia was worthy of further discussion. The fragility of Soviet-Polish relations was evident when the Soviets quickly interpreted this response as Polish intransigence and blamed the lack of progress towards mutual neutrality agreements between Germany and Poland on 'deliberate vagueness' and a general avoidance of addressing 'the real issues'.[5]

By the end of the year, however, the German revolution had run out of steam. Local disturbances failed to ignite a national movement and public opinion veered to the right as a consequence of the abortive communist insurrection taking the country a little further away from the Soviet Union ideologically. The Soviets realised that Germany had been their best hope of exporting the revolution and its failure there initiated a major shift in its foreign policy. Lenin was, by now, very ill and rivals competed to inherit his mantle. Unlike Trotsky, Zinoviev and Radek, Stalin had not been tainted by the failures in Germany and worked assiduously to persuade his Politburo colleagues that he had never believed in a German revolution in the first place. His emphasis was on solving the Soviet Union's internal problems, which meant establishing stable relations with the outside world. This was a little late for Germany, however, who now harboured a sizeable grudge against the Soviets and one that played a large part in the way German foreign policy was to develop under the new German prime minister and the foreign minister, Gustav Stresemann, who had taken office on 13 August 1923.

Chapter 7

THE LOCARNO TREATIES

> He had a wonderful act in which he pretended to be not only fat (which he was) but good-hearted and a little muzzy with beer into the bargain. In reality he was quick-witted and sharp as a buzz-saw.
>
> British journalist Claud Cockburn writing about Gustav Stresemann

The son of an innkeeper, Gustav Stresemann was born in Berlin in 1878. He grew up believing in the spiritual, military and economic superiority of the German people and developed a political philosophy that manifested itself in idealistic sentiment for heroic liberalism and in his romantic style of speech. After the First World War he became one of the most enthusiastic advocates of the political unification of all people speaking German or a Germanic language and, using this argument, supported Germany's claims to Polish and Russian territory in the east and on French and Belgian territory in the west. 'The goal of German foreign policy,' he said, 'must be to strive continually for the revision of the eastern border' and develop close ties between Germany and its minority in Poland.[1] Stresemann's deep desire for the bringing together politically all ethnic Germans in Eastern Europe is a prime example of what was a common aspiration of many German nationalists and one that was exploited to the full by Hitler when he came to power.

Moving to the right politically, he worked closely with the German Supreme Army Command and became their parliamentary spokesman. As leader of the German People's Party, he flirted with revolutionary movements against Weimar but settled down to accept his place in a democratic administration to become one of the pillars of Weimar coalition governments. While he was reluctantly reconciled to the existence of the Polish state, he worked tirelessly to break the bonds of Versailles, especially on the question of revising Poland's boundaries in Germany's favour. At the heart of his strategy to achieve this was a political realism that recognised France as the key to success and that relations with the Soviet Union were of secondary importance. An almost comical figure with his 'beer belly, thick neck, sensuous lips, double chin, bulbous nose, and slanted, almost reptilian eyes', Stresemann was described by the British journalist Claud Cockburn as

> 'entertaining provided that you didn't believe in him' and a man who only pretended to be a 'good European'. Thomas Mann called him 'an extraordinary ... patriotic middle-class businessman' and a 'convinced advocate of imperial conquest ... full of vitality ... and driven by an exemplary commitment to life'.[2]

On the day that he took office, Stresemann received a telegram from Brockdorff-Rantzau, who expressed the fear that Stresemann's west-facing policies risked destroying his own two years of effort to improve German-Soviet relations. If Stresemann was concerned by this warning, he did not show it. He became reconciled to the French occupation of the Ruhr and later stabilised the German currency before agreeing to new reparations terms under the Dawes Plan at Rapallo on 16 August 1924. The Dawes Plan also facilitated huge international loans to Germany through Wall Street bond issues, which, in practice, transferred the burden of reparations from the German state to American banks. In return for the resumption of reparation payments, France, who no longer had justification for the Ruhr occupation, withdrew its troops.

With Franco-German relations now on a much less confrontational footing, Stresemann turned his attention towards Poland, upon whom he planned to exert pressure by weakening its ties to France and exposing it to joint German-Soviet intimidation. To begin with he considered placating Poland with assurances of Germany's peaceful intent and offers of negotiations to formalise their mutual border. He then argued that French commitment to Poland, which encouraged its intransigence, was hindering progress in the resolution of Eastern European boundary disputes. Realising that any German rapprochement with the Western Powers would be received with reservations in Moscow, Stresemann was careful to direct much of his diplomatic effort towards assuring the Soviets of his commitment to friendly relations with them also.

While the Soviets may have been comforted by Stresemann's friendly words, they were certainly not prepared to trust the German government and responded by making overtures to Poland, who were equally concerned, although for different reasons, by any potential weakening of French support. The Poles, however, had little faith in anything the Soviets said and, as usual, were confronted by far too many issues both internationally and internally to give their full attention to any sort of rapprochement. Its hostility, mistrust and fear of its neighbours was almost pathological and was resistant to momentary change of mood or approach from any of them, but it also denied them any chance of making even modest progress in relations. This was most apparent in dealings with the Soviet Union, where suspicions manifested themselves in the delays experienced trying to implement even the most uncontentious agreements of trade and prisoner exchange.

If there had been a tiny window of opportunity for some sort of Soviet-Polish rapprochement, it was soon slammed shut by Stresemann's energetic diplomacy once more prioritising German-Soviet relations over the interests of Poland. The Soviets, willing participants in this patching up of relations with Germany, wanted to ensure that they did not vacate to Western Powers any of the space they occupied in German sentiments. They assured Stresemann that they would never enter into any sort of negotiations with the Poles without the full knowledge and cooperation of Germany. Apart from the diplomatic exchanges, there were now also strong clandestine military ties being established between the Soviet Union and Germany that were proving to be more resilient than the disastrous failed industrial enterprises that had been entered into by German firms such as Junkers in partnership with the Soviet government at Fili.

Chicherin repeated to Brockdorff-Rantzau what Litvinov had told Radowitz, the German chargé d'affaires in Moscow, which was that the Soviet Union was anxious to discuss mutual concerns and arrive at an understanding over international questions ahead of the proposed Geneva Protocol for the settlement of international disputes to be negotiated at the League of Nations, where new governments in both London and Paris allowed for a new approach to the issue of collective security. Despite a grimly unenthusiastic response to this idea from Berlin, Brockdorff-Rantzau, pursuing his own agenda, took the matter up with Kopp and agreed that it might be mutually beneficial to look at their whole relationship through the prism of Poland. Kopp wanted to perpetuate the mood of instability in Central Europe and urged the Germans to vigorously continue their claims on Upper Silesia, which amounted to knocking on an open door.

Brockdorff-Rantzau assured Kopp that Germany would never give up its claims to the whole of Upper Silesia but felt that to pursue the matter at this stage using force would be 'madness'.[3] He was more concerned with the imminent appointment of Jean Herbette, the first post-Versailles French ambassador to Moscow, which suggested a shifting of the sands of European diplomacy and threatened a reappraisal of the Soviet Union's attitudes towards recognising the permanence of Poland's western border with Germany. Kopp parried by wondering how Germany's application to join the League of Nations might impact upon its attitude to Poland's eastern border with the Soviet Union, all of which strongly implied that, for both Germany and the Soviet Union at this time, the Polish question overrode all other considerations. There was an air of urgency in Berlin to ensure that Moscow was well informed about German concerns ahead of Herbette's arrival. Stresemann suggested to Brockdorff-Rantzau that he tell the Soviets that nothing in Germany's membership of the League would give a hard and fast guarantee of Poland's eastern borders but would merely place an obligation on Germany to respect them for the moment. A fine point of interpretation indeed but one that would allow room for obfuscation. With Poland's political boundaries now extending far beyond ethnographic lines there would be ample scope for both Germany and the Soviet Union to continue to agitate for their revision. Clearly Germany was telling the Soviets that they would interpret League Articles as allowing them to remain neutral in any future war between the Soviet Union and Poland while remaining free to supply the Soviets with arms in such an eventuality.

While Brockdorff-Rantzau felt that he had addressed the essential questions raised by Kopp, Chicherin was by no means eager to consider the Polish question in isolation. It seems that Brockdorff-Rantzau had taken Kopp too much at his word and failed to appreciate that his line of argument had been a subterfuge to dissuade Germany from any move towards rapprochement with the West and especially to discourage its application to join the League. The mood became brittle as Chicherin pointed out Germany's only contribution to the discussion was its promise of neutrality but in return the Soviets were expected to be proactive in regard to destabilising Poland's borders. Brockdorff-Rantzau beat a hasty retreat and assured that Germany would join in enthusiastically with any and all attempts to force Poland back to within its ethnographic borders. Chicherin was mollified but not satisfied, citing a number of 'significant differences of opinion' that remained.[4]

At their next meeting on 26 December 1924 Chicherin, under direct instructions from the Politburo, laid out the Soviet position in clear terms. Kopp's previous comments, he said, had to be discounted since he had acted in a personal capacity and had overstepped his authority. At the heart of Soviet thinking was the idea that only by taking into account all concrete political and general questions could the two make any progress on the Polish question. Chicherin emphasised that the Soviet Union and Germany would have to make certain commitments to each other, and each must refrain from entering into any third-party agreements directed against the other, which Brockdorff-Rantzau found a little extreme. Chicherin now came to the issue that was the crux of the matter, namely Germany's application to join the League of Nations. He wanted Brockdorff-Rantzau to agree a coordinated approach, which for the Soviets meant doing all they could to persuade Germany not to join fearing that such a move would isolate them and nudge Germany further towards rapprochement with the West. This now put Soviet strategy directly on a collision path with that of Stresemann but, for the moment, each side was anxious to avoid antagonising the other.

The Geneva Protocol for the Pacific Settlement of International Disputes was an attempt to set up compulsory arbitration of disputes and create a method to identify the aggressor in international conflicts. Despite initial approval by all member states of the League of Nations at the Fifth General Assembly, it was not ratified by Britain and subsequently failed to come into force. This failure had the effect of drawing France into new talks aimed at reducing tensions with Germany in a bid to improve the security of their mutual border and, as a bonus, give Germany an alternative to its current flirtation with the Soviet Union. The position of Poland, France's most important ally and Germany's most implacable enemy, would naturally figure prominently in any discussions. The Soviets started to feel marginalised and tried to keep a diplomatic foot in the door by indicating that they might be willing to take a more conciliatory approach to the Polish question.

Stresemann was facing his first big test that would determine whether he would remain 'a Romantic nationalist (or become) a fiercely realistic, practical (one) … pursuing strictly nationalist goals'.[5] He submitted a proposal to France early in 1925 but was careful not to make any concessions over Polish borders, indeed making it quite clear to Britain and France that Germany was irrevocably committed to their revision. In what he hoped would be seen as an even-handed approach, however, he was careful to keep Moscow informed about the general content of his negotiations with Britain and France, which 'required finesse and involved him in a degree of disingenuousness'.[6] He held talks with the French in which he assured them that Germany would never attempt resolution of the Polish boundaries through war but added, in an aside that he presumably did not tell Moscow about, that he doubted the same could be said for the Soviet Union. Moscow, however, was soon to hear about it through a government-inspired sensational Polish newspaper report, clearly designed to put strain on the German-Soviet relationship, stating that Germany had proposed an alliance with the French in return for the return of Upper Silesia and Danzig to German rule. Stresemann was forced to deny the veracity of the report and tried to placate Moscow by saying that German membership of the League of Nations, which was the ultimate goal of his current strategy towards the West, would be of immense benefit to them allowing Germany to work on the inside and 'hinder any action of the League against (the Soviet Union)'.[7]

Refusing to be placated by Stresemann's assurances, the Soviets sent a warning shot across his bows with a very public statement of a change in Soviet policy towards Poland designed to counterbalance improving Franco-German relations. In a burst of diplomatic disingenuity, Chicherin said that he believed there was much warmth in Soviet-Polish relations that was unfortunately clouded by 'a little bitterness'.[8] Both he and Radek, ignoring for the moment the simmering border disputes, offered support to Poland, which was losing the power struggle with Germany and, perhaps more importantly, losing the support of the French, who now seemed to be more concerned with finding common ground with Germany. Brockdorff-Rantzau took this very seriously indeed and sent a stark warning to Berlin over the dangers inherent in any Soviet-Polish agreement, blaming Stresemann's diplomatic initiative towards France for upsetting Soviet-German relations. His arguments, however, were countered by assurances from ministers in Berlin that although some improvement in Russo-Polish trade was to be expected, the constant violent Soviet border raids, espionage incidents and the complete boycott of Soviet diplomats in Warsaw made fine Soviet speeches unlikely to make any impression on Polish sensibilities. Nevertheless, despite the cool reception to its overtures in Warsaw, Moscow continued to play its 'Polish card' in its effort to prevent Germany joining the League. Litvinov showed Brockdorff-Rantzau a secret French document that seemed to suggest there would be no softening of the Versailles boundaries even if Germany was admitted to the League; in fact there would be no discussion of border issues at all. This was backed up by Soviet threats to 'seek other ways' of protecting itself if German membership was agreed.

Soviet bullying had little effect on Stresemann, whose confidence in his strategy was unshakeable. He did not really believe that Moscow would do anything to seriously damage German-Soviet relations and anyway even if Poland did shift its position towards the Soviet Union, which he doubted it would, the rift that would open up between it and France would not be unwelcome in Berlin. The balance of power in Europe was on the cusp of a seismic shift. If the Soviets were successful in preventing German membership of the League it would put them in a very much stronger position to dictate terms in Soviet-German negotiations but if they failed the Soviets would face virtual isolation in Europe and be forced to watch as Germany went from strength to strength re-establishing itself as a major player in European politics with a concomitant increase in the likelihood of recovering its lost territories in the east. For Stresemann there was really only one possible course of action and that was to gain membership of the League at all costs, but he was not about to pursue it without careful management of its consequences for Soviet-German relations. He was constantly aware of the limitations of German power after Versailles 'consequent on defeat, disarmament and isolation'.[9]

When news came to Stresemann that the British foreign secretary, Austen Chamberlain, in an apparent change of policy wrote in a memorandum to the British cabinet that 'the German-Polish boundary in its present form [could not] remain as it is',[10] confidence in his strategy was confirmed. The French foreign minister, Briand, also retreated from his stance on guarantees for Polish borders, going so far as to say that France would not give unconditional support to Poland and even giving Stresemann advice on how to achieve his ambitions. This was music to Stresemann's ears, but he was careful not to overplay his hand and held back, for the moment, on making any statements about revising Versailles through confrontation, preferring instead to consolidate the concessions he had already won and employ 'trade as an instrument of revision'.[11] Briand was certain, of course, that Poland had no intention of even talking about boundary revision but when Germany joined the League on equal terms to France, together they would be able to exert sufficient pressure to progress that agenda. That was conditional, however, on German guarantees on Franco-German boundaries and, in this regard, Briand was apparently ready to go some distance to support Stresemann in his battle with Brockdorff-Rantzau for control of German foreign policy. The French were determined to bring to a halt to what they saw as a dangerous growth in military and economic cooperation between Germany and the Soviet Union.

Radek stepped in with a piece in the Soviet press containing his usual mix of propaganda, selective half-truths and inspired insights to state the Soviet position. Poland, he wrote, should remember that it owed its independence to the defeat of Germany in the First World War and that had come about as a result of the October Revolution in 1917 and had little to do with the efforts of either France of Britain, neither of whom was particularly interested in what happened to Poland. Britain was now only concerned with fostering friendly relations with Germany to counter the possibility of a Franco-Soviet alliance, while France was realising that its commitments to Poland were becoming a burden as French power was on the wane, leaving Poland without reliable allies in the West. He went on to write that it was now in the interests of Polish security for them to look to the Soviet Union as the only power willing or able to prevent a further erosion of Polish status and influence in European affairs. If Radek expected his views to be taken seriously in Warsaw he was soon disabused of that notion, as was Chicherin when he visited Warsaw on his way to Berlin.

Chicherin was somewhat more diplomatic than the volatile and outspoken Radek when, in late September 1925, he addressed Polish leaders in an effort to 'remove certain misunderstandings' that had soured relations in recent times. He was ready to discuss a non-aggression pact but that met with instant rejection. The Poles evidently had no confidence that any such agreement would withstand the test of reality and be abandoned by the Soviets at any time they chose to do so. The refusal did, however, deny the Poles the chance of sending a subtle message to Berlin that might have had Stresemann looking over his shoulder, but subtlety was not a given where Polish diplomacy was concerned. As it was, when he received Chicherin in Berlin a couple of days later, Stresemann was in a combative mood over continuing Soviet propaganda campaigns trying to stir up proletarian unrest but was more than willing to sign up to a new trade deal and, once again, stressed that Germany was not reorienting its foreign policy in an anti-Soviet direction.

Chicherin was equally blunt when he asked Stresemann to consider why the Rapallo spirit that had seemed to be so important to both countries was evaporating and suggested that it might well be because of Germany's pursuit of a security pact with the West. This was quite contrary to what he had been led to believe, said Chicherin, by reports he had received of a conversation between Kopp and Brockdorff-Rantzau in which Germany's primary goal was seen as working with the Soviet Union to drive Poland back to within its ethnographic boundaries, an assumption upon which Soviet strategy was predicated. This was news to Stresemann who, once again, was at odds with Brockdorff-Rantzau on foreign policy. After requesting a pause so that he could check up on the accuracy of this, Stresemann returned to the talks to assure Chicherin that Brockdorff-Rantzau had been speaking in a purely speculative fashion. Both Chicherin and Stresemann were embarrassed by this explanation, which exposed the extent to which they were both labouring against opposition within their own governments. They then tried to console each other by speaking of the necessity for close and friendly relations in the future.

At their next meeting the following day, however, the conciliatory mood had reverted to a more familiar one as Stresemann accused Chicherin of knowing that it had been Kopp and not Brockdorff-Rantzau who had steered their conversation towards Poland and manipulated it towards an apparent German commitment over boundaries. Chicherin refused to accept Kopp's culpability and argued that even if Kopp might have got the wrong impression and come away with a prejudiced view it had been German diplomats who had broached the subject in the first place. It was all a bit of a messy misunderstanding that had not helped matters ahead of the impending Locarno Conference but it was Stresemann who set out for the conference in a better mood than Chicherin, who had tried and failed to convince the Poles to sign up to a non-aggression pact and had also failed to bring Stresemann onside with a joint initiative aimed against Poland.

The Locarno Conference, attended by representatives of Belgium, Czechoslovakia, France, Germany, Britain, Italy and Poland, opened on 5 October 1925 and was to become noted both for the treaties it adopted and for the spirit of goodwill that overcame difficulties that had wrecked conference after conference in Europe during the previous seven years. Austen Chamberlain claimed that the Locarno treaties were 'the real dividing line between the years of war and the years of peace' but in practice they did little more than paper over the cracks that had been opened up by, and widened since, the Versailles Treaty.[2]

Stresemann's threefold strategy was clear: he would try to avoid any deal that recognised Poland's borders, he would try to prevent France from acting as a guarantor in any arbitration with Poland and, most importantly, he would try to get German exemption from Article 16 of the League Covenant, which would allow it to remain neutral in any new Russo-Polish war. Achieving all three would, he hoped, mollify the Soviet Union and assure it of Germany's friendly relations while maintaining their joint pressure on Poland. His impressive diplomatic skills came to the fore and allowed him to nuance his position depending on his audience. To the League he offered full moral support but claimed that a disarmed Germany could not be expected to give military support to any other member (Poland) in the event of war. To the Soviet Union he gave assurances that, as a member of the League, Germany would act in Soviet interests. To the

British and French, he rejected non-aggression treaties but offered to sign arbitration treaties that considered only peaceful solutions. This obscure distinction left other delegates bemused but allowed them to move on. To his domestic audience, Stresemann called his approach a 'façade' to challenge French insistence that Poland be included in a security pact and implied that there was little of significance in any such arbitration treaty.

Locarno proved to be a triumph for German diplomacy, a failure for the Soviet Union and a disaster for Poland. According to the arbitration treaty between Germany and Poland, if war broke out France would not be able to offer immediate help to Poland unless or until the League of Nations ruled whether or not Germany had been the aggressor. The Polish parliament was in near revolt when Polish foreign minister, Aleksander Skrzyński, came to them for ratification of the treaty.[13] Not only had France failed to consult Poland during negotiations, but it was also clear that, although the alliance was not completely abandoned, France no longer looked to Poland as an important ally in the battle to contain Germany.

Alexander Józef Skrzyński had been born in Austria to an old and wealthy aristocratic family. As Polish foreign minister in 1923 he had secured the Great Powers recognition of, but no guarantees of, Poland's eastern borders. He had worked hard to promote the Geneva Protocol but met strong opposition from Britain, who went on to block Poland's application for a permanent seat on the Council of the League of Nations. While Skrzyński had publicly praised Locarno as a confirmation of Versailles, he privately admitted that it was 'a dagger thrust in the back of the alliance between our two countries [Britain and Poland]'.[14] As a result, he redoubled his effort to bring the Baltic States into a closer union with Poland, including, if possible, the Soviet Union and Finland, but all to no avail. Nothing daunted, he proposed a smaller union between the Soviet Union, Latvia and Estonia that he called an 'Eastern Locarno'. The Soviet Union was naturally eager to prevent Poland from coming under Western influence and forming an anti-Soviet Baltic bloc but, at the same time, found ways of preventing progress on the 'Eastern Locarno' initiative since it did not want to see Poland being elevated to any special position in relation to its Baltic neighbours. Instead Moscow tempted the Poles with the prospect of opening up the vast Russian market to Polish goods but made it clear that this could only happen if Poland curbed its ambitions to play 'the role of manager of foreign relations for all the Baltic States'.[15]

The clear discrimination against Poland and Czechoslovakia in the Locarno Treaties was mainly due to the British, who had refused to include them in a Franco-British security agreement as proposed by the French in December 1921 and later had also refused to sign the Geneva Protocol in 1924. The Protocol, worked out by Skrzyński and the Czech foreign minister, Edvard Beneš, mandated compulsory arbitration of disputes and if this failed, League of Nations members were to come to the aid of any member who was the victim of aggression. Skrzyński, who was the most European of Polish politicians, signed the Locarno Treaties, however, believing that Poland must be part of the European political system, but this outraged Piłsudski, who called him 'that little Locarno bitch' and set himself the goal of redressing them.[16]

It cannot be overstated the extent to which Locarno was a spectacular achievement for Stresemann. He had freed Germany from any obligations to join in League joint actions against the Soviet Union and he had avoided giving any border guarantees to either Poland or Czechoslovakia, thus weakening French alliances with both of these countries. Germany had achieved spectacular success by elevating its strategic position, giving it more freedom to pursue relations with the Soviet Union without antagonising the West while building stronger economic and diplomatic relations with Britain and France without alienating the Soviets. At the same time, it had forfeited none of its ambitions to revise its borders with Poland. The Soviet Union lost much ground in its relationship with both Britain and France as these countries now saw Germany as the nation most worthy of their investment and trade. In another example of Germany's transformed status, apart from its new-found popularity in the West it had also become the only country in Western Europe with which the Soviet Union now had any likelihood of developing substantial economic and diplomatic relations.

For Stresemann, it was clear that, in the immediate future, there was no hope of employing force against Poland to achieve his ambition of the revision of the Versailles boundaries, but Locarno was a first step along the diplomatic route. A second step was to convince the League that the greatest threat to peace in Europe were the 'conditions in the east'.[17] In this way, Germany, with its new-found confidence and connections to the Western Powers, could exploit any future crisis, thereby showing that its resolution was contingent on boundary revision. One of the ways in which Stresemann tried to provoke a crisis that he hoped to exploit was by exacerbating a trade war that had erupted between Germany and Poland.

It had clearly been the ambition of Germany, in the first two years after Versailles, to bring about the ruination of the Polish state and hasten its demise, which had forced Poland to look beyond its nearest neighbour to countries with which to develop economic relations. This soon prompted Germany to change its approach and adopt a policy of cooperation with the Poles to encourage trade, but the damage was done, and it proved difficult for them to gain the trust of Polish businesses. Post-war trade between the two countries had been regulated by Versailles and the Geneva Convention on Upper Silesia of May 1922 but, despite the benefits that German industry and Polish agriculture had both received, it had never been an arrangement that lay easily with either the governments or the people. Versailles had required Germany to give most favoured nation status to a number of countries including Poland, which relied on the tax-free trade to build its economy. One of the terms of the treaty was that Germany was obliged to allow export of specified quantities of coal from the Polish part of Upper Silesia until 15 June 1925. In June 1924, however, a new customs law was passed in Poland, intended to serve as a template for future trade agreements, aimed at protecting Polish markets from foreign competition. When the trade deal with Germany came up for renewal, Poland refused to renew most favoured nation status to German goods. The German press furiously condemned the Poles on 14 June 1924 by saying, 'Poland must be mortally wounded after the trade war. With her blood her strength will flow away as well, and finally her independence.'

Stresemann saw an opportunity to bring economic pressure to bear on the Polish state and suppress its ambitions for growth as an industrial and military nation. In January 1925, Germany halted all purchases of Polish coal and slapped customs duties on all Polish-made products. Warsaw responded by raising tariffs on German goods. When talks began in an attempt to resolve the dispute in Berlin on 3 March 1925, Germany prevaricated by widening the argument and demanding more privileges for the German minorities in Poland as a pre-condition for resumption of the coal trade, but Warsaw refused to allow this to become part of the negotiations. Polish industrial output inevitably suffered, with Upper Silesia feeling the worst effects. The Polish zloty lost value, leading to the collapse of the Grabski government in November 1925. As a result of German pressure, British banks refused to make loans to the Poles and Stresemann refused to engage in any international cooperation to stabilise the Polish economy. In response to a British proposal, Stresemann wrote to the German ambassador in London saying that the recapitalisation of Poland must be delayed until the country was ripe for a settlement of border issues and there was to be no settlement until 'the catastrophe of Poland reached an extreme degree and [Poland] was brought to a state of unconsciousness'.[18]

The Reichsbank president, Hjalmar Schacht, agreed that any economic agreements with Poland must be preceded by Poland's relinquishment of Upper Silesia and the Danzig Corridor to Germany. Britain was only willing to go so far, however, and was not prepared to be used as a pawn in Germany's foreign policy game of chess. It bluntly rejected any linking of Poland's economic and territorial issues and when the US Federal Reserve Bank provided Poland with further loans, Schacht's position crumbled. Paradoxically, the trade war was to have some positive consequences and had the effect of stimulating Polish trade with other countries, not least Britain, which would be very pleased to import Polish coal during the General Strike of 1926. Poland found new trading partners and was forced to initiate a programme of modernisation of the country, but it was also to have political repercussions when a coup d'état of May 1926 brought Piłsudski to power.

Chapter 8

PIŁSUDSKI'S COUP D'ÉTAT

> We want no war waged only with the object of bringing over perhaps some millions of folk to Germany who have no wish whatever to be Germans and who cannot be Germans. We shall never attempt to subject folk who in their hearts only hate us at the price of sacrificing on the field of battle millions of those who are dear to us and whom we love.
>
> Adolf Hitler, 27 May 1933

As a result of Locarno, Germany would go on to become a full member of the League of Nations in September 1926. Polish opposition to the move had been far too weak to counter, what had been for some time, a consensus among the Western Powers that German membership was desirable and inevitable. As a result, Poland, with French support, now tried to negotiate its own membership, which Germany worked hard to prevent. Having seen its erstwhile ally Poland suffer reversals at Locarno, France tried to make amends but struggled to win British support for Polish membership. A compromise saw the General Assembly elect Poland as a non-permanent member, but Germany tried to undermine even this by making incessant complaints of Polish discrimination against German minorities in Upper Silesia and the Danzig Corridor with Stresemann, on occasions, exhibiting his showmanship by angrily pounding the table at council meetings to emphasise his point.[1]

The deep-seated hostility between Germany and France seemed to have ameliorated somewhat after Locarno as Germany voluntarily agreed to settlement of its Belgian and French borders. This boded well for Stresemann's ambitions to dissolve the Military Inter-Allied Commission of Control that monitored German compliance with Versailles and also to demilitarise the Rhineland. Britain, optimistic that a new era of European security had begun, left Locarno with a new confidence in Franco-German relations and held out a friendly hand to Germany. France had strengthened its alliances with both Poland and Czechoslovakia and concluded security pacts with Yugoslavia and Romania that had, in no way, affected its developing relations with Germany. The huge foreign loans that had poured into Germany as a result of the Dawes Plan also inaugurated a period of economic growth and increased trade, which would benefit everyone.

The success of the Locarno negotiations, which, Stresemann had engineered despite the opposition of the Nationalist party in Germany, was a very severe blow to Soviet diplomacy. Moscow felt that, despite all of Chicherin's efforts, Germany had been seduced by Western capitalism and the whole Locarno deal had been directed exclusively to marginalise the Soviet Union. Consequently, in the summer of 1925 when Chicherin faced up to the reality of Locarno, he began planning a diplomatic drive to regain the initiative to counter the Western courtship of Germany.

It was in this light that he came up with a system of neutrality and non-aggression treaties designed to curb the influence of Western capitalists in East and Central Europe and compete with the policies espoused at Locarno. Under the terms of such treaties, a guarantee of benevolent neutrality to the victim of an unprovoked attack was replaced by a promise of active assistance. It seemed timely given the dispute that had erupted between Britain and Turkey, which had raised its profile on the borders of south-east Europe and was the first country invited to sign up to a deal with the Soviets. An ulterior motive that stirred Moscow may well also have been the recent rapprochement between Turkey and Poland involving an exchange of military missions. Turkey initially resisted Soviet overtures but when it was clear that both had suffered rebuffs at Locarno, the Turkish foreign minister, Tewfik Rushdi Bey, wasted no time in meeting Chicherin in the Soviet embassy in Paris, where they signed up to a treaty of neutrality and non-aggression.[2]

This agreement was to act as a template for others concluded soon afterwards, the most important of which was the Treaty of Berlin signed by the Soviet ambassador to Germany, Nikolay Krestinski, and Stresemann on 24 April 1926 declaring that 'the interests of the German people and the peoples of the Government of the Union of Socialist Soviet Republics demand constant and trustful cooperation'. This not only reaffirmed the Rapallo agreement but pledged neutrality in the event of an attack on either party by a third and was to be in force for five years. Stresemann had been encouraged to mend fences with the Soviets by League procrastination during its debate on German membership and by the renewal of the 1921 Polish-Romanian Alliance. To quell Soviet suspicions over Germany's membership and to assuage the League's suspicions over the German-Soviet Treaty of Non-Aggression, Stresemann displayed his trademark panache by pointing out that it was Germany's intention to collaborate closely with the League in the work of the peaceful settlement of European issues and membership would 'constitute no obstacle to the friendly development of Soviet-German relations'. At the same time, the Soviet government could be assured that Germany would oppose any anti-Soviet measures proposed by the League. German diplomacy had once again triumphed by playing the 'Polish card' to great effect. Stresemann had succeeded in removing any possibility of Poland and the Soviet Union reaching agreement on their mutual border that would have allowed Poland to become 'even more arrogant towards Germany'.[3] The renewed Polish-Romanian treaty had reminded everyone of Romania's occupation of Bessarabia, which was such a thorn in the flesh of the Soviets and almost certainly precluded any prospect of progress in Russo-Polish relations. For the Soviets, the benefits of the treaty beyond restraining Germany from moving further towards the West were few but it was hailed domestically as a great success and a sign of growing Soviet prestige in European affairs.

Chicherin, for his part, looked closer to home to find comfort after Germany's dalliance with the West. Poland was clearly in no mood to compromise, so it was to the other Baltic nations, Lithuania, Finland, Estonia and Latvia that he turned. The Soviet Union, he said, desired 'a lasting friendship capable of guaranteeing our frontiers with these countries relations with which had been hampered especially by Poland, who had taken it upon itself to speak for the whole Baltic region'.[4] While this had the effect of weakening Poland's hold over the other Baltic nations, only Lithuania, ever eager to do anything that made Poland uncomfortable, responded positively to the Soviets, who progressed the initiative by suggesting that they would support Lithuanian claims to Vilnius, which had been incorporated into the Polish state. Not only were the other Baltic States unwilling to enter into talks while being subject to endless communist propaganda campaigns from Moscow, but they desperately tried to dissuade Lithuania from succumbing to Soviet entreaties. Poland even suggested that it was ready to talk to Lithuania about a non-aggression treaty but the Lithuanian foreign minister, Mykolas Sleževičius, closed the deal by putting his signature alongside that of Chicherin on 28 September 1922 and even when the

Lithuanian government fell to a coup d'état on 17 December 1922 the new regime chose to honour the treaty.

Piłsudski had refused to allow his name to go forward for the largely ceremonial role of Polish president in the election that was held on 9 December 1922 having been *de facto* chief of state since November 1918 in recognition of his wartime exploits and leader of the armed struggle for independence. His friend Gabriel Narutowicz was elected to the post instead but was in office for only a few days when he promptly fell to an assassin's bullet fired by the rightist fanatic Eligjusz Niewiadonski, who admitted at his trial that his preferred victim had been Piłsudski. As the right-left political divide in the country widened, Narutowicz was succeeded by another friend of Piłsudski, Stanislaw Wojciechowski but, given the febrile political climate, his power was little more than notional and power struggles between more than ten political parties racked the country. By May 1926, there had been thirteen cabinets with ministers rarely in place long enough to get to grips with the country's issues. This left the Sejm, the lower house of the Polish Parliament, appearing to be self-indulgent, irresponsible and quite out of touch with the public desire for a more disciplined and responsible government.[5] The state struggled to respond with east and west provinces still with their own institutions and economic models, having never become reconciled to a central administration. Politicians throughout the country were given no opportunity to gain proper experience of government, leaving bribery and corruption as the only practical forms of political discourse.

Suspecting that it would start a witch-hunt to purge the administration of opponents, Piłsudski had refused to give his support to the Witos government, elected in May 1923. He had resigned as chief of the general staff and ceased to hold any official post in the state, displaying his disgust by even refusing to accept a state pension. Piłsudski's fears had proved well founded when the Witos government wasted no time in dismantling Piłsudski's military systems and arresting two of his close associates on charges of espionage. A smear campaign was inaugurated against the very person of Piłsudski, who described the country as 'sinking into a political and moral swamp'.[6] After only seven months, Witos was ousted from the post of prime minister in favour of Grabski, who was granted exceptional powers to deal with the dire economic situation the country was in, but it was an uphill struggle as international financial institutions shunned Poland and a poor harvest threatened hunger for many. German launched its trade war and minor coalition parties fled the administration. Gold reserves were dangerously low, leaving Grabski no option but to resign on

14 November 1925. Inflation took off as another administration led by Aleksander Skrzyński, one of the architects of Locarno but otherwise an unremarkable politician, tried to bring order. His coalition of diametrically opposed philosophies, however, never had a chance of coalescing.

In April 1926 Polish banks encountered financial difficulties and twenty banks went bust. Demonstrations and riots rocked the main cities. One of the critical issues fuelling the crisis, which had serious political overtones and repercussions, was a devastating loss of morale within the Polish army brought on by the level of civilian control over its high command. The officer corps of the new Polish army had been drawn from several sources. Some were the veterans of Pilsudski's wartime Legions who, like Piłsudski, lacked formal military training before the First World War but believed themselves to be heroes of the independence movement and so merited special recognition by the nation. It was from here that Piłsudski drew his most loyal support, although a number of former Legionnaires supported his rival, Sikorski. Alongside this group was the Second Legion Brigade of former Imperial Austrian army soldiers, led by Generals Stanisław Haller, Stanisław Szeptycki, and Tadeusz Rozwadowski. These scorned Piłsudski's legionnaires as 'incompetent amateurs' but had the reputation of harbouring residual nostalgic devotion to the House of Hapsburg, and hence the new Austrian state, and were generally considered to lack Piłsudski's enthusiasm for an independent Poland.[7] As chief of the military department of the Galician Supreme National Committee (*Naczelny Komitet Narodowy*) during the First World War, Sikorski had come to identify himself with this pro Austro-Hungarian faction of the military and herein lay the root of his enduring animosity towards Piłsudski.

Another group comprised officers from the former Tsarist Russian army who, by and large, were apolitical but Piłsudski's great political interest in the Kresy borderlands, where many of them had originated, saw some drawn towards his camp. Among those who gave allegiance to Piłsudski were General Lucjan Żeligowski, who had seized Wilno for Poland in 1920 and later as war minister in the spring of 1926 helped to lay the ground for Piłsudski's coup, General Wacław Iwaszkiewicz, and General Daniel Konarzewski, who became Piłsudski's vice minister of war after May 1926.

There was also a contingent that had been part of the Blue Army led by General Józef Haller, who was a vigorous opponent of Piłsudski. Haller, of course, had very strong ties to the French military and under his guidance French instructors had been brought in after the war to give formal military education to the Polish army. This resulted in friction within the armed forces between those French-trained regiments under Haller's command and the few Polish officers, whose senior representative was Kazimierz Raszewski, who had previously served in the German-Prussian army.

Up until Witos' first cabinet in 1923, Piłsudski's fellow prisoner in Magdeburg, Sosnkowski, had been the war minister, which had reinforced his control over the army and this had been further strengthened in 1922 when he took the post of chief of the general staff in place of Sikorski, who had been elevated to become premier. During this time of almost total control of the army, Piłsudski tried to reform it in his own image with a significant degree of independence from political control. He formed two overriding military institutions. The first was the Full War Council (*Pelna Rada Wojenna*), an advisory body to discuss and give advice on questions of military training, armaments, mobilisation, communications, technology and fortifications, and other issues on which the president or war minister might wish to consult it. The second was the Inner War Council (*Ścisła Rada Wojenna*), a smaller but more powerful body to prepare operational war plans. This effectively rendered the war minister powerless in relation to the war-operational machinery. Pilsudski could do this because his prestige in the country made him untouchable by the Sejm, who had to seek his approval for every military decision.

When, in November 1925, the financial and economic crisis in Poland forced Grabski to resign, Piłsudski immediately seized the chance of demonstrating his power. He confronted the Polish president, Wojciechowski, with a memorandum, which he obliged the president to sign, cautioning him against permitting any further assaults on the moral interests of the army, which he suggested had been instigated by Szeptycki and Sikorski. The army, he said, could 'no longer permit its honour to be sullied by being made the object of political bargaining among Sejm politicians and ambitious generals'.[8] Wojciechowski admitted that he was powerless to intervene to halt the political and social deterioration within the country.

On the next day, 15 November 1925, a demonstration was held at Piłsudski's country home in Sulejowek ostensibly to commemorate the seventh anniversary of his return from Magdeburg, at which large number of officers from the Warsaw garrison including twenty generals were in attendance. General Gustaw Orlicz-Dreszer addressed the gathering and lauded Piłsudski's achievements as a military leader and 'uncrowned dictator' during the early years of independence and begged him to intervene in the crisis. Pilsudski confessed his deep disappointment with Poland's failures since independence and expressed his conviction that 'justice must be done' without delay. The demonstration infuriated Sikorski, who dismissed Orlicz-Dreszer from his command of the 2nd Cavalry Division in Warsaw and took other extensive administrative precautions against a possible coup d'état.

The show of Piłsudski's strength, however, was too much for Sikorski and in November 1925 a broadly based cabinet was formed under Aleksander Skrzyński with the War Ministry being assigned to General Żeligowski. Sikorski was exiled eastward to command the Lwów Military District and Żeligowski recalled Orlicz-Dreszer to Warsaw, provoking the resignation of General Haller. Skrzyński was, at this time, preoccupied with implementation of the recently concluded Locarno Treaties but on 7 January 1926 he was faced with the question of Pilsudski's return to active political involvement. He was a man not given to confrontation and quickly agreed that Piłsudski's return was essential to secure domestic tranquillity. The right-wing faction of his coalition government, however, vehemently opposed this and caused Skrzyński to prevaricate, forcing the resignation of Moraczewski on 7 February 1926 in protest. Two days later, Piłsudski weakened the government by withdrawing support for Skrzyński and this was quickly followed by war minister Żeligowski's criticism of government policy. The public laid the blame for the crisis firmly at the door of government in general and the right-wing parties in particular as their hopes for return to some sort of order became focused on the return of Piłsudski to rescue the situation. The cabinet was forced to withdraw Sikorski's planned army command project but it was not enough to save the day and the government fell on 5 May 1926. On 10 May, a coalition government of Christian Democrats and Agrarians was formed, again headed up by Witos, but Piłsudski refused to support it and called for the 'cleansing' of Polish politics of bribery and abuse of power for private or party interests. In a press statement, which was immediately confiscated and suppressed by the government, he claimed to be surrounded by 'paid spies' with money available for the advancement of anyone who was ready to betray him.[9]

Żeligowski had started military manoeuvres on 8 May 1926 around Rembertów with Piłsudski in overall charge in a none-too-subtle move to bring pressure on the political situation. During the night of 11 May 1926 a state of alert was declared in the Warsaw military garrison, but some units marched to Rembertów, where they pledged their support to Piłsudski. On the next day, Piłsudski tried to meet Wojciechowski but failed since the president had absented himself to Spała. The government called for the introduction of martial law and the War Ministry declared that Piłsudski was 'not in active service' and had no authority to command any part of the armed forces. Government troops set up machine gun positions and were authorised to fire on any armed units attempting to cross the Poniatowski bridge into Warsaw. Wojciechowski returned later that day and went to the bridge, endorsing the order saying that the government had 'the required power and support of the country'. Piłsudski, with a number of officers, defied the guns and crossed the bridge from the other side, where he urged his old comrade Wojciechowski to dissolve the government 'for the good of Poland'.[10] The president shook off Piłsudski's appeal but did not order his arrest. It was a tense moment where Piłsudski could have turned to the defending troops and, with every likelihood of them complying, order them to stand down. Wojciechowski seized the moment and before that could happen, he called out to them to 'do their duty', turned abruptly and left. Piłsudski recrossed the bridge and retired also to Praga, where he consulted with senior officers and heard the news that firing had broken out in the city with eleven soldiers dead.

Another crossing had taken place at the undefended Kierbedź bridge over the Wisła River and fighting erupted in Castle Square. Piłsudski returned to the city as his men moved towards the Royal Castle, where he joined them, moving through cheering crowds despite gunfire still being heard in the distance. The government authorised the strongest measures, including bombs and machine guns, to disperse the rebels while Piłsudski went into session with government representatives who had called for reserve government troops to be brought up from Kraców and Poznań with orders to 'seize leaders of the rebellion without any attempt to spare their lives'.[11]

On 13 May 1926, there was a general stand-off with sporadic violence as the government scrambled to bring reinforcements into the city. Negotiations between the two sides were mediated by Archbishop Aleksander Kakowski and marshal of the Sejm, Maciej Rataj, but there was no progress. Fighting broke out during which 215 soldiers and 164 civilians were killed, and some 900 people were wounded. The government position was weakened the next day when the Polish Socialist Party declared its support for the rebels and called for a general strike, supported by the Railwaymen's Union (*Związek Zawodowy Kolejarzy*). The strike by socialist railwaymen paralysed communications and prevented pro-government military reinforcements from reaching Warsaw. Huge popular support buoyed the rebel cause and, fearing that a continuation of the crisis would escalate into all-out civil war, near midnight on 14 May 1926, Wojciechowski saw no option but to resign the office of president.

Witos followed up by announcing the dissolution of the government. Piłsudski consulted the French ambassador and a new government was formed under Prime Minister Kazimierz Bartel, with Piłsudski as minister of military affairs.

On 31 May 1926, the National Assembly (*Zgromadzenie Narodowe*) nominated Piłsudski as president. While still considering himself a democrat. he resisted calls for national elections, believing that the country could ill-afford any 'social experiments', but he also declined all calls for a military dictatorship, allowing a free vote for the presidency. When he won the vote, he resigned immediately and Ignacy Mościcki was sworn in instead, but Piłsudski became the real 'power behind the throne'. Piłsudski, however, was a military man first and foremost and had little interest in internal politics. When asked to define his philosophy the best he could come up with was 'the diminution of robbery and the pursuit of honesty'.[12] The new government became known as Sanacja (Sanation) taking its name from its mission to sanitise the body politic of Poland. Its main characteristic was authoritarianism, preaching national interest over parliamentary democracy.

The new foreign minister, August Zaleski, who was a popular choice with the French, established two principles as the foundation of Sanacja foreign policy. The first, governed by Poland's uncomfortable situation between two powerful and hostile neighbours, was neutrality and the second point was maintenance of its alliances with France and Romania. It was Piłsudski's assertion that these two principles, upon which depended Poland's very existence, should never be abandoned. Zaleski, assuring other nations that Poland would continue in the same 'pacific and conciliatory spirit' as before, realised the necessity of collective security through the Geneva Protocol but cautioned against the League of Nations, which should only be involved in extreme circumstances unless Poland wanted 'to be made a fool of'.[13] Piłsudski agreed with his opinion of the League that it would always prioritise collective compromise over individual security, which favoured the stronger states, but believed that neither Germany nor the Soviet Union would be capable of launching an offensive against Poland for at least another ten years.

The Soviet Union was uneasy over the coup, fearing that, at any time, Piłsudski might create border friction to divert attention from Poland's internal problems. The main Soviet foreign policy objectives remained close ties with Germany and a determination to thwart any possibility of a strong Baltic alliance stretching from Finland to Romania headed by Poland. Its efforts to make agreements with these countries in turn failed as each held out for a solution that included them all. Nevertheless, both Zaleski and Patek made overtures to Moscow, to which Zinoviev responded favourably 'in the light of the deterioration of the international position of the Soviet Union'[14] by calling for a settlement with the Polish 'bourgeoisie' and more sustainable trade agreements. However, to his own power base in Moscow he secretly urged continued efforts to undermine the Polish state from within by communist conspiracies. Rykov reiterated his oft-stated view that Poland must, at all costs, be prevented from forming a Baltic bloc under Polish leadership. When Stresemann complained that official statements from Moscow indicated a warming of Russo-Polish relations that were contrary to understandings arrived at between himself and Chicherin, Litvinov assured him that any negotiations were no more than tactical manoeuvres.

Germany saw the new Polish regime as somewhat less adversarial than its predecessors and welcomed signs that Piłsudski seemed to want some degree of rapprochement. However, when the German foreign minister, Karl von Schubert, brought up the issue of revision of the Polish-German border with Zaleski after Poland's accession to the League he got a cold rebuff of 'Never!'. There was a little more agreement on the issue of minorities but that never amounted to very much and it remained a thorn in both of their sides right up to the start of the Second World War. Real progress, however, was made on trade, where both had suffered from the bitter economic war that was raging. While trying to deter any Russo-Polish rapprochement, Germany was quietly responding to signs that Piłsudski was putting 'extraordinary importance on reaching friendly relations with Germany' but doubted that his softer approach heralded any move towards settlement of the border issue, which anyway would require French support if any progress was to be made.[15] Stresemann met Briand at Thoiry on 17 September 1926 and received some encouragement that an answer to the Polish question would follow naturally from closer Franco-German relations. When Chicherin confronted Stresemann over the Thiory meeting he was assured that no concessions had been asked or given by either side. They did, however, discuss the unlikely possibility of Poland conceding the Danzig Corridor in exchange for a chunk of Lithuania. What was agreed was the need for both Germany and the Soviet Union to keep Poland under constant pressure from both east and west, with Germany generally dominating the agenda in relation to Polish matters. However, the fact that Poland was now such an important factor in German-Soviet relations gave it some leverage by playing one off against the other but it was not in Piłsudski's nature to do that and that was a critical oversight.

The Czechs thought that the coup would put Poland on a more anti-Russian track and take Poland closer to Germany. Piłsudski had no love for the Czechs and believed that Czech independence would not stand the test of time. Zaleski, however, had worked closely with Beneš in Geneva, which held out the prospect of some warming of relations, but again they failed to resolve the question of minorities, where each country accused the other of intimidation and discrimination. Furthermore, the Poles harboured suspicions that Prague was still supporting Ukrainian irredentism.

The Polish-Romanian Alliance was renewed for another five years with only a few amendments. Bucharest viewed Piłsudski's return to power favourably, but Piłsudski was not particularly interested in Romania, believing it to lack military credibility that made it irrelevant to the cause of containing German aggression. There was some improvement in the armaments trade, however, which prompted efforts to build a stronger relationship that might have long-term benefits.

The French had little confidence that Piłsudski's leadership would improve Franco-Polish relations but they were surprised by Zaleski's enthusiasm for an alliance as 'an instrument of security and peace'.[16] After Locarno, Briand saw Poland as being of less importance in terms of curbing German revanchism and Piłsudski was quick to realise that. However, there was no sense in taking umbrage at the cooling of French ardour when an alliance, albeit weakened by Locarno, could still act as an insurance policy and there was always the possibility that the new-found rapprochement between Germany and France would fail to stand the test of time, leaving a clear way forward for Germany to rebuild its power and influence. There was a price that Poland had to pay for any support at all from France in international affairs and that rankled. The French now treated Poland as a junior partner and took its interests less seriously, often voting against them in League meetings and demanding humiliating concessions when it chose support. It was usual now for France to make foreign policy decisions without any consultation between French and Polish diplomats.

The coup in Poland was followed a few months later in Kaunas by a nationalist coup to take over the Lithuanian state. The new prime minister, Augustinas Voldemaras, saw relations with Poland as being centred on the return of Vilnius, which was occupied by Polish troops. Lithuania's hatred of Poland was quite on a par with that of the Soviet Union and Germany.[17] The two nations had been officially at war since 1920, Lithuania having previously ended all diplomatic relations with Poland by closing the border, breaking all communications including the rather extreme measures of ripping up thousands of miles of rail tracks and taking down telegraph lines, just in case Poland didn't get the point. There were endless border incidents with casualties, but it was the evergreen issue of minorities that sustained the conflict to the point where 'conflict rather than accommodation prevailed'.[18] Whenever Poland had mooted the formation of a Baltic bloc, it was always Lithuania, encouraged by the Soviets, that had blocked it. Kopp had confidently predicted, on a number of occasions, that when confrontation eventually came with Poland, it would be to Lithuania that the Soviets would look to lead the charge.

The Germans, however, who had their own ambitions where Lithuanian soil was concerned, were a little more circumspect, hoping at some future date to find an excuse to take the Baltic sea port of Memel into the Reich. It should be said that the Soviets were by no means enthusiastic about such a move, which illustrated the limitations to any joint German-Soviet policy towards Lithuania. Indeed, Stresemann was adamant that if the Soviets were to give any encouragement to Lithuania to resist German claims to Memel it would have the gravest consequences for German-Soviet relations, but Litvinov shrugged off any suggestion that Moscow would put Lithuanian concerns before those of Germany. Despite the Memel issue, Lithuania looked for friendly relations, exchanges of intelligence and a joint strategy with Germany in the Council of the League of Nations, especially in relation to their common foe, Poland.

When Piłsudski came to power, he wanted to end the dispute over Vilnius but the Soviet Union kept up its pressure to isolate Poland by claiming that Polish troop movements around Vilnius meant that Poland was going to attack Lithuania. Even though Zaleski dismissed these rumours and stressed the need to reopen normal diplomatic relations, it may well have been the case that the troop movement were designed to pressurise the Lithuanians to formalise relations. It was well accepted that Piłsudski had never become reconciled to an independent Lithuania, and it was not difficult to suggest that, now he was in complete control of Poland, he might be tempted to do something about it. Soviet strategy paid dividends when they were able to negotiate a non-aggression pact with Lithuania on 28 September 1926. With Soviet support Voldemaras, whom Piłsudski derided as having a mentality 'borrowed from an insane asylum', now demanded that the return of Vilnius was the price Poland would have to pay to re-establish relations. Before the Kaunas coup, Piłsudski's had refused to compromise, citing the absence of a responsible Lithuanian government to negotiate with, but now he was anxious to find a resolution and, in secret talks, offered to give up Vilnius in return for the establishment of a Polish-Lithuanian union. Moscow, who with Berlin had no interest in changing the status quo in Lithuania, was unnerved by rumours of a change in Polish-Lithuanian relations and asked the Germans to find out what was going on. Von Schubert doubted that Poland would use force to resolve the issue and categorically assured Krestinski that there was no question of a Polish-German understanding, an assurance that Krestinski took with a pinch of salt judging by the way he put the matter right at the top of his agenda on his next visited to Berlin.[19] Germany's relaxed attitude to the Polish-Lithuanian stand-off had aroused Soviet suspicions that something was afoot that they knew nothing about. Rumour was still rife in Moscow that Germany had sold out Lithuania to the Poles in return for return of the Danzig Corridor.

The Polish-Lithuanian confrontation threatened to spiral out of control when Voldemaras established himself as Lithuanian dictator on 17 December 1926. The whole of Europe held its breath as two nations whose fates rested in the decisions of a dictator and a virtual dictator tried to stare each other down over the border until Britain, whom Germany suspected of acting in direct opposition to German interests in the dispute, stepped in to try and ease the tension. Germany saw this as a ruse to draw Lithuania away from the Soviet camp and into the arms of Poland, which seemed unlikely to happen but just in case they joined the Soviets in making assurances to Lithuania of support should war break out with Poland. However, this was only up to a certain point and the Germans were not giving any ground at all in relation to their claims on Memel.

After Stresemann had been forced to counter Soviet accusations of a secret agreement with Poland over Lithuania with assurances that 'the basic character of [German] relations with Poland will not be touched', he changed his tune twenty-four hours later with a counter-accusation that Moscow had been in contact with Warsaw, without informing Berlin, to arrange a conference to settle the crisis. German-Soviet diplomatic ships had sailed into choppy waters. Stresemann blamed this on meddling by the Western Powers and made it an objective of his strategy to separate Eastern Europe from Western influence as much as possible and leave it to be managed according to joint German-Soviet priorities.

Early in 1927, the French looked at ways of modifying the Polish alliance, not just to have it aligned more with Locarno but to allow it to move away from a policy of alliances as their main avenue of security. Various proposals were put forward by the French ambassador to Warsaw, Jules Laroche, who wanted to restrict the alliance to those terms allowed under the League's covenant. In November 1927, General Louis Franchet d'Esperey visited Warsaw with new ideas for a revision to the military convention but failed to move the Poles, who refused point blank to even consider any changes apart from allowing an increase in French deliveries of war materials.

When the Soviet ambassador to Warsaw, Pyotr Voykov, was assassinated on 7 June 1927, the simmering unease that had pervaded Eastern Europe threatened to boil over. Voykov was accompanying the Soviet ambassador to Britain, Arkady Rosengolts, along the train station platform in Warsaw when a Russia émigré, Boris Kowerda, opened fire in an attempt to kill him, shouting 'die for Russia'. Voykov returned fire as he fled but was hit twice and died in hospital a few hours later. The Soviets accused Poland and Britain of colluding in the assassination and used the occasion to organise communist demonstrations in Warsaw. War fever gripped the Soviet Union, which threatened to mobilise the Red Army. Whilst admitting no responsibility for the incident, the Poles were forced to apologise profusely, but Britain took the dramatic step of breaking off diplomatic relations with the Soviet Union. Litvinov expressed Soviet outrage, accusing Poland of harbouring and even supporting anti-Soviet terrorist organisations. Lenin called Kowerda a Polish agent whose action had been designed to precipitate a military conflict between Poland and the Soviet Union and likened it to the way that Gavrilo Princip's assassination of Archduke Franz Ferdinand had ushered in the First World War.

Tensions rose significantly in the wake of Voykov's assassination. Chicherin chose to point the finger at Piłsudski, who he said was the principal danger to peace and 'a romantic and an adventurer' under strong British influence whose only political idea was to unite Belarus, the Ukraine and Lithuania under Polish control.[20] The normally indefatigable Soviet foreign minister, however, had become ill with diabetes, for which he was treated by German doctors, and so might be excused for his pessimistic fears that France would exploit the situation by manufacturing an incident on the Russo-Polish border to provoke war. Stresemann, who visited him at the Baden-Baden health spa, assured him that France could have no interest in getting into a shooting war with the Soviets over something as trivial as Poland. Few shared Stresemann's optimism, however. France, fearing that the Soviets would send an ultimatum to Poland and Britain, proposed that, in view of his close personal relations with Chicherin, Stresemann should immediately go to Moscow to calm things down. Stresemann thought they were overreacting and merely agreed to consider it. Moscow got wind of this but its interpretation was that they thought

Captured Red Army soldiers after the 'Miracle on the Vistula'

First plenary session of the negotiations in Riga, 22 September 1920

Officers of the Polish Legion interned in Beniaminów

Jozef Haller von Hallenberg

Simon Petliura

French Renault FT tank in Katowice market square on the day of the Upper Silesian plebiscite

Family fleeing Silesia to Germany after the plebiscite

Polish paramilitaries in Upper Silesia

Chancellor of Germany Joseph Wirth with Leonid Krasin, Georgi Chicherin and Adolph Ioffe of the Russian delegation at Rapallo, 1922

Piłsudski (fourth from left) and other coup leaders on Poniatowski Bridge in Warsaw, 11 May 1926

German foreign minister, Gustav Stresemann

Hitler attending a service in Berlin to mark the death of Pilsudski

Anti-Semitic graffiti in Danzig, 1935

German foreign minister Joachim von Ribbentrop (left) with Polish foreign minister Josef Beck

Polish cavalry on exercise, summer 1939

Hitler watches German troops cross the Vistula, September 1939

Stresemann had agreed to send a strong warning to them, which they interpreted as both a provocation and a direct threat that left a sick and weakened Chicherin struggling to defend his current policy to the Politburo. Veiled threats bounced back and forth between Berlin and Moscow.

In September 1927 news broke of an imminent Franco-Soviet non-aggression pact. Stresemann told Brockdorff-Rantzau to find out what was going on, whereupon the ambassador upbraided Chicherin, accusing the Soviets of weakening their commitment to Germany in favour of France. Chicherin, not yet recovered from his illness, was not pleased to be spoken to so bluntly and somewhat enigmatically replied that 'as yet' there was no question of the Soviet Union making a choice between the two. Brockdorff-Rantzau reminded Chicherin that Germany held all the cards in their relationship and could turn away at any time. Chicherin saw the truth of that and became a little more conciliatory, giving assurances that the putative non-aggression pact had been France's idea to stir up trouble against Germany and that the Soviets had no intention of doing anything that was damaging to German interests. Stresemann was not convinced and asked Brockdorff-Rantzau to bear in mind during talks with the Soviets that although German acceptance of a Franco-Soviet non-aggression pact was not entirely out of the question, any attempt to include Poland in any way would be against Rapallo as well as the Berlin Treaty and was to be resisted. The weak Soviet position during these exchanges clearly showed that indeed Brockdorff-Rantzau's assertion that Germany called the shots in German-Soviet relations was not far from the truth.

Any idea of closer relations between Poland and Lithuania received a reality check in late 1927 when Lithuania asked for its quarrel with Poland to be discussed at the League of Nations. The strong Polish reaction threw Berlin and Moscow into a diplomatic spin as the war scare was reignited. Stresemann feared that British and French influences were at work and took the view that the Vilnius issue, which could not under any circumstances be resolved in Poland's favour, must be calmed and this would soon lead to the Western Powers turning their attention elsewhere. Stresemann and Chicherin urged Lithuania to end its long-standing state of war with Poland and in return they would promise to defend Lithuanian interests in the Council of the League of Nations' meetings. Chicherin went so far as to assure the Lithuanians that the Soviet Union would not hesitate to defend them if they came under Polish attack and, at the same time, told Poland 'with greatest emphasis' of the 'immeasurable dangers' that would attend any Polish attack on Lithuanian independence.[21]

Poland meekly replied that it had no such intentions and asked other governments to rein in Lithuanian aggression.

When talks on Lithuania took place in Geneva in December 1927, Stresemann took the opportunity to employ his silky skills in a whispering campaign to suggest that East Prussian paramilitary '*Stahlhelm*' units were poised to move towards Memel and then publicly dismissed the idea as preposterous. Clearly Memel would continue to be unresolved as long as Stresemann found it useful as a tool to influence Lithuanian policy. Others were more anxious to defuse the situation. Piłsudski dashed to Geneva to appear before the council and upbraid Voldemaras as a warmonger. He also had harsh words for the League when it suggested posting troops along the Polish-Lithuanian border, calling the mere mention of such a move 'offensive'.[22] This had the desired effect of forcing Lithuania to declare an end to its state of war with Poland and in return Piłsudski gave a very public affirmation of Polish respect for Lithuanian independence. The Soviets gave little credence to Piłsudski's promise and continued to decry the hypocritical attitude of the League, which was putting up a smokescreen while Piłsudski prepared a war that only the Soviet Union was preventing.

Stresemann took the opportunity to hold a private meeting with Piłsudski at Geneva on 9 December, which proved to be extremely cordial although he was not inclined towards the same level of optimism as the Pole, who had assured him that given sufficient goodwill all Polish-German issues could be settled in six months.

When Stresemann told Briand about the meeting, he was mildly rebuked for not making more of the opportunity to bring up the Danzig and Memel issues and get Piłsudski's detailed views on the border question that France was keen to see resolved. Both France and Britain seemed to believe that Piłsudski was ready and able to compromise on boundaries and that the only question was what he would ask in return but there is no evidence to suggest that their optimism was at all justified.

When Voldemaras went to Berlin at the end of January 1928, Stresemann went to great lengths to convince Poland that the visit should not be interpreted as an anti-Polish move and a few weeks later when he met Piłsudski's delegate Prince Michael Radziwill, it was to emphasise that the time was ripe for German-Polish rapprochement and dangled the carrot of German investment in the Polish economy. The goodwill that was evident between Stresemann and Piłsudski at Geneva persisted through the first part of the year and a number of minor agreements followed between the two countries, but progress was stuttering at best as right-wing elements in Germany, buoyed by the imminent departure of Allied troops from the Rhineland and growing confidence in German prestige, continued to demand that Upper Silesia be restored to Germany. When Zaleski brought up the issue of French guarantees against the prospect of growing German strength, his fears proved well-grounded as von Schubert quickly demanded that the French clarify their position on the matter. Stresemann's strategies were playing out very much to Germany's advantage. No country could now assume that they could make any move in Eastern Europe without taking into consideration the effect it would have on Germany and what it might cost if Germany opposed it. Conscious of this growing power, however, Stresemann was careful to wield it with wisdom and restraint and he was careful to consult other powers before taking initiatives and gave respect and consideration to their views. Neither the Soviet Union nor the Western Powers could now expect to tackle the overriding and perennially troublesome question of border revision without close attention to German sensibilities.

The ever-busy Stresemann, buoyed by his success at Locarno, now met Briand, with whom he had developed 'a truly intimate friendship',[23] to discuss ways in which Germany might play a greater part in European politics. His aim was to eliminate French fears of German aggression and convince Briand of Germany's good intentions which, in turn, would deserve reciprocal action by, for instance, the early withdrawal of Allied troops from the Rhineland. If this could be achieved, then Germany would be completely free to focus its attention on its revisionist campaign against Poland.

Early evacuation of the Rhineland, however, would be against Polish interests. The presence of Allied troops together with the continuing burden of war reparations meant that Germany could not afford to mobilise against Poland, so although Zaleski had to support Franco-German rapprochement it was clear that the withdrawal of troops would strengthen Germany and see the French retreating behind their borders with diminishing enthusiasm for expeditionary adventures. Briand assured him that evacuation would only take place in tandem with further restraints on German disarmament. Zaleski was not convinced and wanted to invoke Article 429 of the Versailles Treaty to force direct negotiations with Germany, Britain and France to arrive at a non-aggression pact. France found a convenient excuse to dissociate itself from such a move by pointing out that Poland could not invoke Versailles to support its action since it had not been part of the Allied delegation at Versailles.

Slowly but surely, France was trying to divest itself of any lingering commitments to Poland. They refused to discuss what mobilisation plans France was putting in place to deal with Eastern Europe contingencies but preparations to build a massive fortification along its border with Germany signalled a move towards unilateralism and a purely defensive posture. All France would offer Poland was a vague promise of military assistance in the form of training and equipment but that would inevitably be hostage to the political whims of constantly changing administrations. The French became increasingly annoyed by what they saw as Poland's constant 'petty and time-consuming' carping to the League of Nations about French reconciliation moves towards Germany that undermined Polish security. Neither were they best pleased by rumours that Poland was talking to Hungary, Italy and Romania, which threatened to isolate Czechoslovakia and Yugoslavia, with whom France was also trying to maintain good relations.

While the Soviet Union was passing through a period of difficulties internally, the Sixth Congress of the Communist International (Comintern) convened in Moscow on 17 July 1928 and chose its platform to denounce the US expansionist policy of 'imperialist aggression'. The leader of the Polish communists, Wera Kosrtrezewa, claimed that his country was being prepared as a 'springboard for attack [by the West and] the occupation of Lithuania was imminent [which would] set on fire the whole world'. For the Soviet Union, Bukharin predicted that the Polish communists would play 'an important role ... in the event of war [to free itself] from the shackles of slavery'.[24] Subsequent analysis shows that Stalin was using the Congress to exaggerate the threat of war to advance his internal agenda both to bring in a policy of industrialisation and also to root out and eliminate opposition to his position. The main consequence for Poland was its renewed repression of the Polish Communist Party.

British-Soviet diplomatic relations were still frozen as they squared up over China and this was felt acutely in Moscow, where it had already suffered a loss of confidence in German support for it against the Western Powers. The Soviets were also uncertain how to deal with Piłsudski, whom they continued to suspect of nurturing ambitions towards Bessarabia and the Ukraine. Despite its doubts about how far it could trust Piłsudski, however, all this encouraged Moscow to look how to reduce tension over the border dispute with Poland. It would eliminate the risk of a Polish invasion and reduce the power of Germany to manipulate tensions for its own ends. A third, not insignificant, benefit would be a warming of relations with France. When the Soviet Union suggested talks about a non-aggression treaty, the Poles this time abandoned their usual dismissive response in favour of tendering counter-proposals that, although unlikely to find favour in Moscow, indicated a significant change in strategy. Chicherin predictably was not impressed but events elsewhere suggested that progress was possible.

On 27 August 1928, fifteen nations signed the Kellog-Briand Pact in Paris, which had initially been a bilateral agreement between the United States and France to outlaw war between them. The US secretary of state, Frank B. Kellogg, had brought his country to the table with France in an attempt to set the scene for wider agreements to outlaw wars of aggression as instruments of national policy. In early 1928, negotiations over the agreement expanded to include other nations including Britain, Poland, Germany and Czechoslovakia, although France, in what must have seemed like a gratuitous humiliation, originally refused to allow Poland to be one of the signatories because it did not consider it to be sufficiently important as a world power. The signatories agreed firstly to reject war as an instrument of national policy and secondly that all signatories would settle their disputes by peaceful means. France saw this as another step along the path to collective opposition to Germany aggression, but Zaleski had overcome French hostility to inclusion and signed simply because he had no choice if he did not want to see Poland being further sidelined on the European stage. Despite being a signatory, Poland had not been consulted at any stage of the negotiations and certainly did not see the Pact as a guarantee of French aid in the event of a German attack.

The Soviet Union reacted to the Kellogg-Briand Pact with contempt. Chicherin saw it as 'a means of isolating the USSR' and condemned it as not having gone far enough in renouncing all methods of aggression.[25] He accused the Germans of betraying the 'spirit of Rapallo' and sacrificing its ties with them for better relations with the West. The Soviets, however, faced with a fait accompli had to make the best of it and so, in December, Litvinov proposed the Litvinov Protocol, which would apply the provisions of the Kellogg-Briand Pact to the relations between the Soviet Union and Poland and by extension, to Lithuania also but not to the other Baltic states. Poland supported the idea but only if the other Baltic states and Romania were included.

Brockdorff-Rantzau died in Berlin on 8 September 1928 from heart disease after contracting a throat infection. His successor, Herbert von Dirksen, shared his commitment to close German-Soviet relations, despite having 'contempt and abhorrence' for communism, but had neither Brockdorff-Rantzau's zeal nor his authority. Although a firm supporter of the secret military alliance that had developed between

Germany and the Soviet Union, this 'unimaginative bureaucrat'[26] lacked the experience and skills to reverse the growth of suspicions and enmities that were beginning to tear it apart. It did not help that Chicherin was also gravely ill, leaving Litvinov to conduct foreign affairs for the Soviets. It was not the best way to start in his new post when von Dirksen's first task was to convey to Moscow Stresemann's deep unease over the Litvinov Protocol. Litvinov had to work hard to assure von Dirksen that it was actually of little significance in the greater scheme of things and had simply been a subterfuge to draw Poland out and, by declaring its position, show its weakness. In any case, he was confident that the Poles would refuse to sign because it was such a disagreeable deal for them and would end with them walking away from the negotiating table, showing them up to be belligerent and troublesome.

Litvinov was wrong, however, because on 9 February 1929 Poland signed up to the Protocol, along with the Soviet Union, Romania, Latvia and Estonia. Even Lithuania eventually signed up two months later. When the Soviets had agreed to include all the Baltic States, the pressure on Poland to agree had become irresistible. Somewhat taken aback by Poland's acceptance of the Protocol, the Soviets immediately began a campaign of undermining it with accusations of Polish non-compliance with and lack of commitment to its terms. Patek, now installed as the Polish ambassador to Moscow, walked out midway through a speech by Rykov in which he had criticised Poland for 'abandoning the spirit' of the Protocol.[27] Beyond the first few weeks after signing, it was clear that the Protocol had done nothing to diminish the deep-rooted animosity that persisted between the two countries. Indeed, a surge in demonstrations, sometimes violent, by crowds on both sides indicated that things were, if anything, worse. Delegates from East Prussia and Danzig were feted in Moscow to show Soviet contempt for Polish sensibilities.

The frostiness of Soviet relations with the Poles was matched by the cooling of those with Germany as Stresemann's strategy of rapprochement with the West was paying dividends. The issue of communist agitation in Germany had never gone away and was now being used by Berlin to justify a number of diplomatic moves designed to extricate itself from the secret military deals with the Soviets that were threatening to become public knowledge and undermine relations with Britain and France. Germany was no longer the outcast that it had been in 1919 and was, once again, taking its place at the high table of European affairs, while the Soviet Union was still knocking at the door. Berlin had started to see its ties with Moscow as an embarrassing liability, but von Dirksen was anxious to maintain an east-west balance by replacing the clandestine activity with more open arrangements that would sustain relations between the two countries in a more conventional way.

German foreign policy was rocked by another death in 1929. This time it was Stresemann, that towering figure of German foreign policy in the 1920s whose relentless and skilful diplomacy had been fundamental to Germany's rehabilitation, who, having suffered ill-health for some time, died suddenly of a heart attack in Berlin on 3 October 1929, aged 51. Stresemann's years of tireless efforts, which had brought him the Nobel Peace Prize alongside Briand for their work on the Locarno Treaty, had been characterised by the intricacy of his strategies but had inevitably required compromises over integrity and sincerity. Julius Curtius, who succeeded Stresemann, was never going to be able to emulate him, but his task was made significantly more difficult as the world economic depression dragged Germany down with all the other countries into a state of instability and social turmoil. It was the time when Nazism started to make an impact of domestic German politics. Stresemann had, in many ways, been a front for Prussian interests and no friend to Poland. Often he had promulgated the impression that Poland was merely a transitory phenomenon that would disappear in time.

The watershed in European politics was further emphasised on 21 July 1930 when Chicherin formally handed over Soviet foreign affairs to the 'ruthless, unsentimental and friendless'[28] Litvinov, who had been preferred to Lev Karakhan, despite opposition from a strong anti-Semitic lobby in the Kremlin. Litvinov's tenure was characterised by a move towards stronger ties with France and a slow reduction in Soviet reliance on Germany in line with Stalin's own growing unease at German rehabilitation. Showing little regret for such a seismic shift in the relationship between their two countries, Litvinov had confided to von Dirksen the previous January that he feared Rapallo was terminally damaged as Germany moved closer to the West with every diplomatic initiative, even as far as suggesting that it was approaching a reconciliation with Poland. While von Dirksen did his best privately to reassure Litvinov, Berlin made no effort to officially refute his claims. After some months of tense negotiations, von Dirksen and Litvinov were able to patch things up a little with an agreement in July that lifted the gloom, but while they agreed on basic aspirations in Eastern European affairs, their individual strategies towards achieving them began to diverge significantly.

In Germany, von Seeckt, although long absent from the political scene, wrote an influential memorandum in which he maintained his faith in strong Soviet relations to stabilise Germany's eastern borders and pursue a strategy of German colonisation and dominance of the 'Slav masses', a theme that was to become more prominent in German politics as the decade unfolded. Central to his argument, which was an echo of his unwavering views since Versailles, was the growing strength of Poland, with whom he saw no hope of a strong, honourable and lasting peace, but by now he had become marginalised and the pro-Soviet lobby in Berlin was losing ground.

Curtius made his first priority to end the tariff war with Poland and came to an agreement to boost trade between the two countries, but when neither parliament saw fit to ratify the deal it foundered, and the trade dispute intensified. This was accompanied by a spate of shooting incidents on the border that brought the boundary dispute back into the full glare of scrutiny. Rallies became a feature of border clashes but in the free port of Danzig also, Nazi sympathisers were stirring up trouble. The Polish press published documents purporting to show German military aid for activists and agitators in Ukraine and East Poland. As tensions rose, a genuine fear, born out of election victories throughout Poland for Piłsudski's followers, that Poland would exploit German internal strife to occupy the German part of Upper Silesia and even East Prussia.

Germany, however, was growing ever stronger and now felt confident enough to ask for armament parity as a priority in the upcoming League of Nations disarmament conference. It was a matter of some concern for Poland that Britain had no strong objections to such a move and France was losing the will to resist German pressure in the Council of the League of Nations. Even the US, which had little active interest in Eastern European affairs, came down firmly on the side of Germany in its argument over revision of the Danzig Corridor.

Chapter 9

THE DEATH OF PIŁSUDSKI

The Litvinov Protocol had failed to improve Russo-Polish relations but Moscow's desire for a non-aggression pact with Poland was promoted in an article in *Izvestia.* However, as so often before, the mood of reconciliation was marred by violence, in this case a bomb incident at the Soviet Legation in Warsaw. It shows the strength of Soviet ambition that this was not allowed to get in the way of talks, especially since Warsaw had secretly instructed Patek in Moscow to pursue a conciliatory agenda and be open to talks over non-aggression. The French got wind of these talks and revealed them to the public, which had both Moscow and Warsaw scurrying to deny that it was they who had instigated them and that they were merely responding to an approach from the other side. Litvinov had trouble convincing Curtius that, although it had not been his idea, 'discussions' but no 'negotiations' had taken place and Soviet-German relations would not be adversely affected.

Litvinov was quick also to scotch the rumour that Moscow was talking to Paris about a similar non-aggression treaty. Again, Litvinov assured von Dirksen that the whole idea had come from the French and had little chance of making progress against Soviet indifference. It can only be imagined, therefore, what von Dirksen made of an official communiqué from Moscow on 12 August 1931 that an agreement with France had been arrived at, even though Litvinov explained that it was designed from the Soviet angle simply to further weaken the Franco-Polish alliance. Any chance of a similar deal with Poland, however, would only be considered if Warsaw dropped its 'traditional conditions'.[1] What Litvinov failed to say was that all the while serious negotiations were taking place in which Poland argued for a collective Baltic non-aggression agreement tied to the League of Nations, while the Soviets insisted on a simple bilateral deal to which the Poles were eventually obliged to acquiesce in order to make any headway at all.

It became almost a Herculean task for Litvinov to reassure von Dirksen that the Polish talks would have no adverse consequences for their relationship, especially in relation to Polish boundaries, but there were other agencies working hard to undermine it. Stalin had secretly responded to the political chaos in Germany by setting up a commission to 'study the possibilities of a revolution in Germany'.[2] Part of the strategy was for the German Communist Party to support the National Socialists in a number of areas, but it was desperately short of funds to finance the organisation of the German proletariat. When the German Foreign Office learned of this, while it may not have been too much of a surprise, it soured relations for several months until the Politburo reversed the policy. Stalin was forced to publicly recant his anti-German line in a speech on 13 December, which did not make comfortable listening for the Poles, when he spoke of 'sympathy for the Germans' and included assurances that any agreement with Poland would not include any guarantees of Polish borders.

The Polish deputy foreign minister in 1930, who became foreign minister in December 1932, was the 'arrogant and treacherous'[3] Józef Beck, who struggled to make a favourable impression with other governments. Beck was very much Piłsudski's man and followed closely the line of self-determination in the face of declining trust in French support. During the previous two years he had progressively supplanted the somewhat ineffective Zaleski, whose lukewarm support for Piłsudski's policies had hastened his departure. Beck's first priority had been to revive negotiations on the Russo-Polish Non-Aggression Pact, that Skrzyński had so assiduously worked on over a number of years. It had been in limbo since before Piłsudski's coup and was now of major concern to the Germans. Beck worked closely with the Soviet ambassador, Vladimir Antonov-Ovseyenko, who had been given significant license by Moscow to improve Soviet–Polish relations in view of the alarming Japanese policy in Manchuria. Where France was concerned, Beck aimed to arrive at a strategy less dependent on them, whom he saw as unreliable, while projecting to the rest of the world the impression that the Franco-Polish alliance was still robust and that no country could sit down to negotiate with Poland without recognising that the French were metaphorically at the table also. Both Piłsudski and Beck expected Poland now to be treated as a great power and looked for an appropriate level of respect from other countries but the reality of Poland's weak position between its two powerful neighbours demanded that, at some point, there would have to be some sort of formal agreement with either or both of them before Poland could move forward.

Beck agreed the Treaty of Non-Aggression with the Soviet Union on 25 January 1932. Poland had dropped its insistence on having the other Baltic States included and the Soviet Union had agreed to sign bilateral agreements with each of them at the same time. It was undoubtedly Polish recognition of the tumultuous political upheavals in Germany that caused Beck to 'foresee grave troubles with her [requiring] a relaxation of tensions with Russia'.[4] The treaty was signed off on 25 July 1932 and included in the preamble a reference to the Treaty of Riga, which it called the basis of undertakings between the two countries. There was no mention of Polish borders, however, which had been stipulated at Riga. For the Soviets, who always saw Poland as a client state of France, the treaty was a not-too-gentle reminder that it would not stand idly by and watch rapprochement between France and Germany with equanimity. Any apparent rapprochement between Warsaw and Moscow, however, was, for both sides, more a short-term tactical move rather than a long-term strategic one.[5]

The Treaty had been concluded after drawn-out negotiations in the face of German diplomatic objections to any new obligations that would recognise Poland's territorial integrity. They objected to Poland receiving any guarantees regarding the current Russo-Polish border, which would reduce tensions there and allow it to concentrate more on issues in the west and threaten to bring about a radical change in the European balance of power. The Soviets ignored German misgivings. The Treaty was seen as a success for Polish diplomacy and clearly stated that the basis of bilateral relations would be the provisions agreed at Riga regarding the two countries' shared border, which was a confirmation of the territorial status quo between Poland and the Soviet Union.

It was significant for Poland that, at the same time, the Soviets concluded similar agreements with Latvia, Estonia and Finland. While negotiations with Romania had ended in failure, due in no small part to the Soviet refusal to recognise Romanian control of Bessarabia, the two sides had at least established diplomatic relations, which was a small step forward. For more than seven years Poland had been angling for a single treaty to include all the Baltic States, which Moscow had viewed as a Polish plan to create an anti-Soviet bloc under Warsaw's leadership and as such had always opposed it. In the end, however, the bundle of bilateral treaties was the best they could get. The normalisation of Russo-Polish relations was further reflected in two other agreements:

on 23 November 1932 the two parties signed a Conciliation Convention, and on 3 July 1933 a multilateral convention.

There is no doubt that the Japanese invasion of Manchuria in October 1931 and Japan's subsequent conquest of it, which threatened the danger of conflict on two fronts for the Soviet Union, motivated them to reach agreements with Poland. However, the main drivers of Soviet foreign policy remained the desire to exploit German revisionism in order to disrupt the European order and to regain territories lost as a result of the collapse of the Russian Empire in 1917. In this regard, the non-aggression pact with Poland was designed to bring pressure on Germany to rebuild Soviet-German relations in the spirit of Rapallo.

Although it did not represent a breakthrough in the true sense, the treaty was the result of prolonged and successful negotiations and seemed to have normalised Russo-Polish relations. Rapallo may not have posed any immediate threat to Poland's security but, at the time, it had indicated that neither Germany nor the Soviet Union was interested in a true normalisation of relations with Poland. That, at least, had changed but it was still the case that the idea of permanent rapprochement or reconciliation with either Germany or the Soviet Union was out of the question for Piłsudski and Beck. The subordination of the Polish state to either one would lead irrevocably to the loss of independence and a violation of Poland's territorial integrity. Poland's foreign policy was a policy of balance and strict neutrality towards both neighbouring Totalitarian Powers. All that would soon be put in jeopardy, however, when on 4 January 1934 Antonov-Ovseyenko, who was enthusiastic about the prospects of improving Russo-Polish relations, received news from Moscow that brought a sharp downturn in relations with Warsaw. The Russo-Polish rapprochement would prove to be little more than a temporary ruse by Moscow, which lost much of its significance when the Declaration of Non-Aggression and Understanding between Germany and Poland was announced.

Before that came about, having achieved the first part of his plan, Beck now turned to Germany, which was in the throes of governmental chaos. Konstantin von Neurath had taken over the Foreign Ministry from Heinrich Brüning on 30 May 1932 amid a general feeling in the Reichstag, which had been stirred up by Soviet propaganda, that Piłsudski was about to take advantage by seizing Danzig. Germany, Poland and the Soviet Union all ratcheted up the rhetoric in a frenzy of claim and counterclaim, lies and accusations, and planned to exploit the chaos for their own advantage. The Reich cabinet member Gottfried Treviranus made a highly emotional and sharply threatening speech about 'the unhealed wounds in the eastern region, that withered lung of the Reich'.[6] In a clear snub, the Polish military attaché, unlike his Soviet counterpart, had been denied an invitation to German military manoeuvres in September 1932 but it was difficult to make much sense of German foreign policy with its internal political situation in flux. There had been little to choose between Stresemann and Brüning in terms of the ultimate aims of German foreign policy. The only real conflict was over the best method of achieving these aims and in the estimation of the time needed for a thorough revision of Versailles. As the economic situation deteriorated, more and more people were turning to the two extremist parties, which fought one another bloodily in the streets.

It seemed beyond doubt, however, that fundamental improvements in Polish-German relations were unlikely. German territorial revisionism was such a powerful motivation in German politics that it was hard to see how it could ever be moderated. Whenever normalisation of relations with Poland was discussed, the German side always demanded territorial concessions that were impossible for Poland to comply with given that its territorial integrity was one of the issues that defined the new state.

By December 1932, Germany was back at the Geneva disarmament conference having won its argument for armament parity. This had only been possible because of French acquiescence that, with the inevitable consequences for the balance of military power in Eastern Europe, was deeply resented by Poland, who saw it as a betrayal of the friendship between France and Poland. The situation at the end of 1932 was summarised by Korbel as follows:

> What France had persistently denied to Germany under a democratic rule, she felt compelled to concede to Hitler's precursors, Papen and Schleidher. England failed to understand the nature of the European crisis and particularly the events in Germany. The Soviet Union perpetually disrupted the constructive efforts of the League of nations and, in fact, gave support to nationalistic forces in Germany. The United States live in complacent isolation. Germany was herself in the grip of the vulgar agitation of the Nazi Party.[7]

Polish foreign policy at this time was focused on challenging four systems of international politics. Firstly, the Rapallo system of German-Soviet cooperation; secondly the Locarno system of the division of Europe into two zones, the west protected and the east lacking any security guarantees; thirdly the Great Powers' hegemony; and fourthly the idea that collective security could be arrived at regionally. With the gradual decline of the Versailles system, two political concepts emerged in a bid to stabilise the European scene: the Four-Power Pact and an Eastern Pact.

The Four-Power Pact between Great Britain, France, Italy and Germany, promoted by the Italian leader, Benito Mussolini, was designed to allow for limited and controlled concessions to aggressor states in the name of maintaining peace. It had been mooted that Poland be invited to be a signatory but German demands for the return of Poznania and Danzig in return for guaranteed borders thereafter soon put a stop to that. No amount of security guarantees by the Western Powers would convince Poland that they would convert into action during a crisis and no number of fine words would ever allow Poland to abandon the principle of the equality of all states under international law. Apart from anything else, Polish diplomats firmly believed that giving in to German demands only invited them to issue further demands. The Soviets feared that the pact would drive them into isolation and saw improved relations with Poland as one way of ameliorating that but the Poles were not inclined to reciprocate. The pact was signed in Rome on 7 June 1933, but France and Germany refused to ratify it after Germany walked out of the Disarmament Conference and the League of Nations in October 1933. The pact never came into full effect.

Failure of the Four-Power Pact led Moscow to put forward proposals for an Eastern Pact (Eastern Locarno), which envisaged the creation of a regional bloc, or security zone, in Central and Eastern Europe including Poland, the Baltic States, Czechoslovakia and the Soviet Union. As a key partner of Poland and Czechoslovakia, France assumed responsibility for promoting the idea but when Pierre Laval became French foreign minister after Barthou was killed in a terrorist attack the idea of 'mutual assistance' was quietly dropped. All signatories would be asked to provide mutual security guarantees and respect the territorial status quo. Poland was drawn to the concept, having concluded that the Western Powers were too remote from the Soviet Union and, claimed Antonov-Ovseyenko, as a consequence considered it a 'distant country' and, furthermore, saw Poland as having 'no world interests'.[8] The Soviet Union saw the Eastern Pact as a way of keeping a foot in the door of European conference rooms and reminding Germany in particular that they had options if they were frozen out. There were, however, powerful arguments against the pact. The weakening bonds between Poland and France, which the Soviets did not seem to fully appreciate, would inevitably lead to Poland becoming more dependent on the Soviet Union, especially given that Germany wanted nothing to do with any Eastern Pact. It was because of this that both Piłsudski and Beck rejected the pact, which had the unfortunate effect of souring Polish relations with both France and the Soviet Union. The Western Powers were rapidly losing all interest in the fate of Poland and actually began seeing it as an obstacle to peace. 'Western Europe does not know Russia, does not understand it, and has never understood it,' said Beck, who saw Poland and the Soviet Union as a 'separate world that cannot be reconciled' and the border between them as 'the border between two mentalities.' The Soviet Union made a great play of blaming Poland for the collapse of negotiations and never altogether abandoned hope that talks might be revived at some point.[9]

Poland, meanwhile, had hoped to reach an amicable agreement with Germany and the Soviet Union but its actions had weakened French influence in Eastern Europe, and when Adolf Hitler was installed as Chancellor of Germany on 30 January 1933 the world had moved on into a new and much more dangerous phase. As an indication of what that meant for Poland, when a resumé of an informal meeting between German and French representatives was issued stating what up until then had been Germany's most extreme demands for settlement of the Polish question, it was given short shrift by von Neurath, who said it was 'on the wrong course' and that the stated terms were 'far short' of actual German terms that would be demanded under the new German government. He rounded off his critique by saying that there could be no question of any guarantee of Polish borders.[10] Tensions rose in Danzig when Polish troops entered the harbour area to challenge restrictions that the city, now under German control, had imposed on Polish traders. Had Germany responded in like manner things could have got out of hand, but Hitler, savouring the first moments of power, was in no mood for a risky foreign adventure at this stage and actually saw in Piłsudski a man with whom he felt able to negotiate. It was always easier for Hitler to deal with men who had the personal power to make decisions rather than the cumbersome machinery of democratic governments. He may have been dismayed, however, had he been aware of Piłsudski's opinion of the Nazis as 'nothing but windbags'.[11]

The rise of Hitler saw a gradual diminution of Prussian influence in German politics. No longer a federation of states, Germany was becoming an *Einheitsstaat* (unitary state). While rearmament was the primary aim of the Nazi administration, it differed in one fundamental way from Prussian militarism, which had, as its dominant characteristic, a chauvinistic desire for domination of the whole life of the nation by members of the Prussian military caste, and the submission of the interest of the country to their narrow interests. The state would henceforth be persuaded to submit to the interests of the Nazis and, in place of the Prussian elite, would be dominated by the personality of a single, distinctly non-Prussian, former corporal. Piłsudski seemed willing to accept that and the general attitude in Poland soon became one of hope for the future in which disputes could be settled and that 'the whole of the ballast which weighed down Polish-German relations during the terms of office of Stresemann which was given such credit in London [could be] dismissed' and Germany would look upon Poland as an equal partner.[12]

Hermann Rauschning, president of the Senate of the Free City of Danzig, investigated the possibility of a Piłsudski-Hitler summit meeting in 1933 and the director of the Port Board in Danzig, Professor Ludwig Noé, raised this matter in 1934 in his correspondence with former prime minister Kazimierz Bartel, but there are no indications that Piłsudski was ever interested in a summit. When a representative of the Polish government asked for an urgent meeting with Hitler on 2 May 1934, his request was quickly agreed. The discussion centred on Danzig and Polish access to the Baltic. Hitler called the present situation 'untenable' but conceded that Poland had legitimate concerns and agreed to conduct all its affairs with Poland 'within the limits of the treaties'. Hitler later told the Polish ambassador that he believed the Danzig Corridor had been established by the Allies knowing full well that it would become a bone of contention that would keep Poland and Germany at each other's throats for some time. Beck seemed reassured and said that his government was doing what it could to dampen down anti-German agitation and press reporting.

It was not anti-German rhetoric that was destabilising the region, however. Rauschning had played a big part in encouraging German culture through the many different organisations designed to foster closer ties and he was a keen advocate of drawing all Germans in Poland, except the communists, into a 'super-party', the *Deutsche Partei* [DP], that would speak for them all. Political representation of the DP in the Sejm pursued a constant and unashamed anti-Polish strategy, resisting any move towards land reform and vigorously supporting moves to return Danzig to Germany. In the western areas the DP soon came to dominate German life, including religious groups also. Its aim was to segregate the German people, making them economically and culturally independent. It constituted a 'serious and divisive irritant in the Polish body politic', ready willing and able to perform whatever duties Berlin saw fit to demand of them.[13]

Seemingly oblivious to all this, Beck and von Neurath seemed to settle down to an amicable relationship, and agreed between themselves that it was time to stop letting the Western Powers play one off against the other. The consequences of war between Germany and Poland, they agreed, would simply be a victory for communism. A number of small agreements over trade and border administrative issues were concluded without difficulty and talks were inaugurated to finally bring the tariff war to an end. Germany, it seems, was making every effort to show its friendly face to Poland, who took advantage by proposing direct talks to resolve 'security factors'. The two countries were further distancing themselves from the collectivist procedures of the League of Nations, which Germany abandoned in October 1933 and which Piłsudski certainly never had any affection for.

It may be argued that, for Poland, there was no alternative to reaching an agreement with Germany. France's international role had been weakened, the post-Versailles order was falling apart and the issue of Poland's contested border with Germany was stifling Polish relations with other countries. Piłsudski was quick to see the benefits of a ten-year agreement whose legal wording, he believed, was much less important than its manifestation of political will.

An official communiqué included details of plans for direct negotiations and Berlin proposed talks on an agreement 'distinctly different from the outworn treaties'. Piłsudski, whom Hitler had called 'a great personality', reciprocated by expressing 'sympathetic recognition' of Hitler, which was interpreted as meaning that he found in the new German Chancellor someone with whom he felt comfortable and not particularly threatened by. He saw Hitler as essentially concerned with Austrian and south German issues and failed to appreciate that he had a wider agenda, his opinion being reinforced when Berlin became reconciled to Polish membership of the League of Nations and raised no objections to its alliances with France and Romania, all of which accelerated agreement on a Declaration of Non-Aggression and Understanding between Germany and Poland that was signed and published on 26 January 1934. The title emphasised the disparity with previous similar agreements and the differences were further demonstrated by its containing no articles. The Danzig issue was bypassed by agreeing a 'hot line' system of communication between Warsaw and Berlin to deal with day-to-day issues that arose. Poland resisted attempts by Germany to develop this understanding into a more formal anti-Soviet alliance, but Berlin was content to see Poland stepping away from a policy of collective security with the Western Powers. Hitler may well have had Poland in his sights as a long-term target, but he was careful, at this stage, to give quite the opposite impression. He had been quick to assess the weaknesses and insecurities of Eastern European countries as a whole and also the growing indifference to their fate shown by Britain and France. It was his strategy, in the early days of his Chancellorship, to play down the idea that Germany was a threat to peace in Europe and that it only wanted to be accepted as an equal with the other major powers. While Eastern European leaders were far from convinced, many, in Britain in particular, desperately wanted to believe it and chose not to raise too many questions.

France had been kept a little in the dark during the latter stages of negotiations and was taken by surprise when the signing was announced, which did nothing to invite its approbation. The Soviets tried to belittle it by suggesting that the Poles had been hoodwinked by German perfidy but Britain, by and large, welcomed it as a move towards a more peaceful Europe. Time would tell which of the two was the better judge of Eastern European political manoeuvrings. Beneš thought the Poles 'incredibly naïve' to think that they had done anything more than give German more time to rearm and claimed that Czechoslovakia had been 'stabbed in the back'. However, it did not prevent him from trying, without success, to get a similar deal with Germany for Czechoslovakia.[14]

A number of prominent and influential historians claimed that overall Polish foreign policy in the interwar period and in particular the 26 January 1934 Declaration of Non-Aggression and Understanding made Poland co-responsible for the outbreak of the Second World War. The renowned historian Hugh Seton-Watson claimed that one of the cornerstones of Polish foreign policy was 'territorial greed' and the agreement was the beginning of German-Polish active cooperation in implementing aggression in Eastern Europe. He characterised Poland of the 1930s as a 'tool of German imperialism'.[15] While many historians see Polish intransigence towards closer ties with the Soviet Union as a serious miscalculation, there are a number of arguments that contradict this conclusion. To begin with, by joining the Eastern Pact Poland would have been unable to continue the policy of normalising relations with Germany on the basis of the agreement signed on 26 January 1934. Furthermore, had the Eastern Pact come into effect, France would have transferred allegiance from Poland to the Soviet Union, giving the Soviets increased powers to subordinate the smaller states to their domination. There would have been few gains for Poland over and above those already acquired through the bilateral non-aggression agreements with Germany and the Soviet Union, and there would have been a significant disadvantage in that an agreement would have given the Red Army a right to march through Poland in the event of war, which would require supplementary military conventions to accommodate as well as being a prospect that made Polish blood run cold.[16]

Piłsudski believed that Poland was still 'trembling for its existence' and faced threats on all sides with the prospect of the European order in the 1930s inevitably heading for breakdown. British and French policy ever since Locarno had, for him, been one long road of appeasement towards Germany and doubted that such policies would guarantee that peaceful relations with Germany would endure for much longer either with Poland or the Soviet Union.[17] Beck told Barthou that,

> Relations in the West have been regulated in the interests of the Western Powers, at the expense of countries in the East, giving the Germans a free hand in this region and the possibility of compensating themselves for concessions made in the West.'[18]

Of Poland's two great neighbours, Piłsudski saw the 'unpredictable' Soviets as the most dangerous. Referring to the growth of the huge military-industrial complex in the Soviet Union at the beginning of the decade, he said, 'The military … in Russia [is] the axis of all state work, while in Germany it is one phenomenon in Nazi ideology but not the primary one.' While he saw that any agreement with Germany could only be temporary in nature, Piłsudski contended that such an agreement was absolutely necessary.

France was still the key to Polish security but after 1934 Piłsudski began to doubt not only France's ability to defend Poland but even to defend itself against a resurgent Germany. He saw France slipping from the heights of its post-war dominance of mainland Europe down the slippery slope of appeasement, with a gentle push from Britain, and adopting a purely defensive mindset as much of the French military budget was being eaten up by construction of the Maginot Line. While Paris made great play of flexing what muscle it had left by trying to build a new system of Eastern European alliances, in reality it was spending rather more time on working out how it was going to come to terms with a resurgent Germany in the West. What trust there had been between France and Poland had been quietly slipping away for some time before 2 May 1935 when Laval, unnerved by the German declaration of rearmament, signed his name next to Litvinov on the Franco-Soviet Treaty of Mutual Assistance. Beck was quick to tell the world that the treaty had placed no obligations on Poland whatsoever.

Piłsudski had, for a number of years been living in semi-seclusion, ruling in a 'dictatorship by proxy' and had been in declining in health, a fact that had been kept from the Polish people. He was a heavy smoker and had suffered from pulmonary emphysema for many years. In 1933 he had caught a severe flu accompanied by some hepatic ailments and began losing weight. In 1935, his liver became enlarged, he started vomiting and was very weak. All medical intervention was ineffective and he died from primary carcinoma of bile ducts at the Belvedere Palace in Warsaw on 12 May 1935, the ninth anniversary of his coup. His body was laid in state in Warsaw Cathedral for a week before being transported 200 miles across Poland in front of continuous lines of villagers to be buried in the crypt of Kraków's Wawel Cathedral.[19] Although Hitler did not go to Piłsudski's funeral and sent his special commissioner for disarmament, the up-and-coming Joachim von Ribbentrop instead, he did attend a special memorial service for him held in Berlin.

Chapter 10

THE RHINELAND CRISIS

> Germany at noon today, when the Reichstag met, sent into the Rhineland zone a symbolic force of troops, a few battalions only, in token of the decision that Locarno is dead and that Germany has the right to militarise it despite the specific ban of the Versailles treaty.
>
> Adolf Hitler speech to the Reichstag, 7 March 1936

Piłsudski was succeeded by General Śmigły-Rydz, who had been chosen in advance by him to become inspector general of the army. This had been in part as a device to keep the army out of politics and to keep politics out of the army, a requirement that was emphasised by the case of Śmigły-Rydz, who was 'a man of few political ideas' and had little aptitude for politics, for which he had neither the intellect nor temperament. Piłsudski's plan to separate army and government had been flawed, however, because the army in Poland was far too central to national affairs not to be involved in politics and Śmigły-Rydz would go on to show just how unsuited he was to the central role he now occupied.[1] The official *Gazeta Polska* called for a collective leadership to meet the challenges of the new Franco-Russian alliance on the one hand and Germany on the other but after Piłsudski's death there was, predictably, a power struggle to fill the huge space at the centre of Polish politics with no single person able to command sufficient support to take his place. The views of Śmigły-Rydz, the armed forces commander-in-chief, General Wacław Stachiewitz, and the minister of defence, General Tadeusz Kaszprzycki, showed that the military were very much in the Francophile camp and tried to undo some of the damage done to the Franco-Polish alliance by Piłsudski's neglect. Śmigły-Rydz in particular felt that Poland had given too much to the cause of German rapprochement, but Mościcki and Beck wore Piłsudski's mantle, and it was they who controlled Polish foreign policy.

When Beck went to Berlin in July 1935, he got the impression that Hitler was looking for improved relations with Poland, which was exactly what he wanted to hear. He saw Eastern Europe stabilised now after the two bi-lateral agreements had been signed to the point where he confidently informed the British ambassador that the agreement with Germany indicated 'psychological changes' in German society that augured a 'permanent change for the better', even though German and Soviet relations would be always riven by irreconcilable differences. Śmigły-Rydz begged to disagree and predicted that after three or four years Germany would have built up its military to the point where it would start a war with Poland over Danzig. It was vital, therefore, in Beck's view to improve relations with Germany and make significant concessions to achieve a better understanding, and for him this meant a flexible approach to the question of Danzig. To this end he cooperated in reducing the authority of the League of Nations' commissioners and turned a blind eye to the Nazification of the city.

Hitler's approach to Poland while his immediate ambitions were focused on his western border seemed to be less confrontational. While the German nationalist movements inside Poland were given new encouragement, on the international stage it was German policy to play down confrontation in the east. One thing at a time seemed to be the policy and the one thing for Hitler in 1935 was to deal with military exclusion from the Rhineland. To ensure that the Polish question did not interfere with his strategy, Hitler chose to exacerbate the differences between two competing philosophies within the German nationalist movements in Poland so that they would be too busy confronting each other rather than causing tensions beyond Poland's borders. There would be a time for unified action but that was not now.

In January 1936, Beck said that the country should focus on Poland and France's common interest, which was Germany, but he saw no need for Poland to subordinate its interest to those of France who, he feared would lack both willingness and ability to aid either Poland or Czechoslovakia in a crisis. To emphasise this, just before his death, Piłsudski had advised Beck to launch a charm offensive towards Britain, upon whom France was becoming more reliant for security, and who he surmised would be influential in supporting Polish efforts to stabilise the Eastern European political structure. Above all else, it proved to be Beck's strategy to 'run with the hare and hunt with the hounds' and in so doing maintain a neutral position between what he saw as the irreconcilable and antagonistic philosophies of communism and Nazism.

During the last few weeks of 1935, persistent rumours were backed up by an increasing flow of compelling intelligence suggesting that Germany was preparing to reoccupy the 50km-wide zone along the east bank of the Rhine, commonly known as the Rhineland, which had been evacuated by French troops after Locarno. This would have huge ramifications for Poland by giving significantly more security to Germany along the French border and allowing it to concentrate its attention much more on its Eastern neighbours. While the politicians bickered over strategy, the French and Polish military grew closer at this time with a number of high-profile visits but the Poles came away with a sense that France was totally preoccupied with its internal politics. They did, however, get a declaration from the French minister of communications that the French would oppose any move by Germany to reoccupy the Rhineland but the French government of the time was little more than a caretaker administration incapable of taking any important decisions and simply holding the fort until elections could be called in the spring. For their part, the British were embarrassed by their own military deficiencies and were unlikely to do anything that might precipitate an armed conflict in Europe.

The commander-in-chief of the German Luftwaffe, Hermann Göring, took the opportunity to visit Warsaw in February 1936 to soothe Polish nerves and managed to sustain a friendly atmosphere throughout the talks by completely ignoring any mention of the Rhineland. Beck had been reassured by Göring's visit and it was his faction that was bringing about a hardening of the Polish line on France. He argued that 'it is better not to talk in [time of] peace of what might happen in [time of] war', but the French military attaché in Warsaw, General Charles d'Arbonneau, warned him that Poland would eventually have to choose between alliance with France or vassalage under Germany.[2] The Polish military's affection for France was, of course, tied up not only with assurances of support but with getting as much military aid as possible to modernise the Polish armed forces, which in turn brought pressure on Beck from Paris to declare what his strategy would be in the event of a German attack on Czechoslovakia or a French move to oppose German incursion into the Rhineland. The French attitude was almost contemptuous of Poland, with barely disguised threats to use Poland as a bargaining chip with Germany. Neither Italy nor Britain seemed particularly interested. Poland was being coerced in no uncertain fashion to 'give practical effect to the alliance [with France] in the event of German aggression in any part of Europe ... in response to [Poland's need for] some form or other of credit arrangement for … rearmament'.[3]

Just after dawn on 7 March 1936, violating Articles 42 and 43 of the Versailles Treaty and Articles 1 and 2 of the 1925 Locarno Treaty, nineteen German infantry battalions and a mere handful of aircraft, entered the Rhineland and by late morning, three divisions were across the Rhine. The British Foreign Office minister Alexander Cadogan saw this as inflicting 'irreversible damage' to Versailles and would later say that this had been the last opportunity to halt German aggression. It is important for understanding the Polish response to look at what the French did or did not do. France appealed to the Council of the League of Nations to mount common opposition to the action but throughout the day not one French boot made any move towards the border. Beck told Léon Nöel, the French ambassador in Warsaw, that Poland would stand behind the French if they chose a military response.[4] On the next morning, a full French cabinet meeting discussed its options and declared, in a supine admission of its lack of will and reluctance to do anything about it, that the German action was 'unacceptable'. It affirmed the decision of the previous day to call on the signatories of Locarno to come to Paris and talk about it while the War Ministry issued a statement assuring everyone that 'there is no question at all of any movement what[so]ever of [French] troops'.[5] When this was followed up by more words from the French president of the council, Albert Sarraut, 'We are not disposed to allow Strasbourg to come under the fire of German guns,' the ambiguity of the phrase (did he mean France would drive the Germans back or try not to provoke them?) failed to reassure anyone inside or outside the country. The talking continued on the following day as the Polish ambassador to Paris, Alfred Chłapowski, repeated Poland's offer of support. In the afternoon Sarraut again called the German action illegal but refused to take unilateral action in the hope, rather than expectation, that the League of Nations would step in with a multinational force to make the Germans evacuate.

Under the circumstances, the terms of Locarno had entitled France to act unilaterally in full expectation of Britain and others giving immediate support, but France prevaricated and ultimately abdicated responsibility for its own security by refusing to make any move without first getting firm assurances of military support. It was 11 March 1936 before any attempt was made to evaluate France's military options, by which time the government had been forced to publicly deny that France had agreed to a 'limited' number of German troops to stay in the Rhineland, but it was this compromise that talks in London came up with on 19 March as an interim measure while further talks were held.

When the Germans ignored any such suggestion and actually reinforced its occupation with more troops it was clear that Hitler's gamble had been a resounding success. It was glaringly obvious that if France was not prepared to face down German provocation on its own doorstep it was hardly likely that any similar action by Germany against Poland would elicit a more vigorous response.

Theoretically, Poland and France had been bound by the military convention of 1921 that obliged each to come to the aid of the other in the event of an unprovoked attack but that had been weakened by the Franco-Polish Treaty of 1925, which replaced a simple automatic commitment by a complex time-consuming procedure engineered by France that was coming to terms, at the time, with its waning dominance of the European scene and becoming more reliant on the concept of collective security bestowed through membership of the League of Nations. In the decade after 1925 a divide had grown between the level of security afforded by agreements over Germany's western border and the almost total lack of progress over sorting out the much more complicated question of its eastern borders. There was a sense that Britain and France had lost what little patience they had started with and allowed their support of an independent Poland to become subsumed under the weight of concern over the growing military power of Germany and the Soviet Union. Although the Franco-Polish agreement remained essentially intact, before his death Piłsudski, in particular, had felt betrayed by the Western Powers and had turned increasingly towards finding accommodation with Poland's near neighbours.[6]

The French were now putting their weight behind a scheme to bind the Poles together with the Czechs and Soviets into a security alliance but for Poland that would mean inevitable subjugation by the Soviet Union, with whom relations had been slowly deteriorating for some time. They could not agree even though their rejection could have the effect of abandoning Czechoslovakia to isolation and if that led to annexation by Germany it would leave Poland facing Germany on both its western and southern borders. France was becoming increasingly anxious that their weakening ties with Poland would eventually result in that country having no option but to come to some agreement with Germany and that would remove any hope of creating an eastern front against Germany in the event of that country launching an attack against France. To reduce the chances of that happening and in the hope of boosting the military faction against Beck, France agreed a security loan to Poland, with no political strings attached, of 2 billion francs, half in cash and half in military materièl. Beck seemed to soften his position and by September 1936 had assured the French that there was still 'a clear tendency to maintain the bilateral alliance [despite] attempts to involve us in [eastern alliances]'.[7] The fact remained, however, that France had suffered a humiliation in the Rhineland on 7 March 1936 and, together with Britain, was shifting its focus from confrontation to appeasement, having been on the receiving end of German revanchist bravado that painfully exposed the paucity of its military capacity to respond. France may still have offered friendship and support, but its military lethargy was less than inspiring and did little to stabilise Eastern Europe.

Hitler was quick to consolidate the huge political gains of his Rhineland gamble and offered the Western Powers a new security deal, which they declined, bringing about the desired effect, from Hitler's perspective, of further exposing their divisions. Seemingly oblivious to Poland's almost pathological hostility to the Soviet Union, France still hoped for a Russo-Polish-Czech alliance, especially given that a left-wing government was poised to take power in Paris. Poland had no confidence that France, becoming ever more reliant on Britain for its security, was now prepared to even consider fighting outside its own borders and Śmigły-Rydz made his military plans accordingly. There was a feeling that the trend towards appeasement would continue in Paris and London until such time as their vital interests were threatened, at which point the whole European political and military landscape would change and Poland would then become an important part of what happened next.

German foreign policy was now being acted out in accordance with Hitler's ambitions. It was no longer a case of whether or not his philosophy expounded in *Mein Kampf* would be given a chance to be realised but a case of who would be the first victim. The ultimate prize was the Ukraine and then the Soviet Union but that could not be won without some sort of accommodation with the Western Powers to avoid a war on two fronts. Weaning Poland off its reliance on French guarantees was seen as an important first step both to weaken French confidence and also to draw Poland ultimately into some sort of alliance with Germany against the Soviet Union. In 1936, however, exactly what form of relationship that would be and how it would be brought about was one of the many details that Hitler had not yet concerned himself with. It was more in his nature to paint his long- and medium-term ambitions with bold colours but little detail while focusing on immediate opportunities with an almost pointillist attention to detail. His great strength was undoubtedly his adroit skill at assessing and exploiting fears and weakness in his adversaries and also his willing to take a gamble, although the latter would also prove to be a fatal weakness.

He simply told Beck, who may have been more Germanophile than Śmigły-Rydz, but was still very aware of the enduring German hostility towards Poland, that there were no insoluble difficulties in the way of closer cooperation. Göring again went to Warsaw and assured Śmigły-Rydz that Germany had no difficulty with the current arrangements over the Danzig Corridor and Hitler began his charm offensive towards Poland with a theme he would come back to again and again by, somewhat hypocritically, emphasising the Soviet Union's lack of 'respect for national borders'. In yet another visit Göring would say that Poland and Germany's interests were 'in total alignment … against Bolshevism' but Warsaw, who continued to see Germany as Poland's 'eternal enemy', remained completely unmoved by such sophistry and continued to be impervious to it. Germany even made informal suggestions that Poland might like to join the German-Italian-Japanese Anti-Comintern Pact in 1936–37 but Beck, whose faith in German goodwill went only so far and no further, had no interest and excused Poland from any talks because of its 'specific location as a neighbour of the USSR'.[8] For their part, the Soviets resented the apparent Polish dalliance with Germany and allowed relations with Poland to lapse into what might be called a cold war or armed peace. When the purges and political trials began in the Soviet Union it was charges of collaboration with Poland that featured prominently on the charge sheets.

With the signing of the Anti-Comintern Pact, Europe was moving towards a fundamental ideological division between the fascist powers and the democracies, with Poland and the Soviet Union hovering somewhere in between. Hitler, of course, was rabidly anti-communist but he understood the importance of economic cooperation with the Soviet Union and also with Poland. Poland had found itself cut adrift from the West and forced to choose between Germany and the Soviet Union. In such a scenario it was the lesser of two evils that would win out but, whichever way it went, the country would find itself between a rock and a hard place. Just as Belgium had become the slaughterhouse of Europe during the 1914–18 war, so Poland saw itself having that role thrust upon it in any new European war but there was no clear path to avoid such an outcome. Beck saw that closer ties with the Soviet Union might encourage the anti-fascists to strike at Germany in the West but more seriously for Poland joining the anti-Comintern bloc could inflame the whole continent.

For these reasons, Poland saw that it might well be that a relatively minor clash of interests over a peripheral issue could escalate rapidly into a conflagration in much the same way that Gavrilo Princip's assassination of Archduke Ferdinand at Sarajevo had done in 1914, and the potential for such was greatly enhanced by the existence of armed and hostile ideological camps. Beck did all he could to avoid having to choose sides. He saw no useful role for the League of Nations, an attitude that irritated Britain enormously, because at no time were Poland's two great antagonistic neighbours members of the organisation at the same time. When the Soviet Union had joined in 1936, Litvinov tried to turn it into an anti-fascist bloc, which is exactly what Poland did not want, and Poland made it quite clear that this was not its intention. When Litvinov accused Poland of being in Germany's orbit, Russo-Polish relation plumbed depths not seen since 1920. Although Beck wanted to sit on the fence, he was incline to lean towards Germany. It was Germany with whom he was forced to find some sort of understanding and a modicum of security as the West retreated into an appeasement strategy.

It was clear, however, that Germany's rapidly growing political and military power would relegate Poland to a minor consideration in German foreign policy, especially after Lord Halifax's visit to the Berchtesgaden, at which time he had indicated that Britain might be amenable to a negotiated settlement of Germany's territorial demands. When Germany provoked Poland with minor cross-border military incursions and got no reaction, the first signs were evident that appeasement over Austria and the Sudetenland would embolden Germany to impose itself on Poland in a most uncomfortable way. Beck had, by now, lost all faith in the French alliance, especially given what he saw as the fragile state of French politics, but clung to his philosophy that only by being 'difficult' could Poland retain any relevance to the Western Powers and retain any inclusion in their agenda. While continuing to wear Piłsudski's mantle of military self-sufficiency, Beck made great diplomatic efforts to maintain a high profile on the European stage, especially in relation to Britain, whose policy towards Poland was crucial. However, when he volunteered Poland as a mediator between Italy and France in 1938, the offer was met with contemptuous silence by Mussolini.

When considering Poland's foreign policy at this time it is important to consider its military situation. Starting from the country's inception in 1918 when its army had no structured training, no traditions and no military doctrine of its own, under the inspired leadership of Piłsudski, this rag-tag of fighters brought together from the remnants of disintegrating foreign armies had smashed the Red Army at the gates of Warsaw and driven it back deep into the steppes. It had only been through the purchase of surplus First World War military hardware from France that any progress at all was made in creating a structured organisation but there was never enough money to modernise or re-equip forces and keep pace with the technologic advances exhibited by either Germany or the Soviet Union. Furthermore, when Piłsudski split the armed forces between the Ministry for Military Affairs as a peacetime command and the Inspectorate General to prepare for future wars he created a logistical and administrative problem that blurred the boundaries of command responsibilities and confused training programmes.

In 1935, Śmigły-Rydz had conducted an in-depth analysis of Poland's overall readiness for war. Because Piłsudski had been over-concerned with the threat from the Soviet Union, the most egregious error that was only now becoming obvious was in the east, where Poland had made most of its investment in defensive infrastructure to the detriment of similar measures along its western border. Both Beck and Piłsudski had agreed with the British foreign secretary, Anthony Eden, that the Red Army was 'very strong and is a factor with enormous potential' but Beck was confident that there was no direct pressure on the Polish border and that Poland was 'handling direct diplomatic affairs with the Soviets perhaps even better than many other countries'.[9] Alongside a new mobilisation plan, Plan 'W', Beck, so as not to alarm Germany, gave secret instruction to make preliminary studies to fortify Poland's western borders. That was all well and good, but the most worrying conclusion of the review was that in terms of equipment and organisation the army had advanced little since 1920. Compared to other armies, it had an over-reliance on cavalry and infantry with few motorised units and the air force was equipped with old, not to say obsolete, French aircraft. Artillery units were far below the numbers required to match Germany and there were no anti-tank units at all. The only tanks in use were small machines suitable only for reconnaissance duties. Perhaps most damning of all, in an age of mobile warfare, communications relied upon First World War equipment that was of little practical use.[10]

Śmigły-Rydz could be forgiven for despairing, especially given the dire state of Poland's economy that had come nowhere close to recovering from the international economic crisis, but he made plans. First of all, he retired most of the top commanders and brought in educated officers as replacements. Then he created a new Committee for the Defence of the Republic (*Komitet Obrony Rzeczypospolitej*) to coordinate the two military organisations to draw up plans for a modernisation programme that, unfortunately lacked strategic objectives. When obsolete aircraft were withdrawn from the air force only 417 machines remained and those were barely usable. Plans to buy and manufacture French aircraft under licence were plagued by corruption scandals. It was always going to be the case, however, that no matter what plans were made for modernisation, mechanisation and expansion, economic constraints were going to severely hamper any progress. Poland, with its low industrial base, simply lacked the resources to compete militarily with other European countries.

It was clear to the Polish leadership that the country was being left behind in the arms race and had no hope of catching up. It could do what it was able to do within its financial constraints but its only real prospect of survival was to either stay out of a war that was now inevitable, which seemed impossible, or align itself with allies that could offer the best protection. A decision about who those allies might be was put on hold while the appeasement strategies played themselves out. In the meantime, a strategy of maintaining some sort of balance between competing forces was Poland's only sensible option. Beck was in no doubt that Poland was right in the firing line of any future war when he said in April 1937, 'armed conflicts most often arise not along the borders of great powers with conflicting interests but rather between smaller states contained within 'spheres of influence'.[11]

Revanchist rallies proliferated and centered around the anniversaries of plebiscites in both German and Polish areas where they had taken place right after Versailles. Each side tried to outdo the other with militaristic parades and bombastic speeches to rouse the crowds into paroxysms of indignation. Borderland myths were perpetuated and widely disseminated in press, radio and film. In areas such as Upper Silesia, the settlement imposed in 1923 was condemned repeatedly as unjust by activists on both sides and continued to be grist to the mill of Sanacja and Nazis alike when trying to invoke patriotism and nationalistic fervour. While governments liked to describe these rallies as demonstrations of 'popular will', it should be noted that, noisy and boisterous as they were, they were organised and supported by only a small percentage of the population. While both sides complained bitterly about the excesses of the other, neither dominated these exchanges and neither could be said to suffer more than the other from the heightening of emotions brought on at such times.

Now that the Nazis were firmly ensconced in Berlin, they began to ramp up the mood against Poland with 'soft' propaganda *Kulturarbeit* in the form of cultural exchanges involving folk song and dance groups. Polish institutions tried to compete with their own touring choral groups and folklore performers, who appeared on the international stage to show the world that, although a new country, Poland was not a backward nation of agricultural insignificance but one that had a rich cultural heritage, giving it credibility as an independent and vibrant state. A cultural war developed in which both Germany and Poland tried to dominate the other through culture. When Poland gave permission for around 4,000 choristers from German minority populations of Upper Silesia to attend a Choral Union Festival (*Sängerbundfest*) in the German city of Breslau they were assured that it was a non-political 'cultural exchange to deepen understanding and closeness between the two neighbouring states'.[12] Presided over by Adolf Hitler himself, it turned out to be the largest and most politicised event and propaganda spectacle in Germany since the 1936 Olympic games. With performers from Germany, Poland and Czechoslovakia in front of an international audience, the festival projected an irridentist notion of pan-Silesia with a common cultural and historical identity that was essentially German. Speeches described Silesian lands as having 'an eternal German face' with 'ancient German heritage' and did not try to disguise a clear agenda to 'recover' the contested borderlands. Performers were lauded as cultural fighters 'mobilised for the struggle' as they paraded before Hitler in traditional costumes. Hitler spoke to them of almost 100 million Germans who 'transcended political borders', and Goebbels gave his own slant on Germans who felt 'an unrelenting bond'.[13] It was as clear a message as one could wish for that the Nazis would try to 'overcome politically imposed divisions' to 'recover' former Prussian provinces and build a new *Großdeutsches Reich.*

Chapter 11

THE ANSCHLUSS

> I am grateful to Mr. Chamberlain for all his efforts. I have assured him that the German people desires nothing else than peace.
>
> Adolf Hitler, 26 September 1938

Following the Upper Silesian plebiscite in 1922 an agreement had been signed between Poland and Germany that provided special protection for minorities on both sides but that was due to expire. It had benefitted both sides but now Poland appeared unenthusiastic about renewing it. This made Germany anxious about the effects on Germans living in the Polish territories, although that was countered by the prospect of the several hundred Jews living in German Upper Silesia coming under Germany's power should the agreement lapse. When von Neurath brought up the subject of renewal with Beck in January 1937, the Pole refused to agree, as he had expected, and so, wanting to avoid any deterioration in relations, he proposed a mutual agreement, less binding than a treaty, to safeguard the interests of minorities.[1]

The other great bone of contention was the port of Danzig, which, in 1937, had actually settled down after a turbulent few years during which tensions had arisen when it was clear that Poland was using the port of Gydnia, which it had started to develop in 1926, in preference to Danzig. As a result, Danzig had suffered a serious drop in revenues and so authorities there took action to prevent any further decrease of the sea-borne traffic passing through the port of Danzig by agreeing a deal with Poland in September 1933 that obliged the administration to cease any discrimination against Polish citizens in the port. The protocol was scheduled to come up for renewal on 30 September 1936.

On 20 June 1933, the National Socialist Party of Germany had been elected to power in Danzig with thirty-eight out of seventy-two seats in the Senate. They had immediately set about remoulding the administration of the port according to Nazi ideology, which led to a period of confrontation. The National Socialist president of the Danzig Senate, Hermann Rauschning, was forced to vacate his office on 23 November 1934 after failing to give sufficient support to the Nazi faction. He was expelled from the Nazi Party and took refuge in Poland. The new administration set about passing decrees that in several instances were found by the Council of the League of Nations to be contrary to the guaranties of the constitution and when a Senate election was held on 7 April 1935, it was declared invalid due to 'unconstitutional' methods employed by the National Socialists. On 18 July 1935, the Polish minister of finance issued an order to the Administration of Customs in Danzig to cease all operations in protest at measures that had been brought in that adversely affected Polish import and export trade through the port. The matter was eventually sorted out and things got back to normal on 11 October 1935, but much damage had been done to relations between Poland and the port authority.

Repeated breaches of the constitution in 1936 forced the issue of Danzig onto the agenda of the League of Nations' high commissioner with the result that, on 4 July 1936 the council appointed a committee of three with representatives from Britain, France and Sweden, to look at accusations that the constitution of Danzig had been 'stripped of all liberally conceived principles'. A new League of Nations' high commissioner for the Free City of Danzig, Carl Jacob Burckhardt, had replaced Sean Lester, whose many protests about Nazi excesses had infuriated both Berlin and Danzig. Hitler assured the Polish undersecretary of state for foreign affairs that Polish rights would be respected under the high commissioner but the new commissioner was under strict orders from Berlin to implement a National Socialist administration with all its concomitant ramifications for suppression of opposition parties and increased threat against the Jewish population, but he was to do it quietly causing as little fuss as possible. The Germans seemed to be getting their way but even they had problems. The president of the Danzig Senate was the 'restrained and thoughtful' Arthur Greiser, a member of the SS, and his nominal superior was Albert Forster, a man of violent temperament and an acolyte of Rudolf Hess. The two men were quite openly hostile to each other. As a matter of principle neither would agree with anything the other did except when opposing Polish initiatives, especially any that attempted to reaffirm the legal status of Danzig or the Danzig Corridor.

Hitler was anxious to avoid friction in Danzig. He did not want the port, or indeed anything associated with Poland, to attract international attention while he advanced his plans elsewhere. Göring made great play of courting the Poles. He made a series of visits to Warsaw and had frequent meetings in Berlin with Lipski, with whom he had established an amicable relationship. It was Göring's great strength as a politician that he was able to hide the ruthless and vindictive side of his character under the cloak of an affable, convivial and amusing host that seemed to distance him from the dour, demonic and distinctly unamusing Hitler, and often made it difficult to visualise him as a serious threat to peace. Berlin had left the two rivals in Danzig to keep each other occupied but the plan backfired when Forster, in a frenzy of Nazification of the port, triggered a number of incidents.

In 1935, elections to the legislative body of Danzig the *Volkstag* returned an absolute majority for the Nazis but still not enough for them to alter the constitution. That did not deter Arthur Greiser, the president of the Danzig Senate, however, who spoke of recent troubles as 'a first offensive in favour of revision of the relations between the League of Nations and the Free City of Danzig'. By the time that the new pro-German Burckhardt took office in March 1937, the Nazis had secured the necessary two thirds majority to amend the constitution and, in effect, in October 1937 the Free City became a totalitarian National-Socialist City. The Nazi leader, Forster, was able to declare in February 1938 that Danzig was now effectively under the control of Berlin and all opposition to the Nazis was removed. 'The Germans in Danzig,' he said, 'will soon be rewarded for their suffering, just as the Germans in Austria and the Sudetenland were rewarded.'

The one incident that gained the most attention and caused much embarrassment for Burckhardt was on 25 May 1938, when Hans Wichmann, a member of the banned Social Democratic Party of the Free City of Danzig, was arrested and questioned by the police. It was claimed that Wichmann was then released but he disappeared from the city. Three months later he was reported to be in Spain but he was never seen again by his family or friends. Investigations later showed that the evidence from Spain was false and it is now believed that a mutilated body found in a sack on the Polish border days after his arrest had been his. Forster had also tried to change the Danzig flag and bring in more repressive measures against the Jews. Burckhardt failed to restrain him and it took a personal intervention from Hitler to bring him under control, and even then only marginally and temporarily. Lipski made strong representation to Berlin over the question of the treatment of minorities in Danzig and resisted all efforts to change the Danzig constitution but even Göring, under pressure from von Neurath not to get involved, was unable to help. The day would come soon, said von Neurath, when Danzig would be returned to the German Reich but that most unlikely of peacemakers, Hitler, intervened in support of Lipski to calm the situation and agreed to make a public statement that included warm words of friendship between Germany and Poland. To keep Danzig out of the headlines on 5 November 1937, Hitler quite disingenuously announced that three principal policies would be applied; there would be no changes in the legal and political position in Danzig, the rights of the Polish population in Danzig would be respected and the rights of Poland in Danzig would be respected.

Unbeknown to anyone in Danzig, 5 November 1937 was also the day that Hitler had held a conference in Berlin, the details of which were included in the secret Hossbach Memorandum, that was in an entirely different vein to his Danzig declaration. Hitler had outlined to his generals a plan for incremental aggrandisement of the German Reich to ward off economic decline and build up strength to oppose 'its two hateful enemies, England and France', who were poised to oppose Germany at every turn. Sometime in the next five years, he speculated, Germany would have to achieve autarky (self-sufficiency) by seizing areas of Eastern Europe to prepare for a possible war with the British and the French.

Hitler again reined Forster in and told him to be patient. The last thing he wanted was for international attention to be focused on the minorities issue in Danzig or Upper Silesia, where arguably German minorities were faring worse than those in Czechoslovakia, lest Poland decide to put up a common front with the Czechs. In the meantime, Beck and Göring made visits to each other's capital, where Austria was discussed. Poland had few interests there except for its exports of coal and Berlin was quick to assure Beck that whatever happened in Austria in the coming months, Polish trade would not be affected and further down the line, if Czechoslovakia came into German sights, there would be some advantages for the Poles as well. Beck also got agreement on restraining Forster's activities in Danzig but the involvement of von Ribbentrop, who had now been catapulted into the role of German foreign minister, in the talks meant that all attempts to initiate discussion about extending current agreements in the port were brushed aside.

Hitler's revanchist propaganda campaign against Poland was ramping up in early 1938 with renewed public demonstrations commemorating the 'heroic' German suffering at the hands of 'invading Polish hordes' during the Silesian insurgencies. Memorials to *Freikorps* and *Selbschutz* fighters were unveiled at the Mount of St Anne in Opole Silesia and Ratibor Borderland Tower, both of which sites were already popular tourist and pilgrimage venues. The German press was playing up incidents that they categorised as persecution of the German minorities and while politicians in the *Bund Deutscher Osten* (BDO) disguised blatant revanchism with calls for peaceful diplomacy, there were numerous incidents of thuggery committed by both sides.

The multinational composition of the Polish state had been one of its most serious domestic problems. The dominance of the Poles in all areas of national life provoked bitter resentment from most of the country's non-Polish inhabitants, who comprised nearly one third of its total population. A major development in international relations had taken place when the Minorities Treaty was signed in 1919, and incorporated into the Polish Constitution in 1922, which was designed to 'protect the interests of the inhabitants of Poland who differ from the majority of the population in race, language or religion'.[2] Throughout the 1920s and up until Hitler's accession to power, Poland was constantly defending itself against charges of minority abuse brought against it by Germany in the League of Nations. In an attempt to bring some sanity to ethnic squabbles after the Geneva Convention expired in 1937, both German and Polish governments signed a declaration to respect the national, linguistic, religious, social, cultural, political, and economic equality and rights of the other's minority. The Polish Germans amounted to no more than 2.3 per cent of the population according to the 1931 census and most of these lived in areas that had once been part of the Imperial German Empire. These small numbers, however, belied the economic power of the ethnic Germans, who benefited from cooperatives, credit unions, land banks, and commercial conglomerates. They also tended to own the bigger and more productive farms and had significant investments in Polish industry. However, throughout the 1930s, as the result of a determined Polish initiative, there was a considerable reduction in German control, especially in heavy industry of Upper Silesia and the farms and forests of Pomorze. Events about to unfold elsewhere in Europe would send a clear signal to the Poles that the rights and privileges of ethnic Germans everywhere would become a tool of German revanchism in a most direct and aggressive way and real or supposed acts of discrimination against them would no longer be tolerated at the government level.

On 12 March 1938, German troops marched unopposed into Austria. The timing of the long-anticipated Anschluss took Warsaw a little by surprise and it took a few days to assess its consequences for Poland. The actual annexation of Austria did not concern the Poles too much and, in fact, within a few days it seemed possible that, while all eyes were focused on Vienna, Poland could settle an old score closer at home without attracting too much attention. Lithuania had long been at odds with its neighbour, with whom it had coexisted for so long within the Imperial Russian Empire. Piłsudski had laboured without success to bring it into a federation and there were voices in Warsaw in 1938 that now saw an opportunity to bring that about by force but calmer counsel urged the establishment of official diplomatic relations as a first step to normalisation of relations. Berlin, hoping for a period of calm after its grab for Austria, had been unnerved by reports of Polish troops preparing to move towards the Lithuanian border, not least because a Lithuania at odds with Poland was a useful pawn to play in German-Polish negotiations. A possible, if not likely, scenario might see Germany agree to the Polish annexation of Lithuania in return for the Danzig Corridor coming back into the Reich. While there might have been advantages for Germany in a Polish-Lithuanian conflict in terms of extending its own influence into the Baltic, especially the tempting prospect of taking back control of the port of Memel, it was not ready for such a move while there was unfinished business in the Sudetenland. Lithuania looked to Western capitals for support but received none and saw no alternative to the exchange of ambassadors with Poland. The example of Poland taking advantage of German adventurism and of Germany happy to brush crumbs off its banquet table for the Poles to pick up was a pattern that would be repeated later in Czechoslovakia. This would benefit both sides, especially Germany, which was anxious to avoid any possibility of Warsaw aligning itself with Prague, a prospect that had never been likely but might be brought about very quickly if sufficient pressure was applied from London and Paris.[3]

On 28 October 1918, Czechoslovakia had been created out of the collapsing Austro-Hungarian Empire by the joining of provinces with no previous historic connections: Bohemia, Moravia, Czech-speaking Silesia, Slovakia and Subcarpathian Ruthenia. Both Poland and Czechoslovakia had been keen to claim the Zoalzie Zaolzie (*České Těšínsko*) region for two main reasons. It was very rich in black coal, which in 1918 had the same significance as oil was to have in the latter half of the century, and secondly the railway station between Bohumín and Košice, which at the time was the only efficient railway connection between the Czech lands and Slovakia. Also, Bohumín had the largest cargo railway station in Central Europe.

The Czechs had contemplated taking the region by force, despite it having been divided between Poland and Czechoslovakia on 5 November 1918 by an interim agreement of two local self-government councils (Czech *Zemský národní výbor pro Slezsko* and Polish *Rada Narodowa Księstwa Cieszyńskiego*), although the central government recognised neither. According to this separation, Poland had got the greater share of coal and control of the important railway station. It then provoked the Czechs by initiating an election in the area to send delegates to the Sejm (Polish Parliament) in Warsaw, which implied sovereignty. There were some Polish troops in the area, but most were heavily involved in the wars with Ukraine while the Red Army was massing for an attack. Taking advantage of Polish distractions, Czech forces invaded and occupied the most important areas, with clashes occurring between opposing forces causing several hundred casualties. After a 'seven-day war', a treaty was signed on 3 February 1919 that put the area temporarily under international control. The attack had annoyed the Western Powers in Paris and caused some embarrassment for Beneš but eventually a decision by the Spa Conference on 23 July 1920, hoping against hope but without much confidence of getting the dispute off its agenda, made a definitive partition of Silesia, giving the Czechs a little more than half of the disputed territory and a third of its population, including Karvina, the coal mines and the railway line. Poland received the territories north of this line. A Polish minority found itself inside Czechoslovakia and Czech speakers remained in the Polish areas of Kladské and Raciborz.

Under Tomáš Garrigue Masaryk the new state of Czechoslovakia had forged a democratic administration and achieved economic stability despite its diverse population, but Slovak, German, Hungarian and Polish nationalism within the republic and outside its territory intensified during the late 1920s and eventually caused weakening of the state's internal and international position. There is no doubt that Czech efforts to assimilate its ethnic minorities had been undermined in the late 1930s by external governments covertly supporting agitators and fomenting discord for their own nefarious purposes. The Polish communities that had chosen to remain in the eastern part of the Czech portion of Cieszyn Silesia (Zaolzie) were mostly reconciled to Czech citizenship, albeit reluctantly, but, like many minorities, they felt that others were treated more favourably.

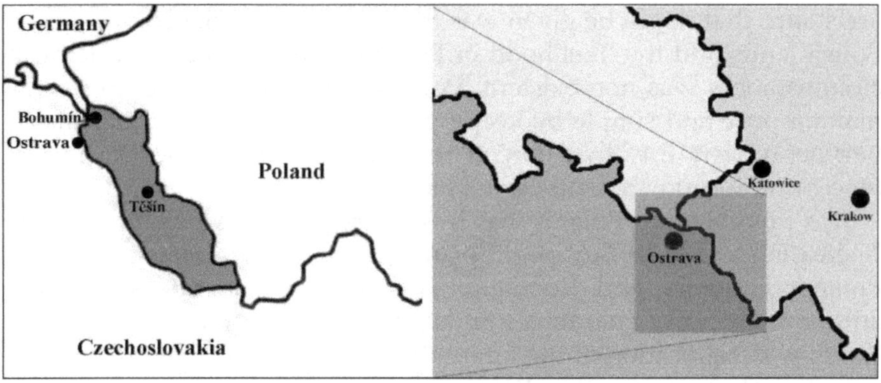

The disputed area of Zaolzie

With Hitler obviously now lining Czechoslovakia up as his next victim in 1938, there was a distinct possibility of a free-for-all when the Czech state came under attack, but in order for Poland to gain maximum benefit from that it would require some nimble footwork from Beck. First of all he had to approach Hungary, the other state with significant minorities inside Czechoslovakia and one that was equally willing to partake of the feast. Hungary's Magyar communities existed all around its borders in Czechoslovakia, Romania and Yugoslavia. There was very little trust between any of the Eastern European countries that constantly looked for ways to revise and expand their borders and so in order to free Hungary up to join any Polish venture it would first have to come to some understanding with Yugoslavia and Romania to ensure that neither of them would take advantage of any diminution of Hungarian forces on their borders. Berlin looked on with general approval. It was a dangerous game for Beck to play, which could only reduce any lingering French willingness to be his saviour. By playing page to Germany's knight, Poland was becoming a hostage to fortune in the hope that, after Czechoslovakia, Germany's territorial ambitions might be satisfied in the short term or at least focus next on the Ukraine. It was a matter of conjecture, however, as to what extent Germany might hold back on its claims to the Danzig Corridor in order to retain Poland as a viable force holding the ground between Germany and the Red Army. In the worst-case scenario, Beck believed that if war broke out France and Britain would see the logic of supporting Poland as a second front against Germany.

It was of significant concern to Poland that the Soviet Union was making no bones about its support for Czechoslovakia in the face of German aggression but the glaring implication of any military assistance that might be given was the transfer of Soviet troops across Polish lands and the likelihood of Poland agreeing to that under any circumstances was non-existent. Poland saw this as Soviet mischief-making pure and simple by keeping its close neighbours in a state of nervous uncertainty that denied them the luxury of mending their fences and forming an anti-Soviet bloc.

It is possible that Poland was less interested in Zaolzie *per se* than in creating a Central European security zone (*Międzymorze*) including Poland, Hungary and Romania. This was a desperate search for additional security guarantees in the face of German rearmament and the slow deterioration of the international situation. It was essentially a continuation of previous Polish foreign policy ambitions first seen in its striving for a Polish-Lithuanian commonwealth and then in Piłsudski's policy in which the Soviet Union would collapse and pave the way for an 'Intermarium' federation of independent states linking up from the Baltic to the Aegean. Beck's version of *Międzymorze* was built upon the dismemberment of Czechoslovakia, which lacked sufficient political cohesion ever to survive as an independent state. Seeing the way in which France and Britain were failing to offer any meaningful resistance to German revanchism gave Beck little hope that Germany's march eastward would be halted by the other Western Powers and so the idea of a broadly based coalition of Central European states at least gave some hope of resistance against the jackboot. The ultimate goal of a security cordon from the Baltic to the Balkans that did not include Czechoslovakia required a common border between Poland and Hungary. However logical and rational Beck may have viewed his strategy, what he failed to take fully into consideration and sublimated to his greater ambitions as he plotted with Hungary was that the destruction of Czechoslovakia would lead to German hegemony over the whole of Central Europe. Germany saw Polish ambitions for *Międzymorze* as being aimed more at them than against the Soviet Union and it is not surprising that German diplomats were under strict instructions to argue against it in all the European capitals, which effectively condemned the project to failure from the start. When Czechoslovakia fell it would be according to German designs not Poland's.

Key to Polish plans was reconciling Hungary and Romania, which had their own historic territorial disagreements, in a 'geopolitical revolution'. Evidence for Beck's ambition is circumstantial and can only be derived from his actions, which were more like those of a 'conspirator' than a government minister in regard to *Międzymorze*. It seems unlikely that he envisaged a written and signed treaty, more an understanding of how the countries might act in concert under certain circumstances that may or may not arise summed up by Beck's deputy Roman Dębicki, who said it was 'about creating a group of friendly nations speaking with each other in a language whose main leitmotif is the need to protect themselves against excessive German expansion'.[4]

Beck paid a visit to Rome at the beginning of 1938, where he met Mussolini and his foreign minister Galeazzo Ciano, who assured him that, while Italian policy led it to proclaim solidarity with Germany, it was also concerned about German penetration of the Balkans and the Danube basin. Poland, they said, was an important part of an unofficial bulwark against German expansionism but it was acknowledged that Hungarian-Romanian rapprochement was a vital part of such a development. When Beck had met Hitler earlier in January 1938, he had come away convinced that he was aiming to move against both Austria and Czechoslovakia and that the Western Powers would do nothing to restrain him. Mussolini left him in no doubt that Italy was equally sanguine about the business despite a previous confrontation when, in 1934, he had sent four divisions of Italian troops to the Austrian border, calling Hitler a murderer after the assassination of the Austrian Chancellor, Englebert Dollfuss.[5] While Poland saw a certain amount of relief as Hitler's gaze was focused on the south-east, the Anschluss brought into relief the reality of Hitler's cavalier attitude to treaties, agreements and assurances. The longer-term ramifications, however, were ominous now that Austrian industrial and human resources were at Germany's disposal.

It was to the Sudetenland that all eyes turned now as the increasing frequency of violent incidents between Sudeten Germans and the Czech authorities opened up possibilities for German intervention. Some in Poland saw the Polish minority in the Zaolzie regions of Teschen and Fryštát as having equally valid claims to secession from Czechoslovakia. Beck had a low opinion of Beneš, who had replaced Masaryk as president, and doubted that the Czech state would survive the growing pressures from without and within. It was no surprise to Beck that Beneš had proposed a 'closer and more lasting' relationship between Czechoslovakia and Germany to supersede any that existed between Germany and Poland and had indicated to France that agreement should be reached to transfer up to 2 million Sudeten Germans to the German Reich.

Poland's co-operation with Germany in the Czechoslovakian crisis became clearly defined after Lipski had talks with Göring on 24 August 1638. Polish-German relations appeared to have reached a high point when they both committed themselves to the break-up of the

Czech state and Polish territorial aims appeared to be accepted. They agreed that both states would seek to resolve their differences over Danzig and then when Lipski saw Hitler on 20 September 1938, if he found him to have received suggestions that German demands over the Sudetenland would be accepted by the British, Lipski had been instructed to reassure Germany of Polish support. He had hoped for some German relaxation of its demands over Danzig in return but Hitler gave no ground on that issue.

Poland had been building up a secret organisation in Zaolzie since 1935 and in the summer of 1938, copying the Sudeten separatism movement, they began organising guerrilla groups in the area. Beck personified Poland's antipathy to Czechoslovakia, which had been evident since the seven-day-war of 1919, and he was not slow to put in a claim for the Polish minority in Zaolzie, which had been accepted in principle on 24 May 1938 to the satisfaction of both Britain and France. When Britain and France had agreed to the outright secession of the Sudetenland at their meeting in London on 19 September 1938 Beck demanded equal treatment for Zaolzie but Beneš, who was scathing of Poland and called it the 'Balkans of the North', would not hear of it. He derided Poland's vision as the 'great policy of the small Republic'.[6] For him, Poland did not have anything like the negotiating power of Germany and he was hoping against hope that the Sudetenland would be the last German demand. To back up Beck's demands, Polish army units crossed the border on 23 September, but the few who did so were driven back by Czech forces. Hungary had followed the Polish request for transfer of territory with its own request on 22 September. The chief of the general staff of the Czech army, General Ludvík Krejčí, reported defiantly that, 'Our army will in about two days' time be in full condition to withstand an attack even by all Germany's forces together, provided Poland does not move against us,' and on 23 September, the Czech military mobilised. On 27 September Poland issued an ultimatum, demanding that Czechoslovakia hand over Těšín, part of the historic Czech lands of Bohemia.[7]

The Treaty of Trianon, a peace treaty signed between the Allied Powers and Hungary, had been prepared by the Paris Peace Conference and was signed in the Grand Trianon Palace on 4 June 1920. The Treaty had stripped Hungary of almost three quarters of the territory previously occupied by the pre-war Kingdom of Hungary, with Czechoslovakia and Yugoslavia being the main beneficiaries. Like other Eastern European countries, Hungary had long harboured ambitions to revise the borders imposed by the Allies at the end of the First World War and recover its lost lands. Having little political or military power, however, it had been forced to adopt a passive role in the hope of opportunities arising as a result of actions by the bigger players. Beck played on these aspirations and tempted Hungary with the prospect of reclaiming Transcarpathian Ukraine and Slovakia.

Hungary had reacted to the Anschluss with approval and Sir Harold Orme Sargent at the British Foreign Office predicted that, thanks to the pro-German policy of Hungarian prime minister, Kálmán Darányi, Hungary would submit its army, economy and foreign policy to German control. There was, however, deep-seated prejudice among senior and junior Foreign Office officials, who were hostile to Hungary after its association with the Central Powers' alliance in the First World War. Hungary's attitude, therefore, provoked wide speculation about the existence of a German-Hungarian scheme to destabilise the region. As a consequence, the British Foreign Office and the cabinet regarded German-Hungarian military cooperation against Czechoslovakia almost as a foregone conclusion. Based on this outlook, the Foreign Office decided that any future Hungarian territorial claims on Magyar-majority territories in Czechoslovakia should be firmly rejected. Budapest would be warned that minority complaints had to be referred to the League of Nations in accordance with the terms of the Treaty of Trianon. While British policy remained outwardly friendly towards Hungary for practical purposes, behind closed door ministers were unhappy about the destabilising effect of its territorial ambitions and viewed the country's foreign policy with distrust.

The British Foreign Office produced two memoranda on Hungary. The first Sargent-Nichols memorandum favoured the limited application of ethnicity, and only recommended the transfer of the Csallóköz, an area south-east of Pozsony and Beregszász, and a town in Ruthenia, right on the Czechoslovak side of the frontier, which both had a higher than 80 per cent Magyar population. A second memorandum, however, which also seems to have been written by Sargent and Sir Philip Nichols, advised the transfer of a significantly larger territory to Hungary. The significance of these documents lies in their ability to reveal British views on Hungarian territorial claims in a period when official opinion was silent for strategic reasons, to avoid arguments with Germany. They also prove that Whitehall did not dismiss frontier revision out of hand, but was certainly aiming to limit its extent to promote stability, and to harmonise with the criteria applied to the Sudetenland.

In August 1938, Hungary signed the Bled Agreement with Czechoslovakia, renouncing the use of force in their mutual relations; an agreement that was greeted with approval by the British press, who reacted positively, but still the Foreign Office was wary. Officials were very suspicious about the fact that the treaty remained unratified. Hungary's prime minister, Béla Imrédy, and foreign minister, Kálmán Kánya, followed a cautious foreign policy and were keen to maintain a delicate balance between Germany and the Western Powers, not least because of Hungary's severe military weakness, and Budapest mostly raised its voice over the protection of Magyar minorities only through the League of Nations.

Romania had played a minor role in the First World War on the side of the Allies but had been forced to sign a separate armistice with the Central Powers in 1917. At the Paris Peace Conference, they were treated not so much according to their contribution to victory, which had been negligible, but for their economic potential. The country was seen as an important buffer state against Bolshevism and was awarded a large part of Hungary to bolster its effectiveness in that regard. During the following years, however, its politics was riven by factionalism and had become increasingly dominated by the fascist Iron Guard. Already in 1937, Romania and Hungary had started exploratory talks aimed at a non-aggression treaty but made little progress. Poland tried to intervene to mediate but such action was frowned upon in Berlin, which had no intention of allowing Poland to dictate events in Eastern Europe. Beck tried to persuade Hitler in January 1938 that no German interests were threatened, but German plans would be made by the Germans and countries such as Poland would play whatever part Berlin decided they would play. Warsaw was not going to be allowed to make plans of its own but it might be allowed to think it could in order to discomfort the Soviet Union, which saw a Polish-Hungarian-Romanian alliance as an attempt to isolate it.

Poland did not fully appreciate the extent to which its ambitions conflicted with German political and economic influence in that region. Beck still believed that Poland had sufficient authority to persuade both the Romanian and Hungarian governments to support his stance and join together to present a common front to Germany, but the influence Germany now had over Romania and Hungary prevented that and diminished Poland's ability to establish itself as an independent power in Central Europe. All Central and South-Eastern relations were being directed from Berlin and while Beck presented his strategy as essentially anti-Soviet, German military leaders saw them as anti-German.

When Beck had met Hitler in January 1938, he had come away convinced that the Führer was aiming to move against both Austria and Czechoslovakia and that the Western Powers would do nothing to restrain him. Poland would have to find its own solution and to do that it would have to be proactive. Then talks in early September 1938 seemed to bring Poland and Hungary closer to an understanding but Beck still thought the Hungarians dangerously passive in the face of German aggression. It was clear by now, however, that Beck had lost all confidence in either France or Britain to take Polish concerns seriously, which may well have been his guiding motivation to avoid taking the matter to the League of Nations, an organisation he had previously held in such high regard. He instructed delegates not to apply for re-election to the council when its three-year term expired.

Hitler and Chamberlain met at Bad Godesberg on 23 September 1938, when the British prime minister presented the proposals that had been agreed with the French. Hitler astounded him by casting them aside, saying he 'could no longer discuss these things ... the solution [was] no longer valid', because of new Polish and Hungarian claims on Czech territory.[8] After the Bad Godesberg meeting, Britain did its utmost to argue Hungary out of igniting a regional war by marching into Slovakia. Although Halifax recommended an immediate decision in the cabinet, during a meeting with György Barcza, the Hungarian minister in London, he warned sharply against Hungary attempting any direct military action. Barcza demanded equal consideration for the Magyars as with the Sudeten Germans. The Halifax-Barcza meeting fully clarified the huge gap between British and Hungarian policies. Regardless of having supported frontier revision earlier out of strategic consideration to limit frictions with Germany, Halifax officially rejected Hungary's demands but knew full well that London would eventually have to accept that the Magyars would receive similar treatment to the Sudeten Germans. British policy shifted from discouraging frontier revision to quietly acceding to some adjustment applying the ethnographic criteria.

Meanwhile, Soviet-Polish relations took a downturn. On 23 September 1938, the acting head of the Polish Embassy in Moscow, Tadeusz Jankowski, was summoned to the Soviet Foreign Office in the middle of the night to be told that if Poland made any move against Czechoslovakia, the Russo-Polish Non-Aggression Treaty would be revoked. This was a reference to Polish troops massing on the Czech border. A visibly shaken Jankowski replied that there were no large-scale military preparations, merely a 'police action' to protect Polish territory from an influx of refugees. The British Foreign Office gave its opinion that Polish demands for the secession of Zaolzie would not in itself constitute an act of aggression by Poland and therefore could not be seen as a violation of Article 2 of the Soviet-Polish Treaty, and fortified by this Jankowski returned to the Soviet Foreign Office later the same day to deliver a note from Beck to say that the Polish government saw no necessity to explain its actions, which were completely legal.

The next day the Czechs were encouraged by the Soviet Union, which supported its determination 'not to yield' to Polish demands. As a show of support, the Soviets mobilised four army corps on combat readiness and moved troops up to the Polish border. Polish reports on 22 September 1938 had recorded 'troops in large numbers which are camped in the woods', with motorised units and stocks of fuel in Belarus waiting to come to Czech aid if the French struck first against Germany. It must be remembered, however, that there was and never had been, any expectation that France would do any such thing. With combat-ready troops marching past the Polish Embassy in the Belarusian capital of Minsk it was obvious that the world was meant to know what was happening. At night Minsk was blacked out.[9] Anti-aircraft drills were carried out the next day and a state of emergency was introduced at noon. At the same time Soviet troops, with aviation and armoured support, moved up to the Polish border in large numbers as mobilisation was ordered in Kyiv and Leningrad. The Czechs expected Soviet pressure to be applied to Poland after it issued its Zaolzie ultimatum to Prague on 1 October 1938 but the deal struck by Chamberlain and Hitler at Munich gave the Soviets no option but to scale down operations and, in effect, abandon the Czechs to their ultimate fate. In November 1938 Beck described the Soviet action during September 1938 as no more than a bluff, but by that time he had the luxury of hindsight. However, all through September Poland had done little to counter the Soviet threat, indicating that it had not taken it seriously.

Although evidence is scarce, there is still the possibility that Stalin was not entirely bluffing. Had Poland gone into Zaolzie in force on 1 October 1938 there is the possibility that the Soviets would have struck across Poland's eastern border confident that Germany would remain neutral and prevent any interference from the West. At the very least, the Soviets could have taken large swathes of Ukraine and possibly hung onto parts of eastern Poland too.

The Munich Agreement was reached on 30 September 1938, which had averted a major crisis, but Poland used the occasion to issue a time-limited ultimatum to Czechoslovakia demanding that Czech troops evacuate Teschen and Fryštát. Beneš was reeling from the body blows of Munich and yielded to Polish troops and civil administrators, which went on to occupy the region. On 2 October 1938 Polish troops invaded Teschen with Hitler's approval. A new border was established along the Ostravice River and the Poles expelled 30,000 Czechs from the region.

These Polish actions had been taken on an opportunistic basis and had not been prearranged in any detail beforehand, but as early as 20 September 1938 Lipski had held talks in Berlin to clarify boundaries in the event of an invasion of Czechoslovakia. He had been anxious to avoid German troops moving into areas touching the Polish border but the map shown to Chamberlain at Bad Godesberg indicating the Czech areas into which German troops were to be sent included the vitally important railway junction of Bogumin, well inside the zone the Poles had hoped to claim for themselves.

On 31 October 1938, von Ribbentrop had presented Lipski with a comprehensive plan for a general revision and settlement of Polish-German relations in which Poland was to be given a guarantee concerning its frontier and the Polish-German Agreement of 1934 was to be extended by twenty-five years. In return von Ribbentrop suggested that Danzig be incorporated in the Reich and an extra-territorial link with Germany be built across Polish territory to East Prussia. This seemed to be a reasonable suggestion but the way in which it had been presented showed a marked change in German attitude towards Poland, especially over the issue of Danzig, where it was clear that Germany was issuing demands and seeking Polish unconditional approval. On 28 October 1938 Marian Stanisław Chodacki, the Polish high commissioner in Danzig, told the Polish state undersecretary, Jan Szembek, that the city was being mobilised and Nazi propaganda was becoming more obvious. The return of Danzig to the Reich was being discussed openly and paramilitary organisations were increasing. Now that Hitler, through the Anschluss, had demonstrated clearly that France nor Britain would facilitate satisfaction of Germany's revisionist claims, Poland's cooperation was of no significance and Hitler saw no reason to take note of Polish sensibilities in his future plans.

Beck and his advisers in the ministry still believed that Germany would not seek a confrontation with Poland, and they decided to seek a means of defusing the Danzig time bomb before it ruptured Polish-German relations beyond repair. Beck proposed to satisfy German demands in Danzig without compromising Polish rights in the city and these efforts at negotiation were to continue well into the following year. He was adamant that Danzig should not become a bone of contention between the two states, and instructed Lipski to seek an interview with von Ribbentrop where he was to make it clear that Poland was ready to hold talks about Danzig and the land bridge between Germany and East Prussia. It was hoped that this would then facilitate a meeting to be held in a spirit of reconciliation between Beck and German leaders in January 1938.

In December 1937, Beck had spoken of 'the process by which the Soviet Union is closing itself off politically and technically from Europe'.[10] The Soviets were in the process of carrying out a forced resettlement of the Polish population from the Soviet part of the Ukraine while, at the same time, removing Poles from the Communist Party apparatus. By order of Nikolai Yezhov, the head of the NKVD, plans were fixed to exterminate over 100,000 Poles who were citizens of the Soviet Union. This criminal order for the 'Polish Operation' is the only known instance of a written order to perpetrate genocide in the twentieth century.[11]

Despite the Soviet self-mutilation of its High Command, the country retained ambitions to regain all territories lost after the First World War, with Poland firmly at the top of its agenda. The Sudetenland crisis had opened up possibilities in this regard as a result of Soviet declarations of support for Czechoslovakia that could only have been translated into action through one of two ways. Either Soviet troops would be afforded permission to march through Poland on the way to Czechoslovakia or east Poland would be occupied by Soviet troops if Germany had invaded from the west. Naturally both alternatives were anathema to Poland but the question is to what extent was the Soviet threat a reality or just a bluff to further aggravate the already tense situation and maybe instigate a war that they would then keep out of.

The Soviets had suffered a blow on 17 March 1938 when Poland had forced a settlement with Lithuania that effectively halted Soviet attempts to exploit the Polish-Lithuania conflict for its own ends and it looked for other opportunities to exert pressure on Poland. Ambassador Edward Raczyński told Chamberlain on 14 June 1938 that despite the purges the Soviet Union was still 'a potential danger' and in Paris the Polish ambassador, Juliusz Łukasiewic, warned that it 'could not remain indifferent' if Czechoslovakia was attacked.[12] Diplomatic exchanges indicate that the Soviet Union was acting in such a way as to escalate the Sudetenland crisis into a wider issue that threatened armed conflict between Germany and the Western Allies.

Since the transit of Soviet troops across Polish soils wound be seen by Warsaw as an act of war, other means of Soviet engagement in Czechoslovakia required the agreement of Romania to allow the passage of Soviet troops or permission to Soviet aircraft to overfly the country. Polish sources believed that negotiations to allow this had begun as early as May 1938 and Warsaw sent a note to Bucharest on 1 June 1938 protesting that any permission for the Soviet Air Force to fly over Romania would be a violation of the Polish-Romanian Guarantee Treaty of 15 January 1931.[13] Indications all through June and July 1938 gave Poland reason to believe that negotiations between Bucharest and Moscow were progressing well despite the Romanian foreign minister Nicolai Petrescu-Comnen's repeated denials that permission would be granted. Eventually King Carol II settled the issue by declaring that he would 'rather see the Germans in Romania as enemies than the Russians as friends'.[14]

Chapter 12

THE DESCENT TO WAR

> I have had the following proposal submitted to the Polish Government:-
>
> (1) Danzig returns as a Free State into the framework of the German Reich.
>
> (2) Germany receives a route through the Corridor and a railway line at her own disposal possessing the same extraterritorial status for Germany as the Corridor itself has for Poland.
>
> In return, Germany is prepared:-
>
> (1) To recognise all Polish economic rights in Danzig.
>
> (2) To ensure for Poland a free harbour in Danzig of any size desired which would have completely free access to the sea.
>
> (3) To accept at the same time the present boundaries between Germany and Poland and to regard them as ultimate.
>
> (4) To conclude a twenty-five-year non-aggression treaty with Poland, a treaty therefore which would extend far beyond the duration of my own life.
>
> Extract of speech by Hitler to the Reichstag, 28 April 1939

After Munich, Poland had been faced with four main options, some more realistic than others. It could fall in with German plans, which would inevitably lead to total subjugation of Poland along with all the other countries from the Baltic to the Aegean. It could ally itself with Czechoslovakia against German ambitions but that would fly in the face of the hostility between the two nations and would require a superhuman effort on the part of France to bring them together. It could declare neutrality and withdraw from active diplomacy, which would leave it totally at the mercy of external forces, or it could try to resurrect *Międzymorze* in some form or another.

While it pondered the merits of each, the Munich agreement was arrived at and the stage was reset for a new act. Poland was quick to exploit the German occupation of the Sudetenland by sending troops into Zaolzie on 2 October 1938 to occupy areas to which it had laid claim since 1920. Beck followed this up by meeting the Hungarian foreign minister, István Csáky, on 6 October to discuss the Hungarian occupation of Slovakia and Carpathian Ruthenia. Beck had no objection to the Hungarian-speaking areas going to Hungary but preferred to see the rest of Slovakia achieving independence but, crucially, as part of the proposed *Międzymorze*. Negotiations with Romania, however, aimed at improving Romanian-Hungarian relations were a little more fraught. Bucharest feared that once the border arrangement inherited from Versailles was altered by military means the whole of the Eastern Europe boundaries would become inherently unstable and Hungary was not well placed to defend its borders. What was required in its view was a 'complete solution' to the Czech issue and not ad hoc changes to its borders.[1] Beck persisted and called on Budapest to state its position clearly. It did and it was clear that while better relations with Hungary would be welcome, Czech border changes allowing Hungary to take over Carpathian Ruthenia were not, even though a small part of the territory would be made available to Romania. It was, furthermore, apparent that Bucharest was not willing to put its name to anything that might be disapproved of in Berlin, which desired to see Eastern Europe remain a collection of independent states. *Międzymorze* suffered its final and terminal rebuff. A frustrated Beck was later to characterise Romania as '*un parfait imbécile*'. Polish diplomats derided Hungary as 'not up to the task [and had] not been able to draw bold consequences from the opportunities that have presented themselves'.[2]

Beck was also disappointed when the hoped-for involvement of Italy did not materialise. Czechoslovakia was far enough away from the Balkans to make Mussolini say 'the existence or non-existence of [Czechoslovakia] does not interest Italy'. While portraying itself as an independent power to be reckoned with, in reality Italy was not prepared to move far from the German position on matters outside its immediate Mediterranean province. Mussolini was content to play diplomatic games with Poland to give the impression that an alternative version of fascism could stand against the power of Germany but Italy was militarily weak in comparison to Germany and its main priority was to maintain the closest possible ties with them.

There was further humiliation for Poland when Lipski was put in his place by von Ribbentrop on 24 October 1938 and reminded that Poland had not been given a seat at the top table. Von Ribbentrop told him that Poland was required to address all the outstanding issues awaiting resolution, which were Danzig, Poznania, access to East Prussia and Poland's accession to the anti-Comintern Pact, and only then would there be an accommodation between Poland and Germany. The implication was clear that the only option for Poland in von Ribbentrop's analysis was for it to become a vassal state to Germany. Things got worse when the Soviet Union dropped ominous hints that its own defence imperatives would not rule out an armed occupation of eastern Poland. A conference was held in Vienna on 2 November 1938, without the Western Powers' involvement, at which Hungary called for arbitration. It was dominated by von Ribbentrop and Ciano, who made the 'first Vienna Award' to Hungary of a wide strip all along the Czech border. Polish failure seemed complete when Beck's efforts to build closer relations with the Baltic States and Scandinavia proved fruitless also. He had suggested some form of security arrangement without any formal obligations, assuming that fear of rising German power would propel them into an agreement. The Scandinavians, in particular, were inclined towards neutrality but they did take part in regional conferences to stay abreast of developments.

With France firmly entrenched in what Łukasiewicz called a 'passive and defeatist', strategy it had lost any will to take the initiative in Eastern European affairs. In Paris the threat of a Polish-Czechoslovakian war seemed a distinct possibility and France had understandings with both but had grown distrustful and weary of their machinations. The French foreign minister, Georges-Étienne Bonnet, had signed a non-aggression pact with von Ribbentrop on 6 December 1938 based on the German-British agreement of 30 September 1938. Controversy surrounded the agreement because von Ribbentrop later made the claim, refuted by Bonnet, that it implied an understanding to give Germany a free hand in Eastern Europe.

Poland and Czechoslovakia had both started out as the progeny of Versailles but Poland had by far the greater claim to nationhood. The Czech state was inherently unstable given the nationalistic aspirations of its multiple ethnic minorities and Piłsudski had believed, from the start, that the artificial construct of the Czech state put it in line to be 'one of the first to disappear from the map of Europe' when the 'inevitable' shocks undermined the international order.[3] Its crucial position left it acutely vulnerable to become the central pawn in the Great Game of European diplomacy where it would be held to ransom by one side or another and eventually written off. Neither did Masaryk and Beneš have any confidence that Poland could retain its 1934 'artificial borders' for very long, with the Danzig Corridor, in particular, described by Masaryk in 1930 as an 'impossibility'. In 1935, Beck had envisaged Austria and Czechoslovakia as 'two states condemned to territorial destruction'.

Animosity between Poland and Czechoslovakia had never really abated. In 1924, France had tried unsuccessfully to persuade the Poles to accept the need for military cooperation with the Czechs but the memory of the 'seven-day-war' made that too bitter a pill to swallow. Despite the Czech claim to be the only functioning democracy in Eastern Europe, Beck called it a 'classic police state [where] liberalism was only a matter of appearance'.[4] This may well have been an exaggeration, and somewhat disingenuous given Poland's own record, but there was no doubt that the Polish minorities in Zaolzie were often subjected to brutal suppression to force them to assimilate. As late as 1936, the Czechs were still petitioning France to use its influence to bring Poland into a 'friendship pact' but Śmigły-Rydz rejected all appeals, seeing how useless it was to align Poland with a state that was daily coming under greater threat from all sides. It is doubtful if this was ever a serious offer anyway given Beneš' declaration that he doubted Poland's usefulness as a barrier between either Germany or the Soviet Union. By the time of the Anschluss it was the Czech view that, 'Until changes are made to the regime in Poland, and as long as Beck is at the head of Polish diplomacy, there is no hope for a Czechoslovak-Polish agreement.'[5]

At the Hossbach Conference, Hitler had made it plain to his generals that the conquest of Eastern Europe was his main objective but there was no clear indication of how he would achieve it. Now the Munich Agreement had opened up the way. The threat of war over his demands for the Sudetenland had abated and so prolonged a period of peaceful conquest where the next battle lines could be drawn. German intelligence was feverishly active disseminating rumour after rumour to keep other countries guessing. At the heart of Hitler's strategy was securing Germany's western borders before implementing his plans to acquire *Lebensraum* in the east. He had tested Western resolve over the Sudetenland and found it wanting but France could still cripple the German economy by retaking the Ruhr and the British Royal Navy was well capable of instituting a naval blockade to German maritime commerce. France, he believed was still a mighty military power, but its forces lacked motivation and its government lacked either stability or resolve. Britain, he hoped, might be persuaded to keep out of any continental war. While he pondered the options, Chamberlain's acceptance of German terms at Munich opened up new possibilities.

The manner in which the British leader had acquiesced left Hitler in no doubt that Britain lacked the will to fight over Eastern Europe, where it had few interests, and that further gains might be made at little cost. It is hard to say how far ahead Hitler planned his moves given that many of them seemed to be characterised by opportunism. In this case the prospect of annexing the whole of Czechoslovakia without Western interference was not only a welcome prospect in itself but created an opportunity to bring pressure to bear on Poland.

At the end of 1938 Polish relations with Germany might be said to have been tolerable if not warm but this belied the enduring ambition of Germany to advance its revanchist ambitions to reclaim the Danzig Corridor or at least coerce Poland with such stringent restrictions on trade that it would be condemned to virtual vassalage. It was clear that France could be relied on to abandon Poland under such circumstances as long as there was no actual war. German control of the Polish economy would then allow it to be exploited to support Germany's greater ambitions and open direct communications to put German troops much closer to the Soviet border. On 24 October 1938, von Ribbentrop put such a scenario to an astounded Lipski at Berchtesgaden in return for a twenty-five-year non-aggression treaty. Lipski saw this as blatant German bullying to get Danzig back and cut off independent Polish access to the sea, while simultaneously further eroding Franco-Polish relations.

As a sweetener to his proposal, von Ribbentrop suggested that Germany might be interested in creating an independent Ukrainian state centred on sub-Carpathian Ruthenia. Poland had long looked on this region of Czechoslovakia with concern, fearing that its rural and poorly educated populace could fall prey to communism, but after Munich the greater fear was that the Germans would imbue it with nationalistic fervour and inflame Ukrainians living across the border with Poland to agitate and destabilise the region. If the region was absorbed by Hungary, which was Poland's preferred option, it would bring about a Polish-Hungarian common border and a breathe new life into *Międzymorze*, but there was no encouragement from Berlin for that option. The whole idea of Ukrainian nationalism was anathema to Moscow, which made the fate of Ruthenia of importance to them also. This resulted in a relative thaw in Russo-Polish relations as Moscow looked to Warsaw for a common strategy for the region. Warsaw took advantage by negotiating a few trade deals and saw the possibility of resetting its strategy of maintaining balance between what it saw as the irreconcilable ideologies of Nazism and Bolshevism.

Sub-Carpathian Ruthenia

On 19 November 1938, von Ribbentrop got his answer. Beck rejected any changes to the Danzig Corridor but offered to discuss a bilateral agreement with German concerns about road and rail communications between Germany and East Prussia up for discussion at the same time. Naturally, Berlin was not pleased by the response, although it can hardly have expected otherwise, but Hitler had, for the moment, every reason to keep the Poles quiescent as he worked out what his next move would be. It didn't stop the Germans from continuing to press for some softening of the Polish position, however, and Beck was invited to meet Hitler in person at the Berchtesgaden on 5 January 1939. Although Hitler had been cordial and had not pressed Beck, the meeting left the Pole with a sense of foreboding knowing that the Danzig Corridor was now high up on Hitler's agenda. He retained, however, the belief that Germany was still interested in maintaining Polish goodwill.

On 26 January 1939, von Ribbentrop followed up with a visit to Warsaw on the fifth anniversary of the non-aggression pact. In a meeting with the Polish president, Ignacy Mosicki, and Śmigły-Rydz, he employed his oleaginous charms to assure them that all outstanding issues between the two countries were eminently resolvable but privately to Beck he emphasised that Hitler was anxious to see some progress in discussions. He once again brought up the possibility of concessions over Ruthenia if Beck would give ground on Danzig, and all the time making clear that it was Germany's wish to build a common front with Poland against communism. It was to no avail, however. Beck sensed the new dangerous mood in Berlin and would not allow Poland to become a German satellite. The German strategy was to continually demand concessions from Poland that it knew would never be agreed to voluntarily and in this way ramp up the tension in a bid to undermine Polish confidence. Beck was right to be worried; in Berlin von Ribbentrop was urging Hitler to complete the takeover of Moravia and Bohemia to raise the stakes against Poland.

The problem for Beck was that he was running out of options to resist the pressure building up from Berlin. France was already looking for a revision to Franco-Polish agreements to reduce French commitments to Poland. The only country that now offered any hope at all of Poland being able to withstand further German coercion was Britain if it could be persuaded to stiffen French resolve. Against a backdrop of street demonstrations in Warsaw during the visit of Ciano in February 1939, Beck asked his London ambassador, Edward Bernard Raczynski, to try and arrange a meeting with British officials in London. The meeting with Ciano did not go well. The Italian foreign minister, anxious not to do or say anything that might displease Hitler, gave Beck no encouragement at all that Polish efforts to stabilise the Danube basin would receive Italian support. In contrast, when the Romanian foreign minister, Grigore Gafencu, visited Warsaw a few days after Ciano, he gave Beck a glimmer of hope by showing great enthusiasm for Polish-Romanian rapprochement but what faint light that had glowed was extinguished emphatically when Hitler entered Prague on 15 March 1939 and forced the Czech leaders to sign a treaty giving him total control of Slovakia.

Hungary had agreed a joint approach with Germany on 12 March in which they would be allowed to seize sub-Carpathian Ruthenia, which they did on 15 March. Not satisfied with the boundary that had been agreed beforehand with Germany, Hungarian troops marched into Slovakia on 23 March. German troops held back and did not become involved as the Hungarians consolidated their gains, which were formalised in a treaty signed on 4 April 1939. A common Polish-Hungarian border had been established that was in line with previous Polish ambitions, but the rest of Slovakian-Polish border was now patrolled by the German army.

Buoyed by his success and deaf to howls of protest from Western capitals, Hitler piled more pressure on the Poles by sending a naval force up the Baltic and forcing Lithuania to cede the port of Memel on 22 March 1939. This German action and the continuous demands by von Ribbentrop, when he had met Lipski on 21 March, for agreement to establish a 15-mile-wide land bridge (what Kornat called a motorway) across the Danzig Corridor to link Germany and East Prussia suggested that the Germans were making plans for further rapid expansion in the east. The British ambassador in Warsaw, Sir Howard William Kennard, handed the Polish Ministry for Foreign Affairs a memorandum saying that Hitler's arrival in Prague showed clearly that 'the German Government resolved to go beyond their hitherto avowed aim to consolidate the German race [and] there is no state in Europe which is not directly or ultimately threatened'. He then proposed that Britain, France, the Soviet Union and Poland offer mutual support to protect international society from 'further violation of the fundamental laws on which it rests'. The Soviet Union supported Britain's initiative but also come up with its own idea for a six-power conference that would include Turkey and Romania. However, Britain waved that aside and pursued its own agenda.[6]

Beck was now coming under attack from his own side, but he did not see any virtue in the British proposal. Antagonising the Germans in this way would not help Poland unless it included firm guarantees of military aid in the event of an attack by Germany. To avoid lengthy arrangements, he asked Raczýnski to put to Britain the idea of a bilateral agreement that could be concluded quickly and run in parallel with the Franco-Polish guarantee.

At the beginning of 1939, Beck was finessing his long-held view that Poland needed better ties with Britain to balance the loss of French support. In doing so he was battling against a significant historical burden. It was clear that Britain had seen Poland as a troublesome state ever since Versailles, when 'doubtful territorial decisions' regarding Danzig had left it with a reputation for discord. Lloyd George had been essentially pro-German when dealing with the Upper Silesian question and little had changed since then, with the British foreign minister, Austen Chamberlain, famously declaring in 1925 that Polish affairs were 'not worth the bones of a [single] British Grenadier'.[7] A successor to Chamberlain, Sir John Simon, whose relations with Beck had been cool at best, went further in 1931 when he had told Zaleski that Poland would have to make territorial sacrifices in order to survive and it was just a question of 'now or later'. Prime Minister Baldwin, responding to the rise of the Nazis in Germany, had said in 1934 that 'the vast majority of public opinion is completely opposed to any policy of alliances on the continent'.

Beck was clearly aware of British antipathy, but he had faith in British institutions and sense of justice, and his ambitions for British aid were not entirely unrealistic. There was a great belief that Britain would not stand aside if France went to war in support of Poland, even though French resolve in Poland's cause had weakened significantly. Beck's approach to Britain was characterised by his avoidance of appearing to be a petitioner and never to overplay his hand by asking favours. His approach, whether to Eden, Halifax or Chamberlain, was to lay out in detail the role of Poland as a stabilising force in Eastern Europe. He freely admitted that Britain did not have the will to invest resources there but hoped that by impressing Britain then Britain would encourage the French to be more proactive in support of Poland. It was understood also that if not actually an alliance then at least strong friendship with Britain might give Germany pause for thought before making any aggressive moves. Beck seems to have made progress because by 1936, Eden, who consistently opposed the policy of appeasement, had said that 'times have changed since Lloyd George in terms of England's view of Poland' and called for a 'common language' in relations.[8]

Just how much they had changed was questionable when Halifax had tentatively agreed to a German solution for Danzig as long as it did not involve the use of force, and then after Munich any sympathy that Britain had felt for Poland was challenged by Poland's action against Czechoslovakia. It was still the foundation of British foreign policy at the beginning of 1939 that there would be no possibility of entering into obligations on the continent beyond those towards France. The British military was fearful of a land war and not slow to say at every convenient moment that German demands were essentially rational and largely justified. Opposition in Britain to intervention on the continent had not been helped either when, during the September 1938 negotiations over the Sudetenland, Poland, fearful of German reaction, had prevaricated when pointedly asked by Halifax if Poland would support Britain if it went to war with Germany over Czechoslovakia. During the first weeks of January 1939, Beck had thought it prudent to conceal German demands over Danzig from the British for fear of the British concluding that Hitler was looking to the east for his next move and that might have caused both Britain and France to retreat into a neutral stance.

The Polish Foreign Office summed up the situation on Hitler's entry into Prague on 15 March 1939 by firstly recognising that Europe had come immeasurably closer to war and a failure to react would only give Germany an incentive to take further steps at Poland's expense. A German drive through Hungary, Romania and eventually Lithuania was not thought impossible and required immediate action to strengthen Polish ties to all these countries to avoid complete encirclement. As a matter of urgency, the anti-German mood in Western Europe was to be exploited to the full. Raczynski noted with satisfaction that Chamberlain appeared to be at last showing some resolve as British military expenditure estimates were being increased.

On 17 March 1939 in a speech in Birmingham, Chamberlain was clear that Hitler had broken the Munich Agreement but the manner of doing so had introduced an entirely new dimension. Whereas in previous actions in the Rhineland, Austria and the Sudetenland, 'there was something to be said for the necessity for a change' it was certainly was not the case in Bohemia and Moravia, which was an example of 'blatant Imperialism'.[9] In his speech, Chamberlain tried to give the impression that his views were simply a continuous progression, albeit an accelerated one, of the way he had approached the issue of German expansionism over the previous months. However, when on 3 April 1939 he called it 'a new epoch in the course of foreign policy' one is left to assume that his views had changed abruptly. Von Dirksen attributed the change of approach to the way that public opinion had shifted and influenced the cabinet, but many politicians of the time have made it clear that it was Chamberlain alone who changed the course of British foreign policy. In cabinet on the following day, the prime minister described Poland as 'the key to the situation' and followed up with a move to consult 'a select group of European countries [the Soviet Union, Poland, Yugoslavia, Turkey, Greece and Romania]' to find common cause against aggression. The omission of Hungary and Bulgaria was significant.

When Kennard put a British four-party plan to Beck on 21 March 1939 it was not well received. The substance of the British initiative was that Poland should join Britain, France and the Soviet Union in a declaration of commitment to consult each other in the event of aggression taking place and with the aim of opposing it. Britain was now the key to Polish strategy and involving other countries in talks would inevitably slow down negotiations and inevitably introduce matters that Poland thought peripheral to the critical issue. Beck was optimistic, having detected a 'truly revolutionary' change in British attitudes to cooperation. However, any signs of increased British readiness to engage with Poland inevitably carried with it a threat that Germany would strike pre-emptively and unilaterally before a firm commitment could be arrived at but at least it was a recognition of Poland's importance as the key to the situation in Eastern Europe. Beck, however, had no grounds for believing that by abandoning negotiations with Germany he would then automatically get British support. Still believing that he had some influence on events, Beck indicated to the Germans the limits of Polish concessions in the hope that a show of resolve would be taken seriously alongside a reaffirmation of Polish goodwill over discussions about Danzig and the East Prussian land bridge.

It was the Romanian envoy, Viorel Tilea, however who changed the dynamics of the negotiations by claiming, falsely, that the Germans had issued an ultimatum to Romania. This was met by an outcry in the British press, which inevitably influenced government thinking and resulted in a commitment made to Romania on 26 March 1939. At the same time rumours started circulating, not least from US ambassador to Britain, Joseph Kennedy, that a sudden attack on Poland was imminent. The well-informed *News Chronicle* journalist Ian Colvin, who had many contacts in Berlin, confirmed this to Halifax on 29 March. The British view initially was that it could do nothing in reply, face a ruinous war or face Hitler down with a coalition of Britain, France and Poland.

The situation now was such that a move by any country in eastern Europe could start a chain of events in which each country would take whatever unilateral action was considered necessary to protect its vital interests. The Soviet Union might take the opportunity to invade Romania, and Hungary or Bulgaria might do the same. It became vitally important that Germany was deterred from making any move against Poland but a threat of retaliatory action by Britain might risk the full force of the Luftwaffe filling the skies over London if the bluff failed and the Germans launched all-out war. Chamberlain still thought that further concessions over, for instance, Danzig might satisfy Hitler but he was flying in the face of the reality that Poland was not ready to agree to that. Chamberlain's attitude suggests that he was still not reconciled to the fact that, for Hitler, Danzig was not the issue, it was merely an excuse and if the city had been conceded it would have been replaced by another demand that would draw Poland further into vassalage until he would have got his *lebensraum* in Poland and then turned to the Ukraine, Romania, Hungary and eventually the Soviet Union. With time running out, Chamberlain was left with few options. Turning British foreign policy on its head, he told the House of Commons on 31 March 1939 that:

> in the event of any action which clearly threatened Polish independence, and which the Polish Government accordingly considered it vital to resist, His Majesty's Government would feel themselves bound at once to lend the Polish Government all support in their power. They have given the Polish Government an assurance to this effect.

> I may add that the French Government have authorised me to make it plain that they stand in the same position in this matter as do His Majesty's Government.

It was not at all clear what Chamberlain meant by his 'assurance' and it seemed that this ambiguity split British opinion, which was not fully behind him. The Beaverbrook press was quick to point out that the reference to 'independence' did not necessarily extend the guarantee to Danzig and the Danzig Corridor that, it was assumed, would inevitably be returned to Germany in the fullness of time without war.[10] *The Times* piled in with its own critique, which asked its readers to look closely at the wording of the declaration and reminded them that, '[Britain] has never been an advocate of the encirclement of Germany.' Raczýnski assumed that the press statements had been officially endorsed by Downing Street and went straight to the British Foreign Office to protest that the government was already backtracking on its commitment. The British press, however, did not speak with one voice. Other papers declared that the warning to Germany was 'completely without reservation or qualification' and that it was up to Poland to decide what did or did not represent an attack on its independence. The Foreign Office was obliged to issue a clarification in which it expressed 'surprise' that attempts had been made to 'minimise' Chamberlain's statement, which was 'perfectly clear and categorical'. Since the Foreign Office had failed to mention either Danzig or the Danzig Corridor in its statement it was anything but a clarification.[11]

The guarantee was seen by many as a reckless gamble to think that Poland could stand up to Germany and should have been preceded by an understanding with the Soviet Union before any thought of making a guarantee to Poland, but Chamberlain had been strongly supported in his views from across the Atlantic. The US ambassador to Britain, Kennedy, had told him on 25 March 1939 that the United States had great sympathy for the Poles and applied direct pressure by urging Britain to go to war with Germany if the Danzig dispute 'blew up'. The US president, Roosevelt, who reputedly doubted Chamberlain's resolve, had meanwhile stiffened the Polish backbone with a message of 'Do not yield.'[12] It is a matter of some dispute as to whether it was Roosevelt's offer of military support that prompted Chamberlain's *volte face* and is worthy of examination.

In his 3 April 1939 speech, Chamberlain actually alluded to Roosevelt as someone who shared his views that 'a challenge ... to dominate one other nation without limits ... must be resisted'.[13] Anthony Eden claimed that Roosevelt was very forceful in trying to persuade Britain to prepare for war and implied that the US was preparing for the eventuality of going to war with Germany also. In a Foreign Policy Committee meeting, Halifax said that a failure to stand up to Germany would be to 'lose the support of the U.S.'. Von Dirksen saw 'American circles working through the American embassy in Warsaw' as actively heightening the crisis, while the German Consul general in San Francisco, Fritz Wiedmann, called Roosevelt 'Hitler's most dangerous opponent [that is] dragging [Britain and France] before her', and made clear his view that it was the US that was behind the drive for a European anti-German alliance.

As early as the beginning of March 1939, the US ambassador to Warsaw, Joseph Biddle, had applauded Poland's 'firmness of attitude [and] steps taken to stiffen Paris and London' and noted that Roosevelt had already agreed to sell war materièl to Britain and France, which was 'music to the ears' of Beck and the Polish government. Kennedy, no friend to Britain, was later reputed to have said 'neither the French nor British would have made Poland a cause for war if it had not been for the constant needling from Washington …' and that Roosevelt had constantly told him to 'put some iron up Chamberlain's backside'.

Roosevelt had, in 1937, already identified Poland as being in Hitler's sights and had urged his ambassadors to promote a strong anti-Nazi stand in European capitals. In a speech published but never delivered, he called for

> sentiment [to be] aroused against governments that show contempt for international decency and justice [and] we should make it possible for other peace-loving nations who are the victims of brutal attack to obtain in this country the munitions and supplies which they require to fight off aggression.[14]

Roosevelt was clearly eager to rouse nations to defend their borders, and was anxious to ensure that US industry should not let slip the chance to profit thereby. He also responded enthusiastically in early April 1939 by clearly speaking out against aggression and German domination and that war would inevitably follow invasion 'of some other nation by Germany'. He followed this up with a direct message to Hitler demanding assurances that Germany would not attack or invade Poland or any other country and urging him 'not to misunderstand the spirit of frankness in which [the message is sent]'. He made a sideswipe at the Italians at the same time in a similar vein.

It is clear that Roosevelt and many in his administration were strongly anti-Nazi but there is no direct evidence to indicate that this manifested itself in pressure on Chamberlain to make his speech of 30 March 1939. However, the number of statements made by a variety of members of his administration make it clear that US encouragement, to say the least, was offered to both Britain and Poland to take a strong stand after Prague but it cannot be ascertained whether it was Roosevelt's influence that finally persuaded Chamberlain to give Poland the guarantee. The president, Calvin Coolidge, is reputed to have said in 1925, 'The business of America is business' and while this is not exactly what he said, the sentiment is correct and it is beyond doubt that war is good for business. Business makes and sells the weapons of destruction and then afterwards invests to rebuild what has been destroyed. With the US the business capital of the world in 1939, one cannot, to some extent at least, help but view Roosevelt's encouragement in this light.

In reality the British guarantee did not significantly improve Poland's position. It made no mention of borders, only 'independence'. On the day before his speech, Chamberlain had expressed a view that Britain should act as arbitrator in the Danzig question but Halifax quietly persuaded him that public opinion would see that as a rerun of Munich. One can only imagine what Hitler would have thought about suggestions that he meet the '*arseloch*' Chamberlain and his damned umbrella again and have to listen to his views on what position Germany should take over Danzig. The complete lack of any operational plan meant that it was far from clear what exactly Britain could do in practical terms if Poland was attacked but Poland had no choice but to accept Britain's offer, even though it would be seen by Germany as a clear provocation. It had been a simple choice between that or having to take Hitler at his word that agreement over the Danzig question would defuse the situation and allow things to calm down, and nobody thought that trusting Hitler would get them very far.

Beck secretly went to London on 3 April 1939 to discuss bilateral guarantees, and there he met Chamberlain and Halifax as well as King George VI and the US ambassador, Kennedy. Halifax tried to limit the terms under which Britain would be obliged to go to Poland's aid when he told the cabinet that he doubted that 'inclusion of Danzig in the Reich would constitute a threat to Polish independence'.[15] When he asked Beck what kind of settlement Poland had in mind for the Danzig question, Beck made it abundantly clear that his country would fight for its independence and reject any German demands for concessions over Danzig and the Danzig Corridor. Chamberlain said that his speech had been designed to prevent a sudden strike by Germany and asked for Polish assurances that the guarantee to Poland must be reciprocated with a similar declaration of Polish support for Britain in the event of a direct attack by Germany upon Britain. Beck asked for time to consider such a proposal. It was still the overwhelming view in Britain that Beck represented a minority anti-German element in Polish politics and that his replacement at any time could bring about a significant change in Polish foreign policy.

As a result of the talks a bi-lateral declaration of mutual guarantees was issued, even though Beck had not consulted the Polish military over the issue. It was accompanied by another, secret, document that included a British commitment to support Poland against any German attempt to undermine Polish independence by any means and an agreement that Britain would come to Poland's aid 'without delay' in the event of an actual military attack. Poland agreed to provide assistance to Britain if Germany first attacked in the west. Both sides were coy about revealing details of this document to the French. Beck saw the agreement as a great success in that it propelled the Danzig question onto a wider platform and opened up the possibility of rebuilding the Franco-Polish alliance through British involvement. 'The road to Paris leads through London,' he said.[16] Working from Chamberlain's vague guarantee of 31 March 1939, Beck had come away from London with a solid foundation for bi-lateral cooperation and mutual obligations with a clear right for Poland to activate the alliance at a time of its own choosing. Britain was slipping inch by inch, almost as if sleepwalking, into the fetid quagmire of Eastern European politics that it had tried so hard for so long to avoid. Just how Britain could help Poland in the event of a German attack, however, was something not even they had worked out.

On the day of Beck's London visit, Hitler, consumed with fury, had instructed the German High Command to draw up plans, in the utmost secrecy, for *Fall Weiß* (Case White), an attack against Poland. Such plans were to be completed to allow for an attack to begin on 1 September 1939. In November 1938, he had already instructed his generals to draw up plans for a surprise seizure of the port of Danzig. It was still, however, a precondition of an attack on Poland that it be first completely isolated politically. His ambition rested on convincing Western opinion that an 'arrogant and treacherous' Poland was being greedy, revisionist, anti-Semitic and pro-German. This was not as difficult as might be thought since Poland had been shown to be opportunistic by colluding with the Germans over Zaolzie and it was rapidly shedding what goodwill was left with the French, whose diplomats abroad were advising Paris to 'terminate once and for all any remaining agreements with [Poland]'. For their part, the Soviets had been provoked almost to the point of war by what appeared to a slow Polish move into the German camp.[17]

Poland, meanwhile, at the end of March 1939 had made its own plans for the defence of the country. If attacked, the army would make a fighting withdrawal from the border to defensible positions along its major rivers, which they would hold until the winter storms came to their rescue, after which they hoped international aid would flow in.

During 1938, Danzig-Polish relations had been good but hardly anyone held out the hope that the port could resist German claims in the long run. There was little international enthusiasm to safeguard its neutrality. There had even been discussion over the reunion of Danzig with the Reich, with Poland being assured of access to the port and all facilities there. Official documents of the Polish Ministry of Foreign Affairs show that Beck was ready to discuss the idea to stabilise relations with a bilateral Polish-German agreement and on 5 January 1939, there followed diplomatic meetings in Berlin on 26 March 1939 and Warsaw on 28 March but these ended only with a Polish refusal to accede to the transit of German troops across the Danzig Corridor. Von Ribbentrop, who complained that relations between the two countries were deteriorating rapidly, did his best to accelerate that trend by complaining to Lipski of Polish treatment of German nationals and members of the German minority in the Danzig Corridor. Harsh words were exchanged with veiled threats on both sides that hostile actions around Danzig would be interpreted as manifestations of national will and would be treated as international incidents. Beck made it perfectly clear that any unilateral German action against Danzig would be seen as an act of war, which made him the very first European statesman to openly threaten Germany in this way. Not that Danzig *per se* was the issue as much as the symbol of Polish borders and independence. The mood in Danzig was febrile and incendiary, with uniformed Nazis seen everywhere and incidents being manufactured between Polish and Danzig customs officials. The anti-Jewish Nuremberg Laws had been introduced in November 1938. Anti-German demonstrations had broken out in many Polish cities such as Warsaw, Poznań, Lwów and Kraków and German activists were routinely arrested.

German Nationalist politicians in Poland had, under strict instructions from Berlin, loudly and persistently proclaimed loyalty to the Polish state at the same time as nurturing a conspiracy against it. All along the borderlands with Germany, intelligence was gathered about Polish fortifications. Incendiary border incidents were manufactured to rouse suspicion and create a mood of insecurity. Berlin actively encouraged migration of German families into Germany to give the impression that they were fleeing persecution. Those who were left were subjected to a concerted programme of Nazification, which even started to bear fruit among the more assimilated minorities in the urban areas who hitherto had been much less inclined to be politicised. While the Germans inside Poland had been as fractious and uncooperative with each other as any competing organisations would be elsewhere and having been a diverse movement ranging from militant to unconcerned, the German Poles, who had for the most part been treated far more leniently than other minorities, started to come together under the Nazi flag in 1939.

Hitler then made a speech to the Reichstag on 28 April 1939 in which he accused the Versailles Treaty of inflicting 'a most severe wound on Germany' by establishing Danzig and the Danzig Corridor in such a way as to prevent understanding between Poland and Germany. The speech was followed up by claims that the 30 March 1939 British statement of support for Poland was incompatible with the German-Polish declaration of 26 January 1934 and had 'arbitrarily and unilaterally' rendered it invalid. This followed a German offer to Poland in early January 1934 to replace the 1934 Non-Aggression Pact with a new Polish-German Treaty of Friendship and Cooperation, which would include mutual border guarantees and an agreement that both countries would coordinate their foreign policies. When Poland rejected the idea, Germany turned the screw, calling the Polish position tantamount to a refusal to talk, and used it as an excise on 28 May 1939 to abandon talks over renewal of the Polish-German Non-Aggression Pact. In spite of this, the Poles persisted in their belief that German actions were really only a war of nerves, and that they still had the option of calling Germany's bluff.

An incident at Kalthof on 20 May 1939, when it was alleged that a German was shot dead at a Polish customs post on the East Prussian border, was used as an excuse by Germany to further escalate tensions in the Danzig Corridor.

Pressure was mounting on Poland but it was not moved to allow Britain to negotiate on its behalf. The British cabinet had intimated that all difficulties could be negotiable but having seen where that had got Czechoslovakia, the Poles had not been prepared to put its faith in Britain, nor did they welcome Britain asking questions about their relations with Germany. Raczynski told Halifax that 'the gravity of the present situation did not arise because of the existence between Poland and Germany of some issues which could be resolved through negotiations', and by stressing the need for Polish-German negotiations, he said that the British government 'exhibits its ignorance of the actual state of affairs'.[18] There was general disquiet in Warsaw over British insistence that Poland should be open to new German proposals to resolve the Danzig issue. The British government continued its efforts to prevent the Poles from declaring that incorporation of the city of Danzig into the Reich was tantamount to a declaration of war.

It is claimed by some historians that by rejecting Hitler's January 1939 demands, Poland made a serious tactical error and assumed culpability for the catastrophe of war that followed, which makes it very important to examine the reasons for the Polish decision.[19] Of fundamental importance was the Polish article of faith that unfettered access to the Baltic was a vital component of national economic viability, without which its independence would vanish, and, despite the emergence of Gydnia as an alternative, the independence of Danzig was symbolic of Polish pride and ambition. It was not clear that discussions over the future of the port had considered what access Poland would have even to Gydnia if the whole of the Danzig Corridor was ceded to Germany. Furthermore, the German call for the establishment of a 15-mile wide 'motorway' under German control joining Germany and East Prussia came burdened with numerous issues of sovereignty, security and terms of use in time of war but the Poles made a number of studies of how it might operate and had actually come up with concrete proposals. The German demands were laid in such a way that, taken as a whole, they were almost certain to be rejected by Poland. It is surprising, therefore, that the Polish Foreign Ministry seemed ready, by this time, to give the matter serious consideration but the Polish military establishment saw any concessions as a humiliation. They seemed to know what Beck failed to fully understand, which was that negotiations would show weakness and any concessions would be seen everywhere as an act of subjugation. Beck did, however, admit that 'none of Hitler's demands were final [and] always marked the beginning of the next demand' but he saw no option but to continue negotiations and keep searching for a way forward.[20]

Hitler's strategy was to isolate Poland rather than provoke it into a violent reaction. The British guarantee of 30 March 1939 had given him pause for thought and a false move at this stage might strengthen the British-Polish alliance, but he was gambling that British resolve would fade. It was still the case, however, that his next move would be to apply the tried and tested routine of fomenting internal rebellion to justify German occupation, as seen in Austria and the Sudetenland, but this time against Danzig and the Danzig Corridor. Poland was to be cut off from all of its lifelines and left to wither on the vine, leaving it ultimately powerless to further resist German demands for the return of Danzig to the Reich. The ever-present threat of force still underlay everything and Hitler was reconciled to outright war if that is what it took. However, again it was vital to isolate Poland first and rob any potential allies of the will to intervene. German diplomats were instructed to avoid discussion of Poland to diminish its importance in European politics. It was not perceptions of Poland, however, that would influence Western actions in the coming months as reaction to German behaviour in Paris, London and Washington.

In his negotiations with Romania in April 1939, it is clear that Beck had an over-optimistic opinion of Polish military strength and an under-appreciation of Germany's, which he thought 'exaggerated'. Polish military hubris had blinded him to the reality that pride, tradition, courage and skill in the use of cavalry would not be enough to halt the panzers, motorised infantry and air force that would be hurled against them. When he met the Romanian foreign minister, Gafencu, in April, they discussed a mutual defence pact that, Beck seemed to believe, would be capable of deterring a joint German-Hungarian attack.

With one foot now metaphorically stuck in the European mud, Britain was in danger of getting the other one similarly compromised when it was forced to respond to developments in the Balkans. On 7 April 1939, Italy had invaded Albania, which threw the whole Aegean and Balkan theatre into chaos. Yugoslavia refused all Western offers of support, no doubt calculating that Germany and Italy, with whom it had recently improved relations, were very much closer physically and required very careful handling diplomatically. Greece, on the other hand, accepted British guarantees made by Chamberlain to Parliament on 13 April, at which time he also, somewhat reluctantly, extended them to Romania as well. France followed suit, with reaffirmation of its guarantee to Poland thrown in for good measure. A day later, Roosevelt, from his vantage point 3,000 miles away, sent a message to Hitler and Mussolini in which he hoped they might avoid all-out war.

Hitler's speech to the Reichstag on 28 April 1939 began with a somewhat sarcastic response to Roosevelt's letter, which he claimed had been seen by the whole world through a press release before he had received a copy. He would now respond in kind but before coming on to that he showed further disrespect by relegating his reply to later in the speech after giving his usual detailed personal interpretation of German history and the many injustices to which he believed his country had been subjected. He went on to blame Versailles, especially its solution for Danzig, for preventing an understanding between Germany and Poland. 'Danzig is a German city and wishes to belong to Germany,' he declared. He described his recent offer to Poland to recognise all Polish economic rights in Danzig, to ensure Poland of a free harbour in Danzig of any size desired, giving completely free access to the sea, to accept at the same time the present boundaries between Germany and Poland and to regard them as final to conclude a twenty-five-year non-aggression treaty with Poland, a treaty therefore that would extend 'far beyond the duration of my own life', and to enter into a guarantee of the independence of the Slovak State by Germany, Poland and Hungary jointly – which meant in practice renunciation of any exclusive German hegemony in this territory. In return he had demanded that Danzig be returned to the framework of the German Reich and that Germany be given a route through the Danzig Corridor and a railway line for herself with the same extra-territorial status for Germany as the Danzig Corridor itself currently had for Poland. 'The Polish Government has rejected my offer,' he told his audience, 'and has declared itself prepared only to negotiate concerning the question of a substitute for the Commissioner of the League of Nations, and to consider facilities for the transit traffic through the Corridor.' He lamented that Poland's 'incomprehensible attitude' was 'a matter of deep regret'.

Hitler then came to the issue of Roosevelt's telegram, to which he responded in extraordinary length. To Roosevelt's reminder of the terrible consequences of war, Hitler said that no nation knew that better than Germany. To an appeal for peaceful settlement of disputes, Hitler said that it had always been 'an exponent of this view'. He called Roosevelt's 'tide of events' threatening war to be no more than newspaper chatter and blamed the leaders of nations for failing to 'control their newspapers'. While his assertion that 'the German people have no desire for war' might well have been true, his stunningly disingenuous follow-up that he personally had 'expressed his abhorrence of war and, no less of warmongers' certainly was not.

Responding to the speech, Poland felt the need to mobilise four infantry divisions and one cavalry brigade but could hardly afford the drain this placed on their fragile economy. They were forced to take their begging bowl and trawl European capitals for loans. Britain offered to finance arms purchases but had little to sell since its own demand for armaments had grown to manic proportions. A deal much smaller than the one sought was eventually agreed but Britain and France, which had also agreed a limited loan, seemed to be in no hurry to make the necessary arrangements and it would take several months before it could translate into actual aid. In any case, events were moving so fast that it was doubtful if Poland would see any benefit before its perilous situation became critical. The laggardly

Western response was seen in Berlin as an indication that British-Franco commitment to Poland was weakening after their impetuous guarantee on 31 March 1939.

The Polish politicians could not conceivably have hoped that Britain would support Polish interests in Danzig and elsewhere, nor that Britain would place its resources at Poland's disposal. Up until the German entry into Prague, there had existed no trust, no unity of interest, no common ground, between the Poles and the British.[21] They were not going to be abandoned by the French, however, who still had the greater residual ties. Urgent exchanges of military delegations between Warsaw and Paris discussed the practicalities of strategic coordination, required by the new guarantee, should Poland be attacked. The French, however, like the British, were in no hurry to make any further rash promises and prevaricated on the pretext of holding talks with the Soviets first. The French army had not been enthused by a political commitment to 'act vigorously ... in the event of German aggression' and worked towards a 'more flexible interpretation'. The result was an agreement that was taken to mean different things by each side. The Poles believed that they had got 'promises' of French support but chief of the French army staff, General Maurice Gamelin, refused to acknowledge any military commitment until it had been endorsed by a political protocol and this Bonnet was reluctant to sign. British support came in the form of repeated statements of their determination to aid Poland, designed to impress Berlin, and extended talks with the Polish military but only vague assurances that the RAF, the only one of the services able to give any sort of help so far from home, would be deployed in the event of an attack by Germany. The Royal Navy, which might have been used to secure Polish shipping lanes, was apparently far too busy looking after Britain's imperial sea routes. It was clear that Britain had few means of backing up its promises to Poland with practical measures if Germany was to launch a sudden attack and so the government made great efforts to draw the Soviet Union into a coalition to preserve the peace.

Soviet Foreign Policy, however, became unclear when on 3 May 1939 Litvinov was 'relieved [of his duties] at his own request', as the US chargé in the Soviet Union, Alexander Kirk, reported it to the US secretary of state, and replaced by the outwardly dull but inwardly astute Vyacheslav Molotov as foreign minister. Moscow denied that the new man would change the direction of policy but it was noticeable that German diplomatic attacks against the Soviet Union were significantly reduced after Molotov's appointment. This implied that there had been a sea-change in relations between Germany and the Soviet Union, the preparations for which had preceded Molotov's appointment, and it was later claimed by Soviet ministers that Litvinov had been removed because of his lack of enthusiasm for Moscow's pro-German initiative. The Soviet commissariat of foreign affairs was purged at the same time as Litvinov's removal. The Polish-American historian, Anna Cienciala, claims that Soviet-German talks had begun as early as 17 April 1939 but were conducted at arm's length from official channels so that they could be repudiated if the Soviets chose to ally with the West. However, after Litvinov's exit 'German-Soviet relations began to warm up immediately'.[22] While this puzzled Western governments, it was not necessarily seen as of great importance given the still gaping ideological chasm between the two countries. Only the US took it seriously and that was because it was significantly better informed about events in Moscow. Kirk had cabled to Washington on 4 May 1939:

> There is an obvious inclination ... to explain this step at the present time on the basis that it portends some change in the direction of Soviet foreign policy. This change might constitute a step away from the principle of collective security and one towards the establishment of relations with Germany in conformity with the indication contained in Stalin's speech to the Eighteenth Party Congress ... and in this connection unconfirmed rumours have recently been current in Moscow of some German approach to the Soviet Government presumably to counteract Franco–British influence ... This action is generally regarded as of major significance in Soviet foreign relations.

When the French ambassador to Berlin, Robert Coulondre, reported to Paris on 7 May 1939 that 'the dismissal of Litvinov as Soviet foreign commissar had caused much comment in official circles in Berlin, and that according to his sources Germany was planning to invade Poland that year and was willing to sign a pact with the Soviet Union to achieve that goal', he was virtually ignored and his warning never reached London or Warsaw. It is worth noting that in meetings with Molotov and his deputy Vladimir Potemkin during May, Polish officials reported 'an unusually good atmosphere' and the new Soviet ambassador in Warsaw, Nikolai Sharonov, was warmly welcomed.[23]

It is hard to say what motivated British and French reaction to rumours of a thaw in German-Soviet relations. They desperately wanted the Soviet Union to join them in an anti-Nazi pact, even though Poland was adamant that it would not be part of any four-party arrangement, and it may have been that they simply refused to acknowledge the possibility of a German-Soviet rapprochement that would drive 'a coach and horses' through the frail edifice of their aspirations. Even when it became apparent that Moscow was employing delaying tactics in negotiations with Western delegates, the reason was assumed to be fear of aggravating Germany and it seems not to have been noticed that parallel talks were going on with Germany. It was also the view of Poland and the Western Powers that the Red Army High Command had been so eviscerated by the Moscow purges of 1937 and 1938 that it was in no state to risk war with Germany by signing up to the Four-Power deal. Beck was convinced that a German-Soviet rapprochement was 'impossible', especially having received what he thought to be assurances from Potemkin, on 10 May 1939 that Poland could count on Soviet support if attacked by Germany, although the Soviet version of the meeting was that Potemkin had only 'hinted' at such an understanding.[24] It should have been plain to Western negotiators that the Soviet terms for joining an anti-Nazi deal, which included the right to free passage of Soviet troops through Poland and dissolution of the Polish-Romanian alliance, would never be agreed to by Warsaw. The Poles saw little benefit if they escaped German aggression only to succumb to Soviet occupation. Moscow, well aware of its critical role in any four-party deal, was using the negotiations to see how far the Western Powers would go towards endorsing the subordination of its near neighbours. As early as 11 April 1939, Ivan Mikhailovich Maisky, the Soviet ambassador to Great Britain had urged Halifax to persuade Poland and Romania to adopt a 'reasonable attitude'.[25] While the British ambassador in Moscow, Sir William Seeds, and his French counterpart in the negotiations, André Beaufre, battled on, Francis Herbert King, a British Foreign Office cipher clerk, was passing copies of secret Foreign Office documents related to the talks in Moscow to the NKVD, Soviet Intelligence, who in turn edited them and passed them on to Berlin.[26] This, naturally, gave Germany an important advantage in their own negotiations with Moscow.

Poland and Romania remained adamant that any deal with the Soviets was likely to precipitate war with Germany, and even if it didn't Beck reasoned that it would sour relations between Berlin and Warsaw, making any negotiated settlement of outstanding issues difficult. However, both British and French public opinion was running in favour of some sort of deal with the Soviet Union to thwart further German aggression. The Polish government, in particular, viewed bargaining with the Soviets as shopping in an 'oriental Bazaar' where a devious merchant was constantly upping the price. Halifax called it 'quite infuriating … it frays everybody's nerves'.[27]

Chamberlain viewed an alliance with the Soviet Union as necessary to prevent a German–Soviet pact, rumours of which were rife, but negotiations were becoming stalled over the issue of Polish and Romanian refusals to accept Soviet guarantees. The Germanophile British ambassador in Berlin, Nevile Henderson, summed up the mood of many British diplomats towards the Soviets by pointing out 'the unwisdom of putting one's faith in the Slavs'.[28] Stalin may well have been prompted to play for time by British press reports on 22 July 1939 to the effect that Chamberlain's man, Horace Wilson, had been in negotiations with Göring's representative Helmuth Wolthat, over a non-aggression pact and a substantial loan to Germany. If this could be agreed, it would at a stroke release Britain from its tortuous and protracted dialogues over any Eastern European guarantees. Wilson's name in this context implies that Chamberlain was at least marginally interested in such a possibility, but it was certainly not a major element of his strategy. The Moscow negotiations had worn down British and French delegates to the point where they had accepted almost all of the Soviet demands in principle and the next stage was for a joint Franco-British military mission, headed by the French general, Joseph Doumenc, and British admiral, Sir Reginald Aylmer Ranfurly Plunkett-Ernle-Erle-Drax, to meet Marshal Voroshilov in Moscow. Berlin was apprised of this mission on 21 July 1939 through its 'reliable source' (King of England, George VI) even before the British delegates in Moscow, who received their instructions on the 25 July. As a result, the Germans stepped up their own negotiations with the Soviets, which were taking place in Berlin ostensibly over a trade-credit arrangement. Eager to conclude a wider deal, Berlin made significant concessions over territorial issues in order to outbid Britain and France for the prize of a Soviet alliance. In early August 1939 the Germans insisted to Moscow that they had limited interest in the Baltic or the Ukraine, and even said they would be ready to see eastern Poland come under Soviet occupation, but progress with any discussion on these matters could only be made as long as there was no military or political agreement between the Soviets and the Western Powers. The pressure for a Soviet-German agreement at this stage was coming from Berlin and all Molotov would say was that Moscow was 'interested', no doubt waiting to see what further inducements Berlin might be ready to offer.[29]

On 7 August 1939, Stalin learned of rumours circulating in the German military that plans had been laid down to invade Poland on any day after 25 August and of Hitler's attempt to make personal contact with Chamberlain. This intelligence probably came through the German diplomat and Soviet agent Rudolf von Scheliha, who had extensive contacts in the higher echelons of German military and government and worked in the German embassy in Warsaw. While this report emanated from gossip rather than any leaked official decision, it prompted the Soviets to take a more urgent approach to talks. It is unlikely, however, that Hitler had settled on a specific date for an attack at this stage while details of any pact with the Soviets had still not been finalised, but his insistence that von Ribbentrop go to Moscow in person suggests that he was eager to arrive at an early and positive conclusion of the talks.

Meanwhile, in an attempt to exploit the cracks in British politics, Göring had used the Swedish diplomat Birger Dahlerus to bring some of his British contacts to Berlin, where the Reichsmarschall, oozing bonhomie and reasonableness, assured them that Danzig and the Danzig Corridor were the last German territorial claims, but it had little effect. The British and Polish governments were moving steadily towards agreeing the terms of a mutual assistance treaty. The British-Franco military mission arrived in Moscow on 7 August 1939 and Stalin instructed Voroshilov how to handle them. 'Ask them whether they have full powers to sign a military convention,' he said 'and if they say no ask them why they have bothered to come at all.' If the delegates answered yes then Voroshilov was to ask them what their plans were to defend their allies against German aggression. If there were plans then it would be necessary for the delegates to explain how they would guarantee the passage of Soviet forces through Poland and Romania because if that was not agreed upon then they should be under no illusions that the whole strategy was 'doomed to failure'. Under no circumstances was Voroshilov to permit the delegates to inspect any Soviet defence installations. Stalin had made sure that the talks would fail.

Voroshilov duly asked on 14 August 1939 how Soviet troops would be expected to take part in a war against Germany if the Red Army was not allowed to pass through either Poland or Romania. Two days later he suspended the talks, citing British and French prevarication, but was also probably because Stalin had received a request from Hitler for an urgent meeting between Molotov and Ambassador Schulenberg. On 17 August, apparently reliable rumours circulated to the effect that Poland was willing to give ground on the troops issue, but, although urgent talks had taken place in Warsaw after which Beck sent Halifax a draft of the mutual assistance treaty, it seems that the stories were started by the Soviets in order to galvanise the Germans into making more concessions in their negotiations. Schulenberg told Molotov that the Baltic States were of no concern to them and suggested that von

Ribbentrop come to Moscow to put the final touches to a non-aggression pact, which had been drawn up in draft form and shown to Schulenberg on 19 August. Schulenberg touched upon German ideas for a secret protocol to go with the pact but did not elaborate on it. Details of the draft, which Molotov accepted in principle, indicated clearly that the Soviet Union had no objections to a German attack on Poland.[30]

A German-Soviet credit and economic agreement was signed on 19 August 1939, which accelerated demands for von Ribbentrop to go to Moscow. European capitals viewed this as a significant development in German-Soviet relations but none had any real idea of how it had altered the landscape. Given that economic treaties, in themselves, were of little interest to the Soviet Union and normally no more than a means to an end, it might have been apparent that there was something much bigger behind the rapprochement. Two days later talks between the British, French and Soviets were resumed but lasted only six hours before they were adjourned *sine die*. During the evening, the French premier, Édouard Daladier, informed Moscow that France would not object to the passage of Soviet troops across Poland. He claimed to have consulted the Poles beforehand but when they refused to agree he went ahead with a French guarantee anyway. The Soviets were not particularly impressed by this gesture since it was not accompanied by an equivalent British offer. This was remedied on 24 August 1939, when Drax was authorised to 'associate himself with Doumenc' on the matter, but by then it was too late. It mattered little because Voroshilov, quite rightly, said that such agreements were worthless without Polish consent.[31]

For months Hitler had made up groundless accusations of Polish perfidy and suppression of the German populations in Poland hoping to break down its will to resist his demands or make some catastrophic error that would cast it adrift from its Western backers. But now all that was over. The time had gone for such games. Hitler's bold initiative to woo the Soviets had paid dividends. All the pieces were falling into place and Poland was staring down the barrel of a howitzer.

Having played both sides against the middle, the Soviets had made their choice. British and French negotiators were humiliated. On 22 August 1939, Chamberlain proposed that the British Parliament pass the Emergency Powers (Defence) Bill and sent a note to Hitler explaining that:

> These steps were rendered necessary by the military movements which have been reported from Germany, and by the fact that apparently the announcement of a German–Soviet Agreement is taken in some

> quarters in Berlin to indicate that intervention by Great Britain on behalf of Poland is no longer a contingency to be reckoned with. No greater mistake could be made.

He called for direct negotiations between Germany and Poland. Hitler replied that, 'Germany was prepared to settle the problem of Danzig and of the Polish Corridor by a very generous proposal, made once only, and by means of negotiations' and in reference to British military mobilisation, he added that 'in the event of such military measures being taken, I shall order the immediate mobilisation of the German armed forces'.

On 23 August 1939, von Ribbentrop flew to Moscow and signed the Treaty of Non-Aggression between Germany and the Union of Soviet Socialist Republics, commonly referred to as the Molotov-Ribbentrop Pact. The terms were briefly as follows:

- the two countries agreed not to attack each other, either independently or in conjunction with other powers
- not to support any third power that might attack the other party to the pact
- to remain in consultation with each other upon questions touching their common interests
- not to join any group of powers directly or indirectly threatening one of the two parties
- to solve all differences between the two by negotiation or arbitration.

The pact was to last for ten years, with automatic extension for another five years unless either party gave notice to terminate it one year before its expiration. On the same day Albert Forster, the Gauleiter of the National Socialist Party at Danzig, became head of state of the Free City of Danzig under a decree adopted by the Senate. When mass arrest of Poles was started, fears of a Nazi coup in the port were taken very seriously in London. Arms and 'tourists' had been pouring in from East Prussia for weeks and it would take only the slightest provocation for the Nazi paramilitaries to find an excuse to rise up. Britain protested but was careful not to do anything further to aggravate the situation. When Lipski saw Göring, whose menace was cloaked in geniality, he was told that it was the interfering British who were at the root of the problem in Danzig, and Göring repeatedly told him that when it came to the crunch, Britain was in no position to do anything to help Poland.

Outwardly Beck appeared to greet the news of the pact calmly, interpreting it as a sign that the Soviet Union was distancing itself from European affairs, but, in private, Lipski found him 'distraught'.[32] Unaware that the pact had included the, somewhat unconventional, clause that it would stand even if one of the parties was attacked by a third party, they believed that it had not destroyed hope that the British and French negotiations could be resumed, and actually assumed that it left open the possibility that the Soviet Union would help Poland if it was attacked by Germany. When this was put to Voroshilov, he took two days to reply and then said that talks could not continue because 'political conditions had changed'.[33]

The secret protocols accompanying the pact were finalised and signed on 24 August 1939. Lipski feared that it would scare Britain and France from making any further guarantees to Poland, and might even weaken the existing ones. With poignant sorrow and overtones of fatalism he wrote, '[Our] two great adversaries shook hands against us,' but Beck put on a brave face and said that nothing much had changed since he had never put any faith in Soviet assistance in the first place. Many in the Polish government were relieved to see Britain and France walk away from the negotiating table, thus closing down all talk of agreeing to allow Soviet boots on Polish soil.

On the following day, there was signed an agreement between the government of the United Kingdom and the Polish government regarding mutual assistance. The two countries agreed to aid each other if either was attacked by another European country. In a secret protocol, the pact specifically named Germany as the likely aggressor. The pact signalled failure of the German strategy to separate Poland from its Western Allies and took Hitler by surprise. This initiated a flurry of activity, during which Henderson was called in and asked to convey to the British government a proposal that Britain withdraw from its Eastern European commitments in return for agreement on a new disarmament treaty. At the same time, Hitler told the French ambassador how distressed he was at the sad state of Franco-German relations and how needless was the animosity that had grown between them. The order to attack Poland was hastily rescinded while Hitler made one last desperate attempt to prevent British and French interference in his invasion plans.

The halted order, however, came too late for the German infantry in the Carpathians, who had already started their attack, and for secret police who had taken over the Polish Consulate in Kwidzyn (Marienwerder) in East Prussia. Hasty retreats and apologies followed but large-scale troop movements continued all along the German-Polish border. The German battleship *Schleswig-Holstein* had entered

Danzig harbour and sat there ominously with its guns pointing at Polish naval installations on the Hel peninsula.

Halifax, somewhat over-optimistically, told Raczýnski that Hitler's order to 'stop everything at once' had been precipitated by his temerity at Western firmness and he would now be amenable to further negotiations.[34] Raczýnski was not impressed with Halifax's naïve interpretation and told the British foreign secretary that he had no doubt that it was Hitler's objective to 'break the resolution of the Western Powers'. Dahlerus came into the picture again on 27 August 1939 when the proposals he had brought to Chamberlain were discussed in cabinet and, as usual, possible solutions to the Danzig situation were suggested in blatant disregard of the fact that it was clear that the Poles would never agree to them. Dahlerus had even suggested that Göring might come to London to hold last-minute talks to avert war but nothing came of that. Beck saw British suggestions as bearing 'the stamp of appeasement' but was forced to agree to 'consider' the proposals.

On 28 August 1939, Poland proposed 'the initiation of direct discussions between the German and Polish Governments on a basis which would include … the safeguarding of Poland's essential interests and the securing of the settlement by an international guarantee'. The Germans replied that they had no intention of attacking Poland and would welcome a British intermediary with diplomatic powers in Berlin for discussions. Halifax and Cadogan told Dahlerus that they thought Hitler was 'in a fix' and a firm stand at this point would allow them to work for 'a peaceful solution on proper terms'.[35] Halifax urged the Poles to come to the table and have regard for 'world opinion'. Chamberlain told the US ambassador, Kennedy, that he found the Poles a lot more difficult to negotiate with than the Germans. Acting on Mussolini's suggestion, the papal nuncio in Warsaw, Monsignor Filippo Cortesi, weighed in by urging the Poles to give ground on the Danzig question.

Berlin agreed to draft proposals for a solution and make it available for the British government before the Polish negotiator and the British intermediary arrived. In Berlin, Henderson told the German minister for foreign affairs that it was unreasonable to expect the Poles to respond at such short notice. At midnight on 30 August 1939, von Ribbentrop, in a somewhat excited state, met Henderson and read aloud, in German and at top speed, a lengthy document containing the German proposals, a copy of which he refused to give to Henderson, claiming that it was already too late. The Polish ambassador went to see von Ribbentrop and told him that Poland was considering favourably the British suggestion of direct negotiations and would make its formal reply in a few hours. At 9.00 p.m. on 31 August the German radio and newspapers broadcast a communiqué containing the German proposals in the sixteen points that had been hurriedly read to the British ambassador the night before and which were published by the German Foreign Office. The broadcast and communiqué asserted that the German government had 'waited two days in vain for the arrival of an authorised Polish delegate' and could 'not but regard their proposals as having once more been rejected in effect'.

Halifax made one last attempt by sending a telegram to the British Embassy in Warsaw suggesting that the League of Nations be brought in to mediate in talks over Danzig. The telegram was still being decoded at 4.30 a.m. on 1 September 1939 when Hitler's Directive No. 1 for the Conduct of the War (against Poland) was put into effect. Without any declaration of war, German armies crossed the Polish frontier in simultaneous attacks from the north, west and south and the Luftwaffe launched indiscriminate air raids on military objectives, open cities, villages and roads.[36]

Both the British and French governments warned the Germans that, unless German armies were withdrawn from Poland, they would fulfil their obligations to Poland. They received no reply and so at 9.00 a.m. on 3 September 1939 Britain and France gave Germany one last ultimatum. At 11.00 a.m. Chamberlain delivered the following speech to the world by radio:

> I am speaking to you from the Cabinet room at 10 Downing Street. This morning the British ambassador in Berlin handed the German government a final note stating that unless we heard from them by 11 o'clock that they were prepared at once to withdraw their troops from Poland, a state of war would exist between us. I have to tell you now that no such undertaking has been received, and that consequently this country is at war with Germany.
>
> You can imagine what a bitter blow it is to me that all my long struggle to win peace has failed. Yet I cannot believe that there is anything more, or anything different, that I could have done and that would have been more successful. Up to the very last it would have been quite possible to have arranged a peaceful and honourable settlement between Germany and Poland. But Hitler would not have it. He had evidently made up his mind to attack Poland whatever happened, and although he now says he put forward reasonable proposals which were rejected by the Poles, that is not a true statement. The proposals were never shown to the Poles, nor to us, and though they were announced in the German broadcast on Thursday night, Hitler did not wait to hear comments on them, but ordered his troops to cross the Polish frontier the next morning.

> His action shows convincingly that there is no chance of expecting that this man will ever give up his practice of using force to gain his will. He can only be stopped by force.
>
> We have a clear conscience. We have done all that any country could do to establish peace. But the situation in which no word given by Germany's ruler could be trusted, and no people or country could feel itself safe, had become intolerable. And now that we have resolved to finish it, I know that you will all play your part with calmness and courage.

On 17 September 1939 Stalin informed Berlin that Soviet troops were about to enter Poland. Molotov presented a note to Grybowski, which he refused to accept but it was delivered to the Polish Embassy anyway. The note read:

> The Polish-German war has revealed the bankruptcy of the Polish state. In ten days of hostilities, Poland has lost all its industrial region and cultural centres. Warsaw no longer exists as the capital of Poland. The Polish government has collapsed and shows no sign of life. Therefore the treaties concluded between the Soviet Union and Poland have ceased to operate ... the Soviet government [cannot] remain indifferent when its blood brothers in the Ukraine and Belarus living on Polish territory ... are left without protection ... the Soviet government has instructed the High Command of the Red Army to order troops across the frontier and to take under their protection the lives and property of the population of Western Ukraine and Western White Russia ... the Soviet government intends to ... deliver the Polish people from the disastrous war into which they have been plunged by their unwise leaders, and give them an opportunity to live a peaceful life.

NOTES

Introduction

1 Polak-Springer, Peter, *Recovered Territory* (Berhahn, 2015), p.4

Chapter 1 National Renewal

1 Seton-Watson, Hugh, *Eastern Europe Between the Wars 1918–1941* (Harper and Row, 1945), p.320
2 Ibid., p.46
3 Allen, Erin, *Library of Congress Blog, Restoring Poland* (2017)
4 Lenkiewicz, Antoni, *Józef Piłsudski Hero of Poland* (Winged Hussar, 2019), p.58
5 Leslie, R.F., *The History of Poland since 1863* (Cambridge University Press, 1983), p.110
6 Snyder, Timothy, *The Reconstruction of Nations* (Yale University Press, 2003), p.58
7 Davies, Norman, *God's Playground* (Oxford University Press, 2005), p.40
8 Ibid., p.41
9 Leslie, p.122
10 Davies, p.284
11 Ibid., p.285
12 Ibid., p.284
13 Sands, Philippe, *East West Street* (Weidenfeld & Nicolson, 2016), p.71
14 Wandycz, Piotr S., *France and the Russo–Polish War, 1919–1920* (The Polish Review, 2017), p.4
15 Korbel, Josef, *Poland Between East and West* (Princeton University Press, 1963), p.18
16 Sands, p.68
17 Snyder, p.62
18 Davies, p.288
19 Ibid., p.291
20 Korbel, p.22
21 Zatonski, Mateusz Zygmunt, *Re-drawing the Central European Map after the First World War* (University of Bath, 2018), p.3
22 Ibid., p.5
23 Buttin, Felix, *The Polish-Czechoslovak Conflict over Teschen Silesia (1918–1920)*, p.74
24 Rothschild, Joseph, *The Ideological, Political, and Economic Background of Pilsudski's Coup D' Etat of 1926* (Political Science Quarterly, 1963), p.27
25 Zatonski, p.9
26 Ibid., p.10
27 Polak-Springer, p.29
28 Buttin, p.70

29 Ibid., p.77
30 Kozon, Martin John, *Sanacja's Foreign Policy and the Second Polish Republic, 1926–1935* (University of Wisconsin-Milwaukee, 2015)
31 Bostwick, Darwin, *Diplomacy in Defeat: Germany and the Polish Boundary Dispute in 1919* (Historical Reflections, 1977), p.23
32 Ibid., p.29
33 Ibid., p.36
34 Ibid., p.39

Chapter 2 The Russo-Polish War

1 Wandycz, p.6
2 Materski, Wojcirch, *The Secnd Polish Republic in Soviet Foreign Policy 1918–1939* (The Polish Review, 2000), p.333
3 Wandycz, p.7
4 Korbel, Josef, *Poland Between East and West* (Princeton University Press, 1963), p.25
5 Wandycz, p.9
6 Korbel, p.31
7 Litauer, Stefan, *The Rôle of Poland Between Germany and Russia* (Royal Institute of International Affairs, 1935), p.655
8 Korbel, p.40
9 Ibid., p.44
10 *New York Times Current History*, July 1920, p.633
11 Biskupski, M.B., *Paderewski, Polish Politics, and the Battle of Warsaw, 1920* (Slavic Review, 1987), p.504
12 Debicki, Roman, *Foreign Policy of Poland 1919–1939* (Pall Mall Press, 1962), p.33
13 Korbel, p.47
14 Davies, Norman, *Sir Maurice Hankey and the Inter-Allied Mission to Poland, July–August 1920* (The Historical Journal, 1972), p.556
15 Ibid., p.560
16 Korbel, p.49
17 Erickson, John, *The Soviet High Command 1918–1941* (Macmillan, 1962), p.93
18 Ibid.
19 Ibid., p.94
20 Zamoyski, Adam, *How Poland Saved Europe from Bolshevism* (Polish History website)
21 Zamoyski, Adam, *Poland A History* (William Collins, 2015), p.296
22 Zamoyski, Adam, *How Poland Saved Europe from Bolshevism* (Polish History website)
23 Korbel, p.54
24 Davies, p.558
25 Ibid., p.560
26 Leslie, R.F., *The History of Poland since 1863* (Cambridge University Press, 1983), p.138
27 Wandycz, Piotr S., *France and the Russo–Polish War, 1919–1920* (The Polish Review, 2017), p.15
28 Dąbrowski, Stanisław, *The Peace Treaty of Riga* (The Polish Review, 1960), p.4
29 Ibid., p.6
30 Snyder, p.64
31 Dąbrowski, p.16

32 Wandycz, Piotr S., *The Treaty of Riga: Its significance for interwar Polish Foreign Policy* (The Polish Review, 1969), p.35
33 Dąbrowski, p.18
34 Wandycz, p.35
35 Snyder, p.68
36 Davies, p.297

Chapter 3 Upper Silesia

1 Lesniewski, Peter, *Britain and Upper Silesia 1919–1922* (University of Dundee, 2000), p.21
2 Tooley, T. Hunt, *German Political Violence and the Border Plebiscite in Upper Silesia, 1919–1921* (Cambridge University Press, 1988), p.59
3 Lesniewski, p.41
4 Ibid., p.28
5 Lesniewski, p.31
6 Ibid., p.47
7 Tooley, p.58
8 Lesniewski, p.50
9 Davies, p.291.
10 Lesniewski, p.57
11 Ibid., p.71
12 Ibid., p.99
13 Ibid., p.109
14 Ibid., p.29
15 Lesniewski, p.134
16 Tooley, p.9
17 Ibid., p.71
18 Ibid., p.83
19 Lesniewski, p.153
20 Tooley, p.94
21 *Polish Character of Upper Silesia*, published by the Central Polish Plebiscite Committee, Warsaw, Diet Building, May 1921
22 Campbell, F. Gregory, *The Struggle for Upper Silesia, 1919–1922* (Journal of Modern History, 1970), p.376
23 Ibid., p.377
24 Tooley, p.306
25 Ibid., p.311
26 Campbell, p.382
27 Polak-Springer, p.29
28 'Poland's Campaign Against Russia: Warned by Powers Against New Transgressions of Legitimate Boundaries–Peace Negotiations Transferred to Riga', *Current History (1916–1940)* (University of California Press, 1920)

Chapter 4 Danzig

1 *Poland, Germany, and Danzig* (Bulletin of International News, 1939), p.8
2 Ibid., p.3
3 Ibid.
4 Allyn, Emily, *Polish–German Relations in Pomerania and East Prussia* (Polish Institute of Arts & Sciences of America, 1944), p.834
5 Kornat, Marek, *Poland and the Origins of the Second World War* (Peter Lang, 2021), p.316

6 Debicki, p.47
7 Korbel, p.69
8 Ibid., p.72
9 Ibid., p.73
10 Ibid., p.74
11 Ibid., p.78
12 Ibid., p.83
13 Ibid., p.86

Chapter 5 The Treaty of Rapallo

1 Gąsiorowski, Zygmunt J., *Poland's Policy Towards Soviet Russia, 1921–1922* (Modern Humanities Research Association, 1975), p.231
2 Korbel, p.111
3 Gąsiorowski, p.231
4 Gąsiorowski, p.232
5 Sands, p.155
6 Gąsiorowski, p.239
7 Korbel, p.115
8 Ibid., p.116
9 Ibid., p.118
10 Ibid., p.124
11 Hodgson, Robert M., *George Chicherin* (The Slavonic and East European Review, 1937), p.698
12 Ibid., p.700
13 Gąsiorowski, p.244
14 Debicki, p.46
15 Ibid., p.53

Chapter 6 The Ruhr Crisis

1 Miller, David Hunter, *The Occupation of the Ruhr* (The Yale Law Journal, 1924)
2 Korbel, p.130
3 Ibid., p.134
4 Ibid., p.136
5 Ibid., p.140

Chapter 7 The Locarno Treaties

1 Wright, Jonathan, *Stresemann and Locarno* (Contemporary European History, 1995), p.110
2 Korbel, p.153
3 Ibid., p.156
4 Wright, p.111
5 Ibid., p.123
6 Korbel, p.161
7 Ibid., p.162
8 Wright, p.112
9 Korbel, p.168
10 Wright, p.111
11 Ibid., p.109
12 Korbel, p.188

13 Kozon, Martin John, *Sanacja's Foreign Policy and the Second Polish Republic, 1926–1935* (University of Wisconsin-Milwaukee, 2015), p.131
14 Ibid., p.191
15 Cienciała, Anna M., *A Forgotten Foreign Minister of Inter-War Poland* (The Polish Review, 2007)
16 Wright, p.126
17 Korbel, p.199

Chapter 8 Piłsudski's Coup d'État

1 Korbel, p.202
2 *The U.S.S.R. System of Neutrality and Non-Aggression*, Bulletin of International News, 1928, p.6
3 Korbel, p.194
4 *The U.S.S.R. System of Neutrality and Non-Aggression*, p.8
5 Rothschild, Joseph, *The Ideological, Political, and Economic Background of Pilsudski's Coup D' Etat of 1926* (Political Science Quarterly, 1963), p.231
6 Ibid., p.236
7 Ibid., p.242
8 Ibid., p.256
9 Lenkiewicz, Antoni, *Józef Piłsudski Hero of Poland* (Winged Hussar, 2019), p.202
10 Ibid., p.203
11 Ibid., p.204
12 Leslie, p.159
13 Kozon, p.37
14 Korbel, p.208
15 Ibid., p.211
16 Kozon, p.46
17 Korbel, p.223
18 Kozon, p.49
19 Korbel, p.227
20 Ibid., p.219
21 Ibid., p.234
22 Ibid., p.240
23 Ibid., p.184
24 Ibid., p.237
25 Kozon, p.63
26 Korbel, p.251
27 Ibid., p.253
28 Ibid., p.258

Chapter 9 The Death of Piłsudski

1 Korbel, p.268
2 Ibid., p.269
3 Overy, Richard, *The Road to War* (Vintage, 2009) p.10
4 Korbel, p.273
5 Materski, p.337
6 Helbich, Wolfgang J., *Between Stresemann and Hitler; The Foreign Policy of the Brüning Government* (World Politics, 1959), p.27
7 Korbel, p.278
8 Kornat, p.32
9 Materski, p.340

10 Korbel, p.280
11 Leslie, p.183
12 Litauer, Stefan, *The Rôle of Poland Between Germany and Russia* (Royal Institute of International Affairs, 1935), p.667
13 Wynot, Edward D., *The Polish Germans, 1919–1939* (The Polish Review, Winter, 1972), p.53
14 Kornat, p.173
15 Seton-Watson, p.189
16 Kornat, p.35
17 Kornat, p.37
18 Ibid., p. 32
19 Ogg, Frederick A., *The Passing of Pilsudski* (University of California Press, 1935), p.433

Chapter 10 The Rhineland Crisis

1 Leslie, p.187
2 Sakwa, George, *The Franco-Polish Alliance and the Remilitarization of the Rhineland* (The Historical Journal, 1973), p.134
3 Ibid., p.136
4 Kornat, p.60
5 Parker, R.A.C., *The First Capitulation: France and the Rhineland Crisis of 1936* (World Politics, Cambridge University Press, 1956), p.357
6 Sakwa, p.126
7 Kornat, p.63
8 Ibid., p.73
9 Ibid., p.226
10 Drzewieniecki, Walter M., *The Polish Army on the Eve of World War II* (The Polish Review, 1981) p.59
11 Kornat, p.92
12 Polak-Springer, p.125
13 Ibid., p.126

Chapter 11 The Anschluss

1 Weinberg, Gerhard H., *German Foreign Policy and Poland 1937–1938* (The Polish Review, 1975) p.8
2 Wynot, Edward D., *The Polish Germans, 1919–1939* (The Polish Review, Winter, 1972) p.24
3 Weinberg, p.15
4 Kornat, p.137
5 Ridley, Norman, *Reading Hitler's Mind* (Frontline Books, 2021), p.80
6 Kornat, p.165
7 Ridley, p.137
8 Ibid., p.135
9 Kornat, p.258
10 Ibid., p.234
11 Ibid., p.235
12 Ibid., p.240
13 Ibid., p.245
14 Ibid., p.250

Chapter 12 The Descent to War

1 Kornat, p.149
2 Ibid., p.151
3 Ibid., p.167
4 Ibid., p.170
5 Ibid., p.176
6 Debicki, p.137
7 Kornat, p.391
8 Ibid., p.394
9 DeFraga, Matthew, *America's Guarantee to Britain March 1939* (UC Santa Barbara 1994), p.13
10 Foster, Alan J., *An Unequivocal Guarantee? Fleet Street and the British Guarantee to Poland, 31 March 1939* (Journal of Contemporary History, 1991), p.35
11 Ibid., p.36
12 Herzstein, Robert Edwin, *Roosevelt and Hitler: Prelude to War* (Henry Regnery, 1952), p.286
13 DeFraga, *March 1939; America's Guarantee to Britain* (UC Santa Barbara, 1994), p.16
14 Ibid., p.25
15 Kornat, p.415
16 Ibid., p.451
17 Overy, pp.10–11
18 Prazmowska, A. J., *Poland's Foreign Policy: September 1938–September 1939* (The Historical Journal, 1986), p.869
19 Kornat, p.314
20 Ibid., p.351
21 Prazmowska, p.865
22 Cienciała, Anna M., *The Nazi-Soviet Pact of 1939* (Ideology, Politics and Diplomacy in Eastern Central Europe, 2003), p.165
23 Materski, p.343
24 Debicki, p.149
25 Cienciała, Anna M., *The Nazi-Soviet Pact of 1939* (Ideology, Politics and Diplomacy in Eastern Central Europe, 2003), p.170
26 Ibid., p.166
27 Ibid., p.179
28 Ibid., p.184
29 Ibid., p.196
30 Ibid., p.207
31 Ibid., p.209
32 Kornat, p.526
33 Cienciała, Anna M., *The Nazi-Soviet Pact of 1939* (Ideology, Politics and Diplomacy in Eastern Central Europe, 2003), p.211
34 Cienciala, Anna M., *Poland in British and French Policy in 1939* (The Polish Review, 1989), p.214
35 Ibid., p.216
36 Debicki, p.162

SOURCES

Allen, Erin, *Library of Congress Blog, Restoring Poland* (2017)
Allyn, Emily, *Polish–German Relations in Pomerania and East Prussia* (Polish Institute of Arts & Sciences of America, 1944)
Biskupski, M.B., *Paderewski, Polish Politics, and the Battle of Warsaw, 1920* (Slavic Review, 1987)
Biskupski, M.B., *Poland in American Foreign Policy, 1918–1945* (Polish-American Sudies, 1981)
Blanke, Richard, *Orphans of Versailles: The Germans in Western Poland, 1918–1939* (Premier Books, 1998)
Blanke, Richard, *The German Minority in Inter-War Poland and German Foreign Policy – Some Reconsiderations* (Journal of Contemporary History, vol. 25, no. 1, 1990)
Bostwick, Darwin, *Diplomacy in Defeat: Germany and the Polish Boundary Dispute in 1919* (Historical Reflections, 1977)
Buttin, Felix, *The Polish–Czechoslovak Conflict over Teschen Silesia (1918–1920)*
Campbell, F. Gregory, *The Struggle for Upper Silesia, 1919–1922* (Journal of Modern History, 1970)
Cienciała, Anna M., *A Forgotten Foreign Minister of Inter-War Poland* (The Polish Review, 2007)
Cienciala, Anna M., *Poland in British and French Policy in 1939* (The Polish Review, 1989)
Cienciała, Anna M., *Polish Foreign Policy 1926–1939* (The Polish Review, 1975)
Cienciała, Anna M., *The Nazi-Soviet Pact of 1939* (Ideology, Politics and Diplomacy in Eastern Central Europe, 2003)
Dąbrowski, Stanisław, *The Peace Treaty of Riga* (The Polish Review, 1960)
Davies, Norman, *God's Playground* (Oxford University Press, 2005)
Davies, Norman, *Sir Maurice Hankey and the Inter-Allied Mission to Poland, July–August 1920* (The Historical Journal, 1972)
Debicki, Roman, *Foreign Policy of Poland 1919–1939* (Pall Mall Press, 1962)
DeFraga, *March 1939; America's Guarantee to Britain* (UC Santa Barbara, 1994)
Dziewanowski, M.K., *The Bolshevik Revolution and Eastern Europe* (The Polish Review, 1969)
Erickson, John, *The Soviet High Command 1918–1941* (Macmillan, 1962)
Foster, Alan J. *An Unequivocal Guarantee? Fleet Street and the British Guarantee to Poland, 31 March 1939* (Journal of Contemporary History, 1991)
Gąsiorowski, Zygmunt J., *Poland's Policy Towards Soviet Russia, 1921–1922* (Modern Humanities Research Association, 1975)
Gatzke, Hans W., *Russo-German Military Collaboration During the Weimar Republic* (Quadrangle Books, 1972)
Helbich, Wolfgang J., *Between Stresemann and Hitler; The Foreign Policy of the Brüning Government* (World Politics, 1959)
Herzstein, Robert Edwin, *Roosevelt and Hitler: Prelude to War* (Henry Regnery, 1952)

Hodgson, Robert M., *George Chicherin* (The Slavonic and East European Review, 1937)
Kimmich, Christopher M., *The Weimar Republic and the German–Polish Borders* (The Polish Review, 1969)
Korbel, Josef, *Poland Between East and West* (Princeton University Press, 1963)
Kozon, Martin John, *Sanacja's Foreign Policy and the Second Polish Republic, 1926–1935* (University of Wisconsin-Milwaukee, 2015)
Lenkiewicz, Antoni, *Józef Piłsudski Hero of Poland* (Winged Hussar, 2019)
Leslie, R.F., *The History of Poland since 1863* (Cambridge University Press, 1983)
Lesniewski, Peter, *Britain and Upper Silesia 1919–1922* (University of Dundee, 2000)
Litauer, Stefan, *The Rôle of Poland Between Germany and Russia* (Royal Institute of International Affairs, 1935)
Materski, Wojcirch, *The Secnd Polish Republic in Soviet Foreign Policy 1918–1939* (The Polish Review, 2000)
Miller, David Hunter, *The Occupation of the Ruhr* (The Yale Law Journal, 1924)
Moll, Marilyn Senn, *Count and Democrat; Brockdorff-Rantzau as the Weimar Republic's first Foreign Minister* (Student work, 1967)
Moorhouse, Roger, *Poland 1939* (Basic Books, 2020)
Munholland, J. Kim, *The French Army and Intervention in Southern Russia 1918–1919* (Cahiers du Monde Russe, 1981)
Ogg, Frederick A., *The Passing of Pilsudski* (University of California Press, 1935)
Overy, Richard, *The Road to War* (Vintage, 2009)
Polak-Springer, Peter, *Recovered Territory* (Berhahn, 2015)
Prazmowska, A.J., *Poland's Foreign Policy: September 1938–September 1939* (The Historical Journal, 1986)
Ridley, Norman, *Reading Hitler's Mind* (Frontline Books, an imprint of Pen & Sword Books, 2022)
Roberts, Geoffrey, *The Soviet Union and the Origins of the Second World War* (Macmillan, 1995)
Rothschild, Joseph, *The Ideological, Political, and Economic Background of Pilsudski's Coup D' Etat of 1926* (Political Science Quarterly, 1963)
Sakwa, George, *The Franco-Polish Alliance and the Remilitarization of the Rhineland* (The Historical Journal, 1973)
Sands, Philippe, *East West Street* (Weidenfeld & Nicolson, 2016)
Seton-Watson, Hugh, *Eastern Europe Between the Wars 1918–1941* (Harper and Row, 1945)
Snyder, Timothy, *The Reconstruction of Nations* (Yale University Press, 2003)
Stanisławska, Stefania, *Soviet Policy Towards Poland 1926–1939* (The Polish Review, 1974)
Thimme, Annelise, *Stresemann and Locarno* (Quadrangle Books, 1972)
Thompson, Ralph, *Peace Prospects on the Baltic* (University of California Press, 1935)
Tooley, T. Hunt, *German Political Violence and the Border Plebiscite in Upper Silesia, 1919–1921* (Cambridge University Press, 1988)
Wandycz, Piotr S., *France and the Russo–Polish War, 1919–1920* (The Polish Review, 2017)
Wandycz, Piotr S., *The Treaty of Riga: Its significance for interwar Polish Foreign Policy* (The Polish Review, 1969)
Weinberg, Gerhard H., *German Foreign Policy and Poland 1937–1938* (The Polish Review, 1975)
Wright, Jonathan, *Stresemann and Locarno* (Contemporary European History, 1995)
Wynot, Edward D., *The Polish Germans, 1919–1939* (The Polish Review, Winter, 1972)
Zamoyski, Adam, *How Poland Saved Europe from Bolshevism* (Polish History website)
Zamoyski, Adam, *Poland A History* (William Collins, 2015)
Zatonski, Mateusz Zygmunt, *Re-drawing the Central European Map after the First World War* (University of Bath, 2018)

New York Times Current History, July 1920, p.633
Poland, Germany, and Danzig (Bulletin of International News, 1939)
Poland's Campaign Against Russia (University of California Press, 1920)
Polish Character of Upper Silesia (Central Polish Plebiscite Committee, Warsaw, 1921)
Poland's Campaign Against Russia (University of California Press, 1920)
Polish Character of Upper Silesia Published by the Central Polish Plebiscite Committee, Warsaw, Diet Building, May 1921
The U.S.S.R. System of Neutrality and Non-Aggression (Bulletin of International News, 9 June 1928)

INDEX